Alberta

Alberta: A State of Mind

EDITED BY

Sydney Sharpe

Roger Gibbins

James H. Marsh

Heather Bala Edwards

KEY PORTER BOOKS

"All the future lies before us/Glorious in that sunset land"
For
Christopher, Daniel, Gabriel, Rebeccah, Rielle

Copyright © 2005 by Key Porter Books Limited

Library and Archives Canada Cataloguing in Publication

Sharpe, Sydney
    Alberta: a state of mind: edited by Sydney Sharpe, Roger Gibbins, Heather Bala Edwards and James Marsh.

Includes index.
ISBN 1-55263-720-4

Alberta. I. Gibbins, Roger, 1947- II. Edwards, Heather, 1976- III. Marsh, James H. IV. Title.

FC3661.S52 2005   971.23   C2005-902764-9

The publisher gratefully acknowledges the support of the Canada Council for the Arts for its publishing program.

We acknowledge the financial support of the Government of Canada through the Book Publishing Industry Development Program (BPIDP) for our publishing activities.

Key Porter Books Limited
Six Adelaide Street East, Tenth Floor
Toronto, Ontario
Canada M5C 1H6

www.keyporter.com

Text design: Jean Lightfoot Peters
Electronic formatting: Jean Lightfoot Peters
Printed and bound in Canada

05 06 07 08 09 6 5 4 3 2 1

Contents

Alberta's Next Century: A Wish List

The Honourable Norman Kwong, CM, AOE
Lieutenant Governor of Alberta

Alberta has seen some remarkable changes in her first hundred years. Her population has grown from thousands to millions, and grown more diverse. Her economy has changed from agrarian to industrial. Her culture has become more sophisticated, without losing touch with her pioneer roots. Railroads and horses have given way to automobiles and airplanes.

The Honourable Norman L. Kwong, Lieutenant Governor of Alberta (Office of the Lieutenant Governor of Alberta)

And yet, some things remain constant. Alberta's skies are still a brilliant blue, her rivers and lakes still sparkle, and the Rockies, of course, are eternal—or nearly so, from our perspective. Alberta's people are still innovative, still stubborn, still optimistic, and still generous, in good times and bad. And it is these qualities that will see Alberta through the next hundred years.

The future will, like any other age, be a bewildering combination of old and new, and there will be many challenges. Alberta has enjoyed a remarkable first century, but there is still much to do, many improvements to make, many injustices to be addressed.

So here's my wish list for Alberta's next one hundred years. I'd like to see...

A more diverse and tolerant culture, with love and respect for peoples of all faiths, colours and creeds.

More respect for senior citizens, so that we may learn from them, support them, and cherish their presence in our lives.

More schools and libraries, for a more educated, more innovative, more introspective Alberta.

A healthier, more active culture, for fitness and enhanced quality of life.

A more diverse economy, to protect Albertans from sudden shifts in global markets.

More help for the poor, the disadvantaged, the disabled, so that all Albertans get a fair share of the province's wealth.

A cleaner environment, to safeguard future generations and simply to respect the natural world that gives us life.

A more vibrant, more internationally recognized arts scene, so that our talented artists can flourish.

The resurgence of First Nations cultures, and a stronger voice for native peoples within our province.

And, of course, a few more Grey Cups for the Eskimos and the Stampeders, and a few more Stanley Cups for the Oilers and the Flames.

These changes will not come about without the concerted efforts of every Albertan. We each have a role to play in building a better tomorrow, and if we are to leave a legacy to be proud of for the generations to come, we must embrace our responsibility to play those roles.

Whatever the future may hold for our province, I know that Albertans will face the challenges of the next one hundred years with the same grit, guts and grace that the first Albertans did back in 1905. I wish I could be around to hear the kids in 2105 tell us how we did in Alberta's second century.

What a story Alberta has to tell!

THE HONOURABLE RALPH KLEIN
PREMIER OF ALBERTA

In just 100 years, this province has gone from a long shot on the Canadian frontier to an internationally recognized hotspot for innovation, industrial success, and cultural vitality.

You don't have to take my word for it, either. After all, some would argue my point of view is biased.

Consider instead the fact that Alberta has the fastest-growing population in Canada, or the numerous economic studies that show Alberta to be a national leader in terms of economic growth. Alberta's diversity is its strength. While energy remains a key contributor to Alberta's gross domestic product, manufacturing and business services are quickly gaining ground.

Consider the research being done in Alberta in the health care field, in the agriculture industry, and in the energy sector. Academics and entrepreneurs are being drawn to Alberta, and for good reason. Think of the Canadian Centre for Behavioural Neuroscience at the University of Lethbridge, which has become a world centre for brain and behavioural research. Consider the vibrant tourism sector that sees upwards of 20 million people visiting our national and provincial parks, rural treasures, urban hotspots, and historic sites every year.

All in all, Alberta enters its second century in an enviable position, with a strong economy, no debt, nation-leading rates of growth and employment, a high standard of living, and an enviable quality of life. What a story!

No government can take credit for Alberta's incredible growth. The credit for these successes falls squarely on Albertans themselves—everyone from Alberta's First Nations and the pioneers of the late 1800s and early 1900s, to the students of 2005, the leaders of tomorrow.

The Honourable Ralph Klein, Premier of Alberta (Office of the Premier, Government of Alberta)

While it is government's responsibility to foster a positive business climate, it is the entrepreneurs and business owners who drive the economy, creating jobs and economic security. It is up to government to protect the vulnerable and disadvantaged, but it is generous Albertans who make the real difference by volunteering their time and resources to help those in need. Indeed, each and every Albertan is responsible for the amazing heights this province has reached. This is not to say there haven't been bumps and bruises along the way. Change and growth are never easy. Whether you're raising a family, running a business, or involved in government, your decisions and direction come under scrutiny. But it's that scrutiny and inevitable criticism that often keeps you pointed in the right direction.

Having goals and staying focused certainly doesn't mean you stop listening to those around you. Striving to understand the opinions and perspectives of our critics, while working to have our own point of view understood, has been a winning combination for my government and for the province.

Alberta's success is due in part to an ability to stay focused on its goals, but it's also due to being smart enough—and humble enough—to make changes when necessary. This has certainly been the philosophy of my government over the past 12 years.

It's my hope that governments in Alberta's second century will continue to follow the fiscal principles that have served this province so well: balanced budgets, no debt and low taxes.

Adhering to these principles will ensure the government's ability to provide a favourable business climate, a dependable health care system, a world-class public education system, and a stable social security system to protect Alberta's most vulnerable people.

Given these things, the people of Alberta are unstoppable. Their potential is unmatched.

And that makes me very proud to be Albertan.

Message from the Prime Minister

THE RIGHT HONOURABLE PAUL MARTIN
PRIME MINISTER OF CANADA

I am delighted to extend my warmest greetings to everyone taking part in the festivities surrounding the celebration of Alberta's centennial.

Our country's success depends on our communities as places where people want to plant their roots and raise their families, where they want to invest their energies, hopes, dreams and ambitions. This remarkable milestone for Alberta is a testament to the high calibre of its communities and its extraordinary dedication to maintaining the highest possible quality of life for its citizens. Albertans can also take great pride in having one of the strongest economies in North America. Indeed, Alberta's enthusiastic entrepreneurs have gained an international reputation for excellence, and it comes as no surprise that it is recognized today as one of Canada's most dynamic provinces.

Let me take this opportunity to wish you all the best for a successful celebration of this most notable milestone. I am certain that you will make this special event a most exciting and memorable occasion—not only for the citizens of Alberta, but also for our entire nation.

Please accept my best wishes for a most memorable centennial celebration.

Ottawa
2005

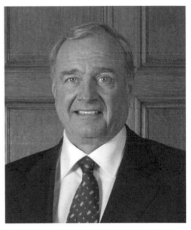

The Right Honourable Paul Martin, Prime Minister of Canada (Government of Canada)

Message from the Leader of the Opposition

THE HONOURABLE STEPHEN HARPER, P.C., M.P.,
LEADER OF THE OPPOSITION, LEADER OF THE CONSERVATIVE PARTY OF CANADA

It is an honour as an Albertan to join in celebrating our province's centennial. For a hundred years, our province has been home to an independent and entrepreneurial spirit, and we can look back with pride at one hundred years that have truly reflected our provincial motto, *fortis et liber*—strong and free.

As we enter our second century, today's Albertans continue to adhere to this spirit. These values are responsible for our success and are making Alberta the envy of the world. More than ever, people from all parts of the country, and from many others, are choosing Alberta as the place to live, do business, and raise families. They will build upon the spirit of our first pioneers and contribute to making Alberta one of the most dynamic, forward-looking societies on the planet.

Alberta's proud and independent spirit has also helped to make it a generous and caring society, and has helped the province to make Canada a better country as a whole. Albertans rely on and help each other. We are proud to be among the most generous donors to charity in the country and to make, on average, the largest contributions. We have used our wealth and good fortune not simply to enrich ourselves, but to build world-class schools and hospitals, to contribute richly to federal finances, and to lay the financial foundations for the future by eliminating our public debt.

At the national level, Alberta's independent spirit has helped ensure a more cooperative confederation. Sir Frederick Haultain's demand for provincial status—the reason we are celebrating this centenary—made Canada a strong federation of provinces from coast to coast. Alberta's efforts to win control of our natural resources helped ensure that Canada's resource wealth would be spread across the country. Today, we see Atlantic provinces

The Honourable Stephen Harper, Leader of Her Majesty's Loyal Opposition (Conservative Party of Canada)

emulating Alberta's quest to control their resources, and Albertans back them in their efforts. Alberta has led the fight for a reformed democratic Senate, which will greatly improve the functioning of Parliament and federalism when it is achieved.

I look forward to Alberta remaining on the cutting edge in the next century. I believe that ideas developed and advanced in Alberta can lead to democratic renewal, and greater cooperation between federal and provincial governments. I am confident that Alberta will lead the way in making the transition from a resource-based economy to a knowledge-based economy, backed by the same spirit of hard work and enterprise that has marked our first one hundred years. Albertans have the strength of character to achieve all of this and more.

Acknowledgements

Thank you, Alberta. The province's centennial is the reason for this book and the people of Alberta are the inspiration. All of us who collaborated felt that there must be an Alberta centennial book that celebrates who we are, where we have been, where we are going and what we are about.

Originally I conceived the book as one that I would write alone. It quickly became apparent, however, that no single author (and certainly not me) could offer more than a pale reflection of the province's enormous variety and energy. After many outlines and shifts and adjustments, the book ignited with its own life and drew in more than 60 collaborators representing a full spectrum of Alberta life and thought.

Gratefully, I became just one of four main editors. Roger Gibbins, one of Canada's foremost scholars and thinkers, came aboard with his characteristic insight, wit and humour. James Marsh, the inspiring editor-in-chief of *The Canadian Encyclopedia* and member of the Order of Canada, lent his enormous vitality and vision. Heather Bala Edwards, writer and editor, plunged in with dedicated enthusiasm, spending many weeks editing first drafts in Calgary, and then launching them electronically to James in Edmonton.

Laura Bonikowsky showed great patience and resolve editing the disparate authors while ensuring that the integrity of the book remained intact. Lorraine Snyder mined the treasures of various Alberta archives to provide the vivid images that bring the book alive. Gerry Thomas and Kate Sheffield both donated their exceptional photographs.

Most of all, this project is a collaboration of passionate Albertans who have given their very best to this province. Their writing, and the work of the editors, has been donated in the Alberta spirit of

EDUCATION

ALBERTA
LOTTERY FUND

FOUNDATION

Alberta Centennial

sharing. All of them would have been offended by an offer of money, if we'd had any to offer. The collaborators are the heart and soul of the book.

Anna Porter, former CEO of Key Porter Books, embraced the province's centennial through this book as if she were an Albertan. Sheila Evely exhibited her usual patience with anxious authors. Clare McKeon miraculously put the book into form under the pressure of an impossible schedule.

A copy of this book will be made available free of charge to junior and senior high schools, as well as community libraries in the province through the generous support of Alberta Education (formerly Alberta Learning) and the Alberta Lottery Fund Community Initiatives Program of Alberta Gaming, with special recognition to Helen Wilson for her patience and professionalism.

I'd like to thank a hundred individuals, but space only allows me to name a few: Jock Osler, for his early support and encouragement when hardly anybody seemed to notice the centennial was coming; Ken King, president and CEO of the Calgary Flames, who envisioned the sports section with his typical slapshot style; former Learning Minister Hon. Dr. Lyle Oberg, for recognizing how valuable this book will be to schools; his successor, Education Minister Hon. Gene Zwozdesky, for following through; and the volunteer board of the non-profit Alberta Experience Society: Jeannette Nicholls, Patricia Leeson, Phoebe Heyman, and especially Don Hobsbawn, whose dedication to non-profit action is unmatched in the province.

The Canada West Foundation, under the leadership of Roger Gibbins, generously lent its office for numerous meetings and its staff to write and track down statistics. The Canadian Association of Petroleum Producers, especially Stephen Ewart, also provided essential statistics. The University of Calgary and University of Alberta and their libraries were always helpful. The Glenbow Museum and Provincial Archives of Alberta were particularly generous in providing images from their prodigious collections.

Sydney Sharpe
Calgary
June 20, 2005

Introduction:
Alberta State of Mind

SYDNEY SHARPE

Alberta is three million people, a thousand places, a dozen climates, a score of landscapes, and an endless array of attitudes, opinions and lifestyles. Our province ranges from the lakes of the north to the arid badlands of the southeast, from the flat prairie of the eastern regions to the mighty peaks of Jasper, Banff and Kananaskis. Alberta in this Centennial year is the summer rodeo in dozens of small towns and big cities, the theatre in tiny Rosebud, soaring operas in Edmonton and Calgary, the risky work on oil rigs, the mammoth industrial operation of the Athabasca oil sands, the world-class cancer research in two of Canada's finest medical schools, the annual struggle with climate and economics to raise crops and animals on the land. Modern Albertans are citizens of the world: we were born in Vietnam, India, Pakistan, Lebanon, Israel, Russia, Britain, Chile, Haiti, China, the United States, Ontario, Saskatchewan and, yes, Alberta. We grew up on native reserves, in tiny rural towns, in mammoth world cities. We speak a hundred languages besides English, including the native tongues heard on the trails and in the forests a thousand years before modern settlement.

Sydney Sharpe (photograph by John Hoon).

Albertans, in short, are virtually impossible to define in narrow ways. If two Albertans declare themselves to be politically conservative, another will shout: "Not me!" For every proud Calgarian there's an Edmontonian who believes her city is better, and a rural Albertan who thinks they're both deluded. The forest ranger roaming the summits of Banff lives a planet away from the business executive looking at the foothills from his highrise office. The rig worker in the north and the Calgary financier who raises money for the worker's employer are bound tenuously by oil, but have little else in common. Often we are as different from each other as we are from any other Canadians.

And yet, we share a state of mind that defines us as Albertans. A century of shared experience in Canada's white-hot political crucible has forged an identity that's clear in our thoughts and those of other Canadians. From one perspective we are the contrarians, the doubters, the wealthy westerners who question national habits and search for other paths. Our image is as sharply etched as Quebec's. In some quarters we are admired for questioning traditional national wisdom; in others, we're disliked and even feared. Oil wealth has made us arrogant, these people say, forgetting that for many decades Alberta was a poor province with no control over its resources. And they fail to recall, too, that in 1980 the federal government attacked Alberta's ownership of its oil and gas with an official ferocity unique in Canadian history. Alberta's public prickliness grows from deep historical roots.

For many Albertans, though, these feelings have softened in the decade leading up to our centennial in 2005. Newcomers raised away from such experiences find the old emotions rather peculiar. Far from fearing the federal government, they now wish it would just get out of the way. They believe the economy has grown so powerful that hostile federal measures would damage the whole country. Only a truly foolish national government would even make the attempt.

Describing the provincial psychology, or attempting to, makes us sound like outsiders and even separatists. We are not. The vast majority of Albertans are loyal, proud Canadians who want nothing more than to take a central role in the nation's affairs. We have close economic ties to America but do not feel like Americans, or want to be Americans. Albertans share the tough, indestructible strand of Canadianism that persists in every province through all our national difficulties. Outsiders sometimes fail to realize that Albertans can still love Canada while disapproving of the way it functions. Preston Manning caught the spirit of the province brilliantly when he coined the Reform Party's original slogan: The West Wants In. Albertans, more than any other westerners, knew exactly what he meant.

While deeply involved in Canada, Albertans are showing a new confidence in themselves and their province. We care less than we did about the opinion of others, preferring to judge ourselves on our own merits. And Alberta is undeniably in the midst of a creative explosion in the arts, business, academics, education and government. Our province leads the way in finding new financing measures for expanding cities; the provincial government was the first to share fuel tax revenue with municipalities. Alberta students score among the highest on world tests. Researchers from Alberta universities routinely make world headlines with medical and scientific breakthroughs. After a wrenching period of cutbacks in major institutions, the province is now pouring money back into universities, schools and health care. Alberta is debt-free and the province has maneuvering room unknown to any other government in Canada—or North America, for that matter. The provincial government's actions will always be hotly debated, but nobody can deny that Alberta's position is enviable. Even the province's most vociferous detractors would love to be in our boots as we begin the second century.

This book attempts to describe Albertans to themselves through the voices of leading Alberta writers and thinkers. All these writers have submitted their work free of charge, as their enthusiastic contribution to the Centennial. To our delight, the list of contributors kept growing as the project went along. They include the lieutenant governor, the premier's spouse, the attendant premier, the current prime minister, the federal opposition leader, two big-city mayors, holders of the Order of Canada, scientists, social scientists, deans, doctors, environmentalists, business leaders, political analysts, journalists and other experts of all sorts. Coordinating the project has been occasionally chaotic but always exciting, rather like the province itself.

Our tone is unabashedly celebratory, without being slavish or uncritical. Alberta has much to celebrate; the province has risen from the deepest backwoods obscurity a century ago to a position of considerable international renown. Much of this was accomplished, in the face of federal indifference and even hostility, with startling bursts of creativity. Alberta has hosted many of the world's greatest sporting events, welcomed (and produced) some of its finest performers and artists, and set world standards in many areas of industry, including energy. We are far from perfect, but in an uncertain world where progress is intermittent at best, Alberta has done extraordinarily well in scores of areas, many of them virtually unknown to the public. How many people realize, for instance, that committees of the Alberta Medical Association lowered deaths of mothers and infants in childbirth to the lowest levels in the world? Beginning in 1936, they examined every single death, interviewed doctors and made changes in medical practice, all with a view to protecting mothers and children. Nearly 70 years after they started, their work is still admired by practitioners around the world.

None of this should be surprising. The Alberta spirit springs from a well of independence and self-sufficiency. Our entire history has been a struggle to make a way for ourselves. As Albertans, we want to control our own destiny. Within this vast and diverse land, we've discovered our unique way of doing things.

Oil sands extraction is an entirely new industry, created by Albertans in Alberta. This dry fact becomes stunning reality for any-one who visits Fort McMurray and sees the two-storey high trucks as they rumble about their work. Nothing on the planet matches the sheer scale of the industry that mines the rich goo that natives used hundreds of years ago to caulk their canoes.

Albertans were the first Canadians to elect a woman to political office—on June 7, 1917. Indeed, the prairies jump-started women's political rights, as Manitoba, Saskatchewan and Alberta, in quick succession, recognized women's right to vote in early 1916.

Alberta homesteaders relied on the ingenuity and hard work of Aboriginals already residing on lands that often seemed foreboding. While the federal government had negotiated treaties with First Nations and provided reserves that too often were inhospitable, the Métis were left to fend for themselves. Alberta uniquely recognized the contribution of the Métis people by passing the Métis Population Betterment Act in 1938, thus giving the Métis nine of their own settlements in northern Alberta.

Albertans often march to their own beat, but when they hear the drums of war, their commitment and gallantry know no bounds. The two world wars of the twentieth century robbed the small towns of their young men—and women, too. Today, all that's left in many of these rural places is the promise of the past and the cenotaph.

In Alberta, there is a communal pride of place and a deep-rooted sense of responsibility. That's why Albertans are such fervent volun-teers. In other parts of Canada where there are high levels of government intervention through subsidies and grants, the notion of volunteering often appears alien. Why volunteer? Why not get paid? Albertans never even ask the question. Volunteering is part of the Alberta psyche and it helps lure countless world-class events because organizers know they'll succeed.

Albertans cooperate of their own volition. They don't act because they're told or forced to do so. When a problem pops up, and a nasty dust-up seems inevitable, just leave Albertans alone and they'll come up with a solution—and it's often innovative. Whether it's a cooperative group like the Sundre Petroleum Operators Group (SPOG) or a dispute resolution process, most will try to hammer out a workable compromise.

Alberta has become an urban province, as more and more people move into urban areas for the big-city jobs. This also brings the big-city problems of congestion, crime and growing apathy. Yet Alberta cities have so far been highly successful at managing growth and environmental challenges. Crime rates are actually falling. Although few Canadians would suspect it, the City of Calgary has the best national record of reducing emissions under the Kyoto Accord on greenhouse gases.

We will consider Alberta on its own terms, not those imposed by others. The book will ponder alienation, but not in the old and tired configuration that elicits rolling of eyes rather than wracking of brains. Every part of Canada is alienated, except perhaps Toronto and Ottawa. Alberta is not unique in its alienation from the federal seat of power. But its response is unique.

This is a book about the Alberta way as an impetus for doing and for being who we are. Why are we like this? In part it's a function of our dynamic history, our unique economy, our distinct politics, our growing society, our disparate geography, our extraordinary environment.

Some outsiders stereotype the spirit of Alberta as narrow, but do so only from the confines of a comfortable political pew. In reality, Alberta is expansive. The province has a deep sense of itself in the world, and can find the confines of the Canadian border very constricting. After Quebec, Alberta is probably the most ambitious province internationally. Yet Alberta's quest, unlike Quebec's, is international cooperation and economic prosperity, not independence. Alberta makes its international initiatives within the rules of Confederation.

It is also the province that has the most open and uncomplicated relationship with the United States. That stems in part from its history of north–south immigration, especially after Alberta opened its homesteads to its American neighbors. Alberta's economic link to the United States through agriculture and energy has only strengthened the traditional ties. The irony is that Ontario, which depends far more on the American economy for its prosperity, is far more anti-American.

Alberta encourages its people to think not just outside the box, but beyond the mountains and the plains. And they do, with unique gusto.

The spirit of Alberta is very strong and highly contagious. Why do Albertans do what they do? Why do they think and feel unique, distinct, and different? In a spirit of celebration, this book will explore those questions as it defines the spirit of Alberta as a state of mind, and will attempt to shine a small light on the province's future.

Alberta and its Politics—From Prophesy to Progress

SYDNEY SHARPE

The hothouse of Alberta politics and its frequent isolation from the federal system have produced some of Canada's most fascinating political experiments. They include Social Credit, the Progressive Party, the Co-operative Commonwealth Federation (CCF, founded in Calgary, in 1932), as well as the Reform Party and its offspring, the Canadian Alliance.

Despite this proliferation of parties, Alberta's political life is anything but unstable. Albertans elect the same party through many elections, always preferring to make their governments change rather than change their governments. And those governments, whatever their stripe, have often been strikingly original in their solutions to provincial and national problems.

Alberta has also spawned some of the most intriguing and influential politicians this side of Newfoundland. Home-spun religion topped with a chicken in every pot pushed William Aberhart's nascent Social Credit Party from the pulpit into the legislature. His disciple, Ernest Manning, spread the message through his own Bible Hour radio broadcasts. He indirectly produced a new federal movement, the Reform Party, through his son, Preston, in 1987. Even before Social Credit, the United Farmers of Alberta generated great change and even more striking scandal.

This chapter explains why Alberta's political life seems so different from the rest of Canada's. It also reveals how ground-breaking leaders like Peter Lougheed and Ralph Klein changed both the federal and provincial political landscapes.

Alberta has built its political road one hard rock at a time. Every bit of dust, dirt, and sweat leads to a singular destination: long-term

The program for Alberta's inauguration ceremonies in Edmonton on September 1, 1905, with highlights of the events of the day (Glenbow Archives/NA-1030-28)

Alberta and its Politics—From Prophesy to Progress

Thousands of new Albertans attended the swearing-in ceremony of their first Lieutenant Governor, George Hedley Vicars Bulyea, on Inauguration Day, September 1, 1905 (Glenbow Archives/NA-1297-4)

governments by parties that constantly reshape themselves to suit the public mood. Since 1905, only four parties have governed. The shortest run for any of them was 14 years, when the United Farmers ruled between 1921 and 1935. Alberta's road is paved with originality, tough-mindedness and pragmatism. Shaped by the code of the frontier, this is a road cemented in trust and sealed with a handshake.

Alberta is the only jurisdiction in Canada, North America and, arguably, the western world, where most elections seem virtually uncontested. A major reason for this is that Alberta governments have the capacity to respond to what the people want and change themselves from within.

There is certainly opposition in Alberta politics, much of it coming from the Liberals and New Democrats who toil gamely on the opposing benches for one generation after another. The opposition that often matters more, however, grows from the ferment that builds gradually within the governing party over several terms. The brawls behind closed doors reflect the issues in the cities, towns and rural areas of the province. Governing parties have learned to be very flexible, shifting from cost-cutting to spending, or Ottawa-battling to federal-provincial co-operation, depending on the mood of the day.

The ruling rhetoric is almost always conservative, but government practice is intensely pragmatic and finely tuned to current needs. The Progressive Conservatives, for instance, often acted almost like classic Canadian liberals in the 1970s, when they kick-started enterprises with public money and even bought an airline. By the 1990s this same party was widely believed to be deeply and ideologically conservative as it made radical cuts to spending, privatized services, and reduced the size of the civil service. With the debt crisis resolved by the end of the decade, the Conservatives under the same premier, Ralph Klein, once again started behaving like a typical Canadian government, pouring money into health care and education.

Our history shows that these agile shifts satisfy the majority of voters over several terms, until finally there comes a tipping point that topples the governing party. That moment is always a long time coming, though; the average time in government over our first century is 25 years for each of the four parties that have ruled Alberta. Social Credit lasted 36 years and the Progressive Conservatives, so far, have been in power for 34.

During such long stretches in office, Alberta governments have the luxury to be experimental and original. Large cushions of public support allow them to tinker, adjust and correct over several years, even decades, without fear of losing an election. Social Credit flirted with the laws of Canada by creating a parallel monetary system and inventing the Alberta Treasury Branches in the 1930s. In the new century, Premier Klein's government constantly tests federal rules as it tries to reinvent health care. Such measures always create lively debate both inside and outside the province, but they are part of a long provincial tradition.

Alberta has never felt completely part of Canada, and its geographic and political distance has encouraged original thinking. From an initial position of colonial inferiority, Alberta's political culture evolved into one that is unique, assertive and self-sufficient. Albertans feel comfortable with large majorities that can stand up to Ottawa; but they also expect their governments to be energetic and vigorous. This dynamic has persisted through the near-bankruptcy of the Great Depression to today's unprecedented prosperity. "Our original alienation came from powerlessness and our new alienation comes from power," says Dr. David Taras of the University of Calgary.

Indeed, Alberta's alienation has evolved to reflect the province's place as a national decision-maker. The Calgary–Edmonton corridor is now an engine of national economic growth. Former Progressive Conservative Premier Peter Lougheed set the tone in the 1970s by

Alberta and its Politics—From
Prophesy to Progress

The Inaugural Day parade on September 1, 1905, on Jasper Avenue in Edmonton (Provincial Archives of Alberta/B-6717)

Liberal politician Alexander Cameron Rutherford served as Alberta's first premier from 1905 to 1910 (Provincial Archives of Alberta/A10649).

refusing to be paternalized or marginalized by Ottawa and Prime Minister Pierre Elliott Trudeau. When those battles cooled in the 1990s, Premier Ralph Klein created his own brand: the Alberta Advantage. The words neatly caught Alberta's modern mood of pride mixed with touchy independence. Klein's early term cost-cutting became a model for governments all over the country, and when the provinces and Ottawa began to balance their budgets, the premier and Alberta got plenty of the credit. For the first time in our history, Alberta was being widely emulated rather than casually dismissed.

Suspicion of Ottawa remains and is quickly rekindled at the slightest hint of unilateral federal measures. The modern flashpoint is often health care, but the hostility goes back through the National Energy Program of 1980 to the resource ownership battles during the 1920s.

"Now Alberta is growing and it's the same issue," adds Dr. Taras. "Can we trust Ottawa? It's a club and they ignore us. Trust is everything on the frontier." And the majority of Albertans continue to trust their local governments more than any outsider.

Alberta's formal political destiny appeared ordinary enough at the beginning, when Liberal MP Alexander Cameron Rutherford was named the first premier in 1905 at the creation of the province.

Yet it was far from a simple end to the backroom brawls between the Conservative and Liberal MPs in Ottawa. Sir Wilfrid Laurier's federal Liberal government had a strong Minister of the Interior in Edmontonian Frank Oliver, whose influence won his city the status of provincial capital. Rutherford, the MP for Edmonton–Strathcona went the extra mile—and crossed the North Saskatchewan River—to give the City of Strathcona the new University of Alberta in 1908. The two cities merged in 1912, creating a northern powerhouse always ready to take on its southern sister, Calgary.

For 16 years Alberta's political life did not seem very unusual, at least from the outside. The governing party installed by the federal Liberals ran a succession of regimes based largely on party loyalties and patronage decisions. But alternatives started brewing as early as 1909, when the United Farmers of Alberta formed to advance rural interests. Its offshoot, the United Farm Women of Alberta, campaigned energetically for the right of women to vote and hold office, which was granted in 1916 in Alberta, Manitoba and Saskatchewan—the first such right accorded to women anywhere in Canada.

Becoming Persons
Sydney Sharpe

Women on the Alberta frontier were focused and tough. They had no choice. Whether that frontier was geographic, social or political, women persevered to break ground. They often ran the homesteads, clearing and planting the fields while the men worked to make enough money to buy more land, machinery, grain and goods. Women on the farm welcomed the help of aboriginals living nearby who knew how to live and work in a harsh climate.

That quest for survival spilled over into the political realm where women demanded equal rights. The suffragist movement in Canada saw women given the right to vote in 1916, in part because women were integral to the farm economy. Most tasks on the family farm were determined by health and strength rather than gender. As World War I raged across the globe, women also joined the war effort and some found themselves at the front as nurses and aides.

Another important factor that fueled women's suffrage on the prairies was antipathy towards the federal government. More voters

In 1916 Emily Murphy was appointed police magistrate for Edmonton, the first woman magistrate in the British Empire (Glenbow/NA-273-3).

Born into an affluent Montreal family, Henrietta Muir Edwards used her influence to further the social and political rights of women (Glenbow Archives/NA-4035-162).

meant a stronger voice against Ottawa, so Alberta and Saskatchewan quickly followed Manitoba in giving women the right to vote in 1916.

The federal government, under Robert Borden, granted women the vote in 1918, and in 1920 allowed women to be elected to Parliament.

Ottawa had been left scrambling after Alberta's success in 1917. Louise Crummy McKinney was the first woman to be elected and sworn into office in Alberta, in Canada and in the British Empire, with Roberta MacAdams following right behind her as the second. MacAdams, a dietitian who was serving in England as a lieutenant in the Canadian Army Medical Corps was also the first (and only) woman in the British Empire elected by the Armed Services. She continued her trail-blazing by becoming the first woman in the entire British Empire to introduce legislation.

Women had the right to vote and to hold office. What they didn't have was the right to be appointed to the Senate, because they weren't fully recognized as "persons." This was the result of a bizarre rendering of the definition of "persons" under the British North America Act.

In 1916, a male lawyer challenged a ruling of Judge Emily Murphy because she wasn't considered a "person" and thus, he claimed, held her judicial office illegally. A year later, when Magistrate Alice Jamieson suffered a similar embarrassment, Judge Murphy decided the law must

Nellie McClung (left), Emily Murphy (right) and Laura Jamieson (centre) helped lead the feminist cause in western Canada (City of Edmonton Archives/EA10-2070).

be changed. For the next ten years, she and her many colleagues clamored for women's equality, winning little but empty promises.

Then, in 1927, Murphy enlisted four other eminent women to mount a monumental legal challenge: Nellie McClung, the firebrand feminist, author and Alberta MLA; Irene Parlby, Alberta minister without portfolio and the second woman in the British Empire to become a cabinet minister; Louise Crummy McKinney, a teacher, temperance crusader and ground-breaking MLA; and Henrietta Muir Edwards, journalist and artist.

These Famous Five petitioned the Supreme Court of Canada to rule on whether women were "persons" under the BNA Act and eligible to serve in the Senate. The women soon lost, but their arsenal was far from empty.

They, and their many advocates, marched on a wider front to the court of the British Privy Council. It was there, on October 18, 1929 that they finally knew victory. The word "persons," the court ruled, "included members both of the male and female sex ... and that women are eligible to be summoned to and become members of the Senate of Canada." The silliness had stopped. Women were finally legally declared persons.

Yet even as these distinguished women were fighting for equal rights, some of them were actively advocating against rights for others. Emily Murphy, who wrote popular books as Janey Canuck, railed against Chinese, Jews, Blacks and others whose heritage she didn't share. Her book, *The Black Candle*, is riddled with racism.

Vivacious and eloquent, Nellie McClung advanced the feminist cause in her day and publicized the need for the economic independence of women (Glenbow Archives/NA-1514-3).

Following her career as a lieutenant in the Canadian Army, Roberta MacAdams entered politics and became the first woman to introduce a piece of legislation in the British Empire, a bill to incorporate the War Veterans' Next-of-Kin Association (Glenbow Archives/NA-1476-1).

When Irene Parlby was appointed Minister without Portfolio in the new UFA government in 1921, she became the first woman in Alberta and only the second woman in Canada to become a Cabinet member (Glenbow Archives/NA-273-1).

Murphy, along with McClung and McKinney, enthusiastically supported one of Alberta's most notorious pieces of legislation: the Act Respecting Sexual Sterilization. Introduced by the United Farmers of Alberta in 1928, this act wasn't repealed until 1972, after 4725 Alberta women and men were sterilized—most without either their consent or their knowledge.

Murphy believed in the genetic power of white, Anglo-Saxon Christians. These eugenicists were also concerned that physical or mental challenges or deficiencies could be inherited by the next generation.

Indeed, Canadian immigrants were referred to as "stock," in much the same manner as cows and horses. Author Aritha van Herk, in her book, *Mavericks*, points out that "Murphy argued for sterilization as a means to control the 'degradation' of good Canadian stock."

The Famous Five certainly deserve recognition for advancing women's rights. Yet those monumental accomplishments remain tainted by the racism that was common to the age. The next stage of equality, for persons of all races and religions, was an even mightier battle for a later age.

The UFA became more active politically and in 1921 defeated the Liberals. As a government, the UFA was rather cautious, focusing on advances in education and health care. Yet it was the staid UFA that eventually produced both Alberta's greatest victory and its most notorious political scandal.

The UFA's second premier was John Edward Brownlee, the son of an Ontario merchant and devout Methodist teacher, who moved to Alberta in 1909. He became the UFA's first Attorney General in 1921 and premier in 1925. Like many transplanted Ontarians, Brownlee was a spirited Albertan who resented the province's second class status in Confederation. He lobbied tirelessly for Alberta ownership of natural resources, a right always enjoyed by the founding provinces.

From the beginning, when Ottawa created two new western provinces in Alberta and Saskatchewan in 1905, the federal government kept the natural resources for itself. This deprivation, unprecedented in the British Empire, persisted for 25 years. In Alberta it meant there was too little money to pay for the province's administration. The constant plea for more Ottawa subsidies created both anger and a passionate will in Alberta governments to become self-reliant. When oil was discovered at Turner Valley in 1914, the joy was muted, as the well-oiled federal machine proved to be aptly named.

Premier of Alberta John Brownlee negotiated the transfer of control over Alberta's natural resources (Glenbow Archives/NA-145-11).

Premier Brownlee made it his mission to correct the injustice, and he finally won his victory in 1929, with the signing of an historic transfer agreement. Parliament formally assented to the Natural Resources Transfer Act on April 3, 1930.

That one piece of legislation laid the foundation for Alberta's future prosperity, and also for some of its greatest battles, as when the federal government later tried in various ways to control the pricing, trade and revenues from Alberta's oil and gas resources. The Transfer Act was a tremendous legacy for a premier, but the unfortunate Brownlee would be remembered less for this achievement than for the scandal that ended his career.

In July 1933, Brownlee took a longtime friend, Vivian MacMillan, for a ride in his automobile. She was a clerk in the Attorney General's office who was engaged to a man named John Caldwell. Brownlee noticed that his car was being followed, and later discovered that the men in the pursuing vehicle were Caldwell

During the Depression the Social Credit party promised every Albertan $25 per month. After the province defaulted on a bond in 1936, the government introduced a new monetary system and "funny money" certificates were issued. The Supreme Court ruled that this attempt to create currency infringed on federal responsibilities and outlawed the scheme (Glenbow Archives/NA2377-1).

"Bible Bill" Aberhart led the Social Credit party to a landslide victory in the 1935 provincial election (Provincial Archives of Alberta/A2043).

and Neil MacLean, who would become Vivian MacMillan's lawyer.

Two months later, the MacMillan family sued Brownlee for seduction under the Alberta Seduction Act, seeking $10,000 in damages for Vivian and $5,000 for her father. Brownlee countersued, claiming the story had been concocted for gain. In a strait-laced era, the case became a tremendous scandal, especially when a jury found Brownlee guilty of seduction in 1934. A judge overturned that decision, but after many maneuvers and appeals through Canada's Supreme Court all the way to the British Privy Council, Brownlee finally lost in 1940. His political career had ended in shame six years earlier, but to this day it remains far from clear that Brownlee had actually seduced Vivian MacMillan.

By the time Brownlee left, the Great Depression was at its nadir and voters were fed up. In 1935, William "Bible Bill" Aberhart and his Social Credit movement took the reins of power. Social Credit would last for 36 years, evolving from its original dogmatic, religious base into a wider pragmatism, until Peter Lougheed's revitalized Progressive Conservative Party finally chased it from office in 1971.

Social Credit had one thing in common with the UFA—it was primarily rural and agrarian. Rural Alberta was the main source of protest, and it spawned not just the two provincial parties but the Progressives and the Co-operative Commonwealth Federation. This was an incredibly fertile period for the agrarian populism that has always been strong in Alberta. It persists in modern times in the formation of the Reform Party, the Canadian Alliance, and the merged and revived Conservative Party.

Populist parties are like oil wells, tapping reserves of pent-up political energy. Every generation or so they release the anger of Canadians in a geyser of frustration directed mainly at the country's political and economic elites, the people who claim to know best. Populism is always angry, often negative, and never friendly to the status quo, but it is ultimately useful because it forces politicians to get back in touch with the people. No other province comes close to Alberta's record of generating these prairie political tornadoes.

Yet populism can descend into the dark side, too. Religion and populism can become the twins of intolerance if fused together in ignorance and anger. The historical record is very clear about Social

Credit's anti-Semitism, which was nominally purged by Premier Ernest Manning after World War II, and in its eugenics legislation, which was not repealed until 1971.

The federal Social Credit record was just as scurrilous, with Holocaust denier Jim Keegstra elected as a second vice-president of the national party. In 1985, David Bercuson and Douglas Wertheimer wrote in *A Trust Betrayed*: "There is not much left of the federal Social Credit Party in Canada or in Alberta today, but what there is seems to be as anti-Semitic as Douglas Social Credit ever was."

Many populist leaders have been spirited into the political arena through a belief that their mission is divine and inspired by God. As Progressive politician Reverend William Irvine of Calgary wrote in 1920 in *The Farmers in Politics*: "The line between the sacred and the secular is being rubbed out." The same tendency persists today in American politics, with the approval of many like-minded people in Canada.

Premier Ernest Manning speaking at the 1968 leadership convention at which his successor Harry Strom was chosen (Provincial Archives of Alberta/J280-4).

But it was "Bible Bill" Aberhart who took his political calling to a whole new level on his radio program, Back to the Bible Hour, where his nasal voice and booming bombast brought religious revivalism right into the living room. Even before he was elected in the deep Depression of 1935, Aberhart had converted his political successor.

"I picked up this broadcast from Calgary that Mr. Aberhart started that fall of 1925. That was responsible for changing the whole course of my life," Ernest Manning stated in a 1982 archival interview. He became a devoted political and religious disciple of Aberhart, eventually bringing his own Bible program to the radio waves.

Aberhart vowed to fight modernism through his Social Credit movement, which promised every Albertan $25 a month in a credit dividend. He openly railed against Ottawa by passing numerous laws to take Alberta out of the national monetary system. The Alberta Treasury Branches, the only provincial depositor's bank in the country, still stands as a legacy of that period.

Aberhart also passed the Accurate News and Information Act, which commanded every newspaper to publish verbatim any statement by the chairman of the Social Credit Board. Newspapers were also told to provide, when requested, all sources for articles, and threatened with fines and closure if they refused. The *Edmonton Journal* ultimately won a Pulitzer Prize for standing up to this

Alberta and its Politics—From Prophesy to Progress

The "Exit" sign was prophetic, as Harry Strom was unable to fill Manning's shoes and stave off the challenge of the energetic Peter Lougheed (Provincial Archives of Alberta/J947-3).

brazen attack on free speech and backing one of its reporters, Don Brown. Brown had been arrested and tried on the floor of the legislature for misquoting a Social Credit politician. Brown avoided going to jail only when public outrage forced the government to commute his sentence.

Even those sympathetic to Social Credit found Aberhart to be, in the words of writer John Barr, "a strong leader but a poor follower, a confident pilot but a fractious, quarrelsome and sometimes rebellious crew member." He remained popular because many Albertans agreed with his religious convictions and admired his refusal to be cowed by Ottawa.

When Aberhart died in 1943, the new premier, Ernest Manning, worked to bring the party into the modern era through less internecine strife and better connection with the voters. Manning was a follower of Aberhart and had attended his Prophetic Bible Institute in Calgary, but his personal style was more moderate and conciliatory. Manning oversaw many advances in public education, health care and transportation, while always protecting Alberta's interests on the national scene. Manning's tenure took him into the heart of the swinging sixties, and he retired in 1968, just as the Beatles were belting out "A Hard Day's Night."

The Social Credit flame, already flickering, soon fizzled under Manning's successor, veteran cabinet minister Harry Strom. The Socred movement was disintegrating under the pressure of modern times. Strom's party became guilty of the only sin that ever drives Alberta governments from office—it grew unresponsive and resistant to change. Many Socred ministers now lectured rather than listened, and they paid the price on August 30, 1971, when Peter Lougheed's Conservative Party drove them from office.

Lougheed represented an Alberta that was becoming more urban and sophisticated. Harvard educated, he was a lawyer with a powerful sense of Alberta's interests but no fear of the outside world. Indeed, Lougheed saw only opportunity both within Canada and beyond its borders. When the federal Conservative government of Brian Mulroney fought for the Free Trade Agreement with the United States, Lougheed was his most ardent backer among the premiers.

Always an economic activist, Lougheed argued vigorously against any attempt to control oil prices within Canada. His first battles in the early 1970s were fought with Ontario Premier Bill Davis, also a

Conservative, but Lougheed always felt that the real opponent was the federal Liberal government of Pierre Trudeau. The oil-pricing wars of the early 1980s, after the creation of the National Energy Program, became a national constitutional crisis. Alberta cut production and invested heavily in the industry in order to reinforce its negotiating position with Ottawa. In a round of tense meetings, Lougheed's energy minister, Merv Leitch, proved himself a match for his aggressive federal counterpart, Marc Lalonde. Better prepared, more resourceful and dealing from a position of strength, the Albertans eventually forced a compromise agreement. The province didn't win all its points, but it forced Ottawa to retreat. In later years, the National Energy Program was dismantled by the Mulroney government after falling oil prices made it largely irrelevant.

Lieutenant Governor Grant MacEwan looks on as Peter Lougheed is sworn in as Alberta's tenth premier on September 11, 1971 (Provincial Archives of Alberta/J712-2).

Politics and Ethnicity

Raj Chahal

The Canadian Prairies have always been the land of opportunity, the place where new settlers could build upon their dreams. At the turn of the last century immigrants from Europe crossed the ocean and the continent to start new lives. And today immigrants from other countries such as China, India, and the Philippines settle in Alberta to pursue their dreams.

Alberta, like Canada at large, has undergone significant changes to its ethnic make-up over the last quarter century. Not only have Alberta's cultural and economic landscapes been shaped by successive waves of immigration, but the face of its politics has changed dramatically too. We can see this in the participation in public life of people of many different cultural backgrounds.

In Alberta, one need only look at Rahim Jaffer and Deepak Obhrai—Members of Parliament for Alberta ridings who are of South Asian descent and who were born in Africa. As well, other Alberta Members of Parliament are immigrants—John Williams was born in Scotland, and a number of members were born in the United States.

At the provincial level the legislature includes the Minister of Community Development, Gary Mar, of Chinese heritage, Moe Amery

Dr. Raj Pannu, leader of Alberta's New Democratic Party from 2000 to 2004, was twice named one of Alberta's 50 Most Influential People by *Alberta Venture* magazine (NDP).

Alberta and its Politics—From Prophesy to Progress

Rahim Jaffer, MP for Edmonton–Strathcona since 1997, immigrated with his family to Canada to escape persecution in Uganda. Here he mentors Canadian Alliance interns in 2002 (Photograph by Steve Barrett, Conservative Party of Canada).

from Lebanon, Shiraz Shariff from Uganda, Bharat Agnihotri and Dr. Raj Pannu from India, and Wayne Cao and Hung Pham, who are from Vietnam. The late Harry Sohal was one of the first visible minorities to be elected to the legislature and George Ho Lam served as an alderman in Calgary over 30 years ago. As well, there is the Honourable Norman L. Kwong—the first person of Chinese heritage to serve as Lieutenant Governor in Alberta.

Another sign of the importance of ethnic diversity in Alberta is evident in Calgary's six sister cities: Quebec City; Jaipur, India; Daqing, China; Naucalpan, Mexico; Daejeon, Korea; and Phoenix, Arizona. Edmonton has two sister cities: Harbin, China and Nashville, Tennessee.

Alberta's diversity and its generosity of spirit in accepting individuals from all parts of the world, as represented by its elected officials, will serve it well as it develops its relations with the rest of the world.

Ottawa has never since challenged Alberta with such damaging policies as the National Energy Program. Many experts agree that Alberta's economy is now so powerful that hostile measures would hurt not just the province, but the whole country.

Lougheed aggressively promoted economic expansion within Alberta, pressing for oil sands development and other industrial growth. He offended arch conservatives by buying Pacific Western Airlines on the grounds that Air Canada's policies, controlled in central Canada, were inimical to western economic development.

In a reprise of their photo of the "gang of six" from the election of 1967, Lougheed leads his cabinet down the steps of the legislature after their 1975 victory (Provincial Archives of Alberta/J1810-1).

Lougheed was always acutely sensitive to national resentment of Alberta's growing oil wealth. Through the new Heritage Savings Trust Fund, Alberta began to make loans to other provinces at interest rates well below the market.

The constitutional talks of the early 1980s were at least as sensitive and divisive as the oil crisis; and once again, Alberta made a major contribution. At a crucial moment, the province proposed the constitutional amending formula that was accepted by all but Quebec, and stands today. Lougheed's deputy minister of Federal and Intergovernmental Affairs, Peter Meekison, is generally credited with writing it under the premier's supervision.

Lougheed and his nemesis, Pierre Trudeau, attend a 1977 news conference (CP Archives).

Lougheed always refused to get involved in any federal issue without ensuring that Alberta was a major contributor. He was determined to show that the province, while protecting its resources, was a full and creative partner in Canada. This task was always difficult, both at home and in the country at large. More than any premier, Lougheed had to appear tough to Albertans and conciliatory to the rest of Canada. He walked that swaying tightrope without a major slip until his retirement in 1985.

Lougheed was followed by Don Getty, a former Edmonton Eskimos quarterback who had been elected to the legislature with a small group of Conservative MLAs in 1967. Getty also had a strong sense of Alberta's interests and was at his best in federal-provincial meetings. He once saved a crucial session from collapsing when he physically blocked the Newfoundland Premier, Clyde Wells, from leaving the room. Getty played an integral role in developing the Free Trade deal and he was a major player in two failed constitutional deals, the Meech Lake Accord and the Charlottetown Accord.

Within Alberta, Getty signed the first agreement in Canada allowing Métis self-government. His government also pumped money into several industrial ventures that went sour when the economy softened. Getty was fated to govern in a time of declining revenues after oil prices plunged in 1986. The result was escalating annual budget deficits that topped $2 billion. Getty began to deal with the deficits, but there was widespread discontent both within the Conservative party and among the voters. Getty heard the message and announced his retirement in 1992.

Lougheed was a major spokesman for the West and a champion of provincial rights (Library and Archives Canada/PA-182412).

That set the scene for Ralph Klein, the former Calgary mayor who had served as environment minister in Getty's government. In a free-for-all party leadership race, Klein eventually faced off against Nancy Betkowski (now MacBeth), handily winning a runoff ballot.

Famous Five for Tomorrow
Sydney Sharpe

Marilyn Buffalo is a powerhouse who brings Aboriginal issues into the mainstream while also challenging traditional male roles. Her life has been dedicated to human rights as well as raising her own family as a single parent. She has been president of the Native Women's Association of Canada and blazed a trail by running for National Chief of the Assembly of First Nations. Of her 30 years of community activism, she said: "You get to meet varied, assorted people from different nations and backgrounds and, in the end, you find out we're really not that different."

Deborah Grey was a formidable opposition MP, first for the Reform Party, then the Canadian Alliance and finally the Conservative Party. Armed with a bold wit and a refusal to discard her effervescent persona in the face of indifference and outright hostility, Grey persevered.

When a man she was sitting beside on a plane asked her what she did, Grey told him that she was an MP. He said: "Oh, you work for an MP. That must be interesting." Grey replied: "No. I *am* the MP, but I do have a secretary and his name is Robert."

Elaine McCoy is an environmentalist who has devoted her working life to social justice issues. In 2005, she was appointed Senator by Prime Minister Paul Martin. She had been a provincial cabinet minister under Conservative Premier Don Getty and had run unsuccessfully for the leadership of the provincial Tory party. As a cabinet minister, McCoy referred to herself as "an advocate for women."

"Women politicians do make a difference. If more of us take seats in the legislature, at the cabinet table and in the top ranks of the public service, then gradually issues of concern to half the human race will no longer be ghettoized as 'women's issues.'"

Anne McLellan rose quickly as a Liberal superstar, from law professor and assistant dean at the University of Alberta. She became an adept Resources Minister in Prime Minister Jean Chrétien's cabinet, winning over the hard-nosed oil patch with her tenacity and willingness to learn.

Known as Landslide Anne for her slim election victories in Edmonton, she nonetheless became an astute Deputy Prime Minister under Paul Martin. "I feel a tremendous onus to do the best I can because it's also women I'm representing," says McLellan.

Frances Wright brought the Famous Five statues to parliament hill, an honour previously reserved for former prime ministers, monarchs and the fathers of confederation. Wright's achievement finally toasts the mothers of confederation as the Famous Five raise their teacups in respect. Wright's tireless campaign raised awareness, money and ultimately the images of five amazing Alberta women who were instrumental in women being recognized as persons.

"This monument symbolizes one of the most important democratic achievements by Canadians for Canadians. It will recognize the role women have played in building Canada and remind us how we became the country we are today."

Klein quickly established himself as one of the most single-minded and original political leaders Alberta had ever seen. When the public rebelled against high pensions for MLAs, he simply abolished the pension plan. The polls reversed overnight and he handily won his first majority in 1993. Driven by a fundamental distrust of the activist policies of the Lougheed era, Klein immediately embarked on the most aggressive cost-cutting measures in Canadian history. He slashed programs, reduced funding to schools and hospitals, privatized services, and won agreement from public servants to take a five per cent pay cut. Klein's measures were often harsh and led to labour unrest in education and health care; but he remained popular with a large proportion of the electorate. Much of Canada was startled by the actions of a politician who was performing much of the difficult cost cutting that they had avoided. Klein became a role model for other premiers whose provinces faced similar deficits, such as Mike Harris in Ontario. By July 2004, aided by soaring oil prices, Klein could

Joe Clark is one of only two prime ministers to come from the prairie west. The other was Saskatchewan's John Diefenbaker. (Provincial Archives of Alberta/J2456).

announce that Alberta would be completely free of deficit and debt by its centennial year.

During much of Klein's era, Alberta has been blessed by booming prosperity and high energy prices. Combined with the absence of debt, this gives the province economic opportunity unmatched in North America. Alberta has become a magnet for people, companies and capital from around the country. Politicians all over the province face the enviable challenge of managing this unprecedented growth. Klein's government is responding by reinvesting money—surplus cash, not borrowed funds—back into health care and education.

Through prosperity and the crushing Depression, from a rural base or an urban one, Alberta governments of all parties have shared key similarities. They are original and tough-minded. They develop practical responses to political problems and dress them up in partisan rhetoric. They protect both Alberta's national interests and its local sacred cows. When the debt seemed out of control, no government ever seriously contemplated a provincial sales tax, knowing that would spell early political death.

The past decade has brought a fundamental change in provincial psychology. Alberta has become so prosperous and powerful that federal plans don't seem quite so significant or dangerous any more. Ottawa has become less relevant, even as many Albertans start to feel more secure within Canada.

"Alberta is that sweet spot where geology meets geography which meets character," says Jim Dinning, former minister under both Peter Lougheed and Ralph Klein.

"When they designed the boundaries of this province, there was the richness of our resources, the natural bounty of our mountains and our clean water, as well as very productive flat land where you can grow almost anything. Then you throw in the character of the men and women who have chosen to live here. Mostly, people come here by choice—on purpose, with purpose. You mix all that character and bounty in a bubbling cauldron and there is nothing that we can't do when we set our minds to something. We can do almost anything."

"Albertans have a boundless desire and capacity to be great Canadians. There is a love of this country because so many people have moved from their home to Alberta by choice and made Alberta their home. The links across the country are strong—forget Ottawa,

Alberta's first legislative proceedings on March 15, 1906, were relegated to Edmonton's Thistle Roller and Ice Rink near Jasper Avenue until construction of the new Legislature Building was completed in September 1912 (Provincial Archives of Alberta/B3387).

someone always wants a fight with Ottawa—so we still have the desire to reach out. We can't build something on the politics of alienation. Albertans have moved on."

That is the political spirit that carries Alberta into its second century with less swagger but more vision and imagination. The tired stereotype of the redneck Alberta trucker or cowboy is as far from today's reality as William Aberhart's blasts of intolerance during the darkest days of the Depression.

Albertans now can see a future where we can lead rather than struggle to survive.

American designer Allan Merrick Jeffers designed Alberta's legislature building in the Beaux Arts fashion commonly associated with government buildings in the United States, an architectural style consisting of massive columns and domes rising above spacious rotundas (Glenbow Archives/NC-6-1663) .

Alberta and its Politics—From Prophesy to Progress

2 Alberta in Confederation: Thinking Outside the Box

ROGER GIBBINS AND HEATHER BALA EDWARDS

Albertans traditionally have defined themselves politically as far removed from a distant federal government and national political community. A complex and sometimes abrasive relationship with this external political world has shaped Alberta's political culture, its "state of mind." As a consequence, Albertans have seen themselves, and indeed have been seen by others, as outsiders in Confederation. In the process, the rough coal of regional discontent has hardened, and has been polished over the years to a gem-like sparkle.

Albertans have not been content to maintain the status quo; they have tried to "come in from the cold." The traditional viewpoint of existing outside the mainstream could be set aside if Albertans would define their province on its own terms. Alberta, as it enters its second century, could lead by example rather than constructing more walls between Alberta and the larger Canadian community.

The cowboy outsider taming the wild frontier is an image of themselves that many Albertans nurture (Glenbow Archives/NA-777-14).

Outsiders in Confederation

Alberta's outsider status is deeply embedded in the province's political culture. The basic framework of Canadian political life, laid down well before Alberta's creation in 1905, came under almost immediate critical attack within the new province. However, the agrarian radicals and American populists who formed the United Farmers of Alberta governments (1921–1935) failed to find a sympathetic national audience, and Alberta was offside from the get-go. In federal elections throughout the 1920s and early 1930s, Albertans supported the radical arm of the Progressive Party of Canada, while the party's less radical supporters in other provinces were successfully wooed back into the mainstream national tent by Liberal prime minister William Lyon Mackenzie King. When William Aberhart's Social Credit Party won the 1935 provincial election, Alberta voters began to send Social Credit MPs to Ottawa, emissaries who were isolated within Parliament and in turn further isolated the province. In federal elections running from 1935 to 1957, before John Diefenbaker's Progressive Conservative landslide in 1958 transformed the political landscape, 70.5% of Alberta MPs were Social Crediters. Thus Albertans celebrated their golden jubilee in 1955 by marching to their own political drum, Canada's one-province band.

If other Canadians had any impressions at all of Alberta during this time, they were impressions shaped by the dust bowls of the Great Depression. In the years following the Second World War, Alberta perched precariously on the margins of national political and economic life. Being "outside the tent" was a stark reality, not just an internal perception. It would take oil wealth, and more specifically the OPEC-induced price increases in the 1970s, to bring Alberta onto the national stage. The OPEC signal was clear—Alberta could no longer be ignored, and a new breed of provincial politicians led by Premier Peter Lougheed was determined that this would not happen. The outsider was knocking at the country's door, with oil money jingling in its jeans and a chip on its shoulder.

Alberta's ongoing outsider status is most evident in federal elections, where Albertans have an uncanny knack for picking the losing side. True, Albertans picked the winner in 1958 as they and the rest of the country swept John Diefenbaker into office, but then Albertans stayed in the Conservative tent for the rest of the

Great Depression. Although the Depression of the 1930s was a calamity throughout Canada, the prairie provinces were hit particularly hard. Whereas personal incomes in Ontario declined by 44% between 1929 and 1933, they fell by 49% in Manitoba, 61% in Alberta and 71% in Saskatchewan. As western Canadian historian James Gray notes, "[the Depression] was a decade that destroyed men's faith in themselves, mocked their talents and skills, blighted their initiative, and subverted their dedication to the cultivation of their land. It shattered the morale of our inland empire, replaced a whole people's proud search for success with a dispirited search for security." It is not surprising that the Depression experience still ripples through Alberta's political culture.

**Alberta in Confederation:
Thinking Outside the Box**

century—other than a brief flirtation with the Trudeau Liberals in 1968—while the Liberals rebounded elsewhere. From time to time, the rest of the country also supported the Conservatives and thus Albertans ended up, willy-nilly, on the winning side, but they were primarily out of step as Pierre Trudeau, Jean Chrétien and Paul Martin rolled up Liberal wins. When Albertans finally abandoned the Progressive Conservatives in 1993, along with the rest of the country, it was for the Reform Party of Canada, then the Canadian Alliance, and then the new Conservative party. To some extent, therefore, Alberta's outsider status has been self-inflicted.

Now admittedly, others can also lay claim to outsider status. Aboriginal peoples have in many respects been cast as outsiders on their own land, and Quebec, with its francophone majority and distinct society, has a self-evident case for outsider status. When it comes to national politics, however, Albertans have a stronger claim than Quebec to the outsider crown. Wilfrid Laurier, Louis St. Laurent, Pierre Trudeau, Brian Mulroney, Jean Chrétien and now Paul Martin illustrate the national success of Quebec political leaders. Indeed, Quebecers have had a lock on the prime minister's office since 1968, one broken for only a few months at a time by Joe Clark, John Turner and Kim Campbell. Clark's brief tenure was only a blip in the dominance of national leadership exercised by central Canadians Trudeau, Mulroney, Chrétien and Martin.

Outsider status is worn with pride by many Albertans, who see themselves as victims of Confederation. Critics of the federal system point to the fact that Alberta did not receive control of Crown lands until the Natural Resources Transfer Act of 1931, and to a host of national policy decisions that set the province apart. In this context, the 1980 National Energy Program was a defining event in the evolution of Alberta's political culture. The outsider label, moreover, is not just self-perception; Canadians living elsewhere in the country often see Alberta as a fat-cat province frequently at odds with mainstream Canadian values. Thus Albertans, unlike the Canadian norm, are seen as being opposed to gun control, the Kyoto Accord on climate change, and same-sex marriage. Even Alberta's quixotic search for Senate reform isolates the province from the rest. Although outsider status may be a badge of honour within the province, to other Canadians it delivers a mixed message.

Yet here is the paradox and dilemma: if Albertans have been

Confederation's outsiders, they have also been outsiders wanting to come in from the cold, to be part of and perhaps even to lead the national mainstream. The big question facing Albertans, at least until recently, has been how to come in from the cold, and how to do it on their own terms.

The West Wants In

When the Reform Party of Canada was created in the mid-1980s, its founding leader was Preston Manning, son of former Alberta premier Ernest Manning. Not coincidentally, Reform's mantra, "the West wants in," neatly captured the over-arching theme of Alberta's approach to federal politics. The desire to be an integral part of the national community has run through the province's history from the first days of agrarian settlement to Alberta's turbulent relationship with the federal government in the early years of the 21st century. However, while Albertans have wanted a stronger voice in federal politics, their terms for doing so have had little appeal outside the province, thus creating an enduring tension between Alberta and the national political community.

Although Albertans have not designed an explicit collective strategy for influencing the national agenda, a number of implicit strategies can be extracted from the province's first century in Confederation. What they share in common is a lack of success.

Population Growth

Albertans see their province as a land of unbounded growth and opportunity, and in-migration from other provinces supports the perception that the country is tipped east to west, with families and economic opportunities running downhill into Alberta (and even further downhill into B.C., although this is less readily acknowledged). However, the magnitude of demographic change is often exaggerated in popular perceptions. Yes, Alberta is growing, but its share of the national population has increased only modestly from 7.5% in 1971 to 9.9% in 2001. And yes, some other regions are in relative decline, most notably Atlantic Canada (7.6% of the national population in 2001 compared to 9.5% in 1971) and Quebec (down from 27.9% in 1971 to 24.1% in 2001). At the same time, Ontario has increased its share of the national population, from 35.7% in 1971 to 38.0% in 2001. Demographic transformation is a gradual process at

"Most of our parents and grandparents...went out and broke the land, and we inherited a lot of their attitudes. We like frugality; we believe in cooperation; we believe in public health care—a whole lot of things this region has contributed to Canada.... We believe in a populist sort of democracy where everybody is equal; we don't look for elites to accommodate. This is one of the reasons western Canada is very special: we've tried to democratize Canada, whether it's the Senate or whatever, and we will continue to try to democratize Canada." David Kilgour, Independent MP for Edmonton Southwest.

Alberta in Confederation:
Thinking Outside the Box

In 1930, Alberta finally won control over its natural resources. Prime Minister William Lyon Mackenzie King (centre) and UFA Premier Brownlee (to his left) signed an agreement allowing the province to collect revenue from oil and gas royalties (Provincial Archives of Alberta/A10924).

best, and thus while Albertans try to bend the federation to their own political vision, their province remains a relatively small tail trying to shake a much larger and not overly amiable Canadian dog.

Economic Power

From the outside, Albertans appear to be arguing that their province should pack more weight than its population alone would justify, that money should count when population alone is insufficient to command national attention and respect. To some extent, this perception is accurate. Over the past decade, Alberta has been Canada's most prosperous province, and there is little likelihood that its run of good fortune will end soon. Alberta is awash in energy resources—conventional oil and natural gas, the oilsands, coal and coal bed methane—that will continue to enjoy strong continental markets for the foreseeable future. It is not surprising, therefore, that many Albertans believe that this economic capital should be able to buy political capital, that Alberta's contribution to the national economy should yield additional political leverage. Albertans are quick to point out their net contributions to other provinces through both equalization and the redistributive elements of most federal programming. Unfortunately, political history suggests that Alberta's wealth is as likely to attract external hostility as it is to be a positive source of political leverage. Confederation is a very traditional, even old-fashioned, club that looks askance at the *nouveaux riches* from the Alberta oil patch.

Regional Leadership

Albertans have compensated for their province's small population by donning the cloak of regional discontent, by equating Alberta's

Composition of the population of western Canada by province in 2001:		
British Columbia	4,015,266	43.5%
Alberta	3,056,739	33.1%
Saskatchewan	1,000,134	10.8%
Manitoba	1,151,285	12.5%

interests with those of western Canada, now 30% of the national population. Although only one-third of the regional population lives in Alberta, Albertans tend to see the West as Alberta writ large. Provincial politicians, commentators and academics happily speak on behalf of the broader regional community, often to the irritation of British Columbia, Saskatchewan and Manitoba. There is just a touch of regional imperialism in the Alberta political style.

Alberta's self-proclaimed role as regional voice has been re-inforced by energy wealth, long-serving premiers enjoying massive electoral support, and British Columbia's erratic behavior on the national stage. Until recently, B.C. punched well below its demo-graphic weight in national politics, thereby allowing Alberta leaders by default to speak for the West. In the years ahead, however, this regional voice will be increasingly challenged by more assertive political leadership from the other western provinces. It is also inter-esting to note that the federal government now refers to "British Columbia and the West," thus placing Alberta within the smaller prairie community rather than within the larger West. Alberta's regional cloak may be stripped from its shoulders.

Rebuilding the National Party System

Albertans have been particularly inept or stubborn with respect to using the national party system as a means of gaining a national voice. As noted above, Albertans routinely end up on the losing side of federal elections; their steadfast support of the Conservative Party, and variations thereof, has put them at odds with the Liberal governments that have dominated the national landscape. Albertans have contributed far more to the opposition benches in the House of Commons than they have to the federal cabinet. In purely partisan terms, we have been outsiders *par excellence*. Moreover, even when Albertans have been inside the federal tent, as they were during the Mulroney governments from 1984 to 1993, the experience has not

| **Alberta in Confederation: Thinking Outside the Box**

been all that positive; the Alberta-based Reform Party came into existence in the mid-1980s when Alberta enjoyed particularly strong representation in the Mulroney cabinet.

Instead of working within the conventional partisan arena, Albertans, it would seem, will go to any lengths to avoid jumping aboard the Liberal bandwagons that have routinely rolled across the national political landscape. Here it is also important to note the lessons that many drew from the past four federal elections. In each case, an Alberta-led, western Canadian party—first Reform in 1993 and 1997, then the Canadian Alliance in 2000, and finally the new Conservatives in 2004—failed to make significant headway outside the West, and support from the West alone was not enough to win national office. (Stephen Harper came agonizingly close in 2004, but spooked the Ontario electorate in the last few days of the campaign by returning to "the West wants in" theme.) Wave after wave of regional protest has broken apart against the rock of Ontario. The electorate's message, at least as interpreted by the winning Liberals and the national media, seemed to be that there is a fundamental incongruity between western Canadian values—particularly Alberta values as manifested in Preston Manning, Stockwell Day and Stephen Harper—and mainstream Canadian values lodged in Ontario. Albertans have tried to remake the national party system in their own image, but have lacked sufficient political weight to do so. Failure has further reinforced Alberta's outsider role in Confederation.

Institutional Reform

For generations, Albertans have argued that traditional parliamentary institutions fail to reflect adequately regional interests and aspirations. The existing norms of Parliamentary democracy, with tight party discipline and cabinet solidarity, stifle the expression of regional interests, and place political power firmly in the hands of the Ontario and Quebec electorates. Thus Albertans have been leading advocates for parliamentary reform, and for Senate reform in particular. The reform impulse goes back to the early 1920s, continued under Social Credit governments from 1935 to 1971, and then rose again with Alberta's enthusiastic support for the Reform Party of Canada and its successors. It is important to note, however, that this reform impulse is primarily directed outwards, to Ottawa, the national parties, and the parliamentary system. Liberal hegemony in Ottawa is definitely a problem for Albertans, whereas an even more powerful Conservative hegemony in Edmonton is not seen as a threat to democratic values or practice.

By far the most popular institutional remedy for Alberta's outsider status is Senate reform, which speaks directly to "the West wants in." A reformed Senate would provide, or at least Albertans believe it would provide, a more effective regional voice within the national government. It would also provide a regional check on the powers of the House of Commons, and thus the cabinet, institutions inevitably dominated by the two central Canadian provinces. Furthermore, the notion of a Senate with equal representation from all provinces speaks directly to the central role that equality plays in the Alberta political culture, and opposition to a special constitutional status for Quebec. Finally, having Senators elected by the people rather than appointed by a distant prime minister has great appeal to Albertans (and should have appeal to all democrats, we would argue parenthetically). However, Alberta has not been successful in selling its case to the country. Although the province produced the first and only elected Senator, Stan Waters, in the interregnum between the introduction of the Meech Lake Accord in 1987 and its collapse in 1990, the precedent has not been picked up. Despite two Senate "selections" in 1997 and 2004, Senators continue to be appointed by the prime minister with little consultation with the government or people of Alberta.

The failure to advance Senate reform points to a broader conclusion: none of the Alberta strategies has been particularly successful. In a sense, Albertans have been banging their heads against a stump, lacking as they do the necessary political or demographic clout to drive systemic change. Albertans have argued that institutional reform is the only secure route to political inclusion, and hence the quest for Senate reform. Unfortunately, the Alberta cause has been largely dismissed outside the province, thereby reinforcing the internal perception that the deck is stacked, the game is fixed. The brutal reality is that Alberta being "in" is not seen as essential to national unity, whereas the farther Quebec is "out," the greater the wooing by the Canadian community.

It is important to note in this context that Alberta governments, like all provincial governments, have used discontent with Ottawa

In a 2004 survey conducted by the Canada West Foundation, 86.9% of 800 Alberta respondents agreed that "Canada should replace the existing Senate with an elected Senate with equal representation from each province." The level of agreement in Alberta was only slightly higher than for similar size samples in British Columbia (85.0%), Saskatchewan (81.3%) and Manitoba (78.1%). When 800 Ontario respondents were presented with the same statement, 72.0% agreed.

as a strategic resource. (This strategy is routine to the point of tedium in Quebec, is increasingly used by Ontario, and led the Premier of Newfoundland and Labrador to remove Canadian flags from provincial buildings in early 2005.) It is difficult for opposition parties in Alberta to find their footing in political discourse dominated by "them versus us." To side with "us" makes opposition parties seem irrelevant, while to side with "them" borders on treason. Unfortunately, just as governing parties in Alberta have used angst with the national government as a club on opposition parties within the province, so too have the federal Liberals used negative Alberta stereotypes as a strategic resource. Thus opposition opponents such as Preston Manning, Stockwell Day and Stephen Harper can be attacked for not reflecting mainstream Canadian values. How could they, runs the implicit messaging, when they come from Alberta? Thus we have the troubling, albeit understandable, situation where the federal Liberals attack Alberta and the provincial Conservatives attack Ottawa, to their mutual advantage. Whether the interests of either Alberta or Canada are well served in the process is doubtful.

Second Century Strategies

So, where do we stand today in terms of "the West wants in?" Although hard empirical evidence is difficult to secure, we would argue that the mantra "the West wants in" is losing much of its strength. Yelling into the abyss, and getting not even a faint echo in response has less and less appeal. But, if "the West wants in" is losing its appeal, what are the alternative strategies?

Firewalls and Decentralization

Some have reacted by abandoning "the West wants in" in favour of the firewall strategy; if we can't influence Ottawa, maybe we can minimize Ottawa's influence in Alberta. The advocates of an Alberta "firewall" argue that Alberta should follow a Quebec-based strategy and maximize the exercise of its own constitutional space by, for example, creating a provincial police force to replace the RCMP, creating an Alberta pension plan analogous to the Quebec pension plan, and perhaps withdrawing from the Canada Health Act.

Bob Edwards: The Humorous Side of Alberta Politics

Sydney Sharpe

Bob Edwards (1864–1922) was famous for his sharp eye, irreverent wit and wicked wordplay, all of which he used brilliantly in his newspaper, the *Calgary Eye Opener*. He poked fun at the arrogance and zaniness of the times and his favorite targets were fast-talking politicians and businessmen. He championed women's right to vote, as well as the temperance movement, despite, or maybe because of, his own battle with the bottle. Edwards liked to say that his role was to "comfort the afflicted and afflict the comfortable."

His aphorisms resonate today.

Now I know what a statesman is; he's a dead politician. We need more statesmen. 1918

The great man of today in Canada is made up of one part achievement and nine parts printers' ink. 1910

Never trust a man whose dog has gone back on him. 1910

The things that come to the man who waits are seldom the things he waited for. 1912

By the time the average man is old enough to gratify his tastes, he hasn't any. 1915

One kind of hypocrite is the man who, after thanking the Lord for his dinner, proceeds to find fault with the cook. 1916

One trouble with being efficient is that it makes everybody hate you so. 1916

It's as easy to recall an unkind word as to draw back a bullet after firing the gun. 1916

A good man who goes wrong is just a bad man who has been found out. 1917

Prosperity never spoils men that adversity cannot crush. 1917

Too many people salt away money in the brine of other people's tears. 1917

People always laugh at the fool things you try to do until they discover you are making money out of them. 1918

Forgive your enemies, but if you have no enemies, forgive a few of your friends. 1918

It's a waste of time telling a man he is a liar. If he is, he knows it. 1918

Bob Edwards, editor of Calgary's *The Eye Opener*, used satire to expose the follies of big business, self-righteous individuals, and rigid social institutions (Glenbow Archives/NA-450-1).

As one journeys through life and the shadows begin to fall eastward, one reaches the solemn conclusion that too much of the world's wisdom is uttered and too little lived. 1918

Probably the saddest thing about Ottawa is the number of fourth-rate intellects applied to first-rate problems. 1918.

Some men spoil a good story by sticking to the facts. 1919

If it's all the same to history, it need not repeat itself any more. 1919

A girl should never marry until she is fully competent to support a husband and then she shouldn't marry that kind of man. 1920

When a man quits turning around to look at a pretty girl he is old enough, almost, for the Senate. 1920

A little learning is a dangerous thing, but a lot of ignorance is just as bad. 1921

Most of our tragedies look like comedies to the neighbors. 1921

If you want work well done, select a busy man; the other kind has no time. 1922

Many of these quotations are found in Grant MacEwan's definitive biography of Bob Edwards, called *Eye Opener Bob* (published by Institute of Applied Art, Edmonton, 1957). Grant MacEwan's own illustrious career included being Lieutenant Governor of Alberta from 1966 to 1974.

"The West wants in" strategy was true to Alberta's historical circumstances, where the power to shape the Alberta economy—tariffs, banking, inter-provincial transportation—were powers that logically rested with the national government. They could not be decentralized to provincial governments, and therefore influence within the national government—getting in—was essential if the provincial economy were to be protected. Now, however, with trade barriers all but gone (except for inter-provincial trade barriers), with transportation and financial institutions largely deregulated, Ottawa has less and less relevance. In the face of globalization, Albertans are turning more and more to the international environment rather than to the rest of Canada, and NAFTA is increasing north–south economic ties at the relative expense of east–west ties. In a more globalized environment, when many of the most pressing economic powers have migrated to international bodies such as the World Trade Organization or to international pacts such as NAFTA, there is simply not that much of interest in Ottawa to get into. Indeed,

much of Ottawa's remaining relevance comes through financial contributions to areas of provincial jurisdiction, and it is not beyond the
realm of possibility that Alberta soon will be able to say no to such
conditional federal largesse. Thus, while the Quebec strategy of
greater decentralization made little sense for generations past in
Alberta, it may make much greater sense for generations to come.

None of this should suggest, of course, that Ottawa has lost all
relevance. Although its economic clout and relevance have diminished, the federal government's impact on social programming is
steadily expanding. On balance, however, "getting into" the national
government has less utility today than it did in the past.

Waiting for Social Change to Work its Course

Another possibility is that internal transformations within the Alberta
society will lead inevitably to a rapprochement with the larger Canadian
community. For example, substantial in-migration from other
provinces, and indeed from other countries, coupled with the increased
dominance of Calgary and Edmonton on the political landscape, will
inevitably erode distinctive aspects of the Alberta political culture. In
short, we will start to think more like the rest of the country because we
will *be* more like the rest of the country, and the distinctive strains of
regional angst will fade. Albertans will be brought into the national
mainstream, even if kicking and screaming. It is tempting, therefore, for
the national government to do nothing to address regional discontent,
and to wait for social change to transform the province in a way that will
bring Alberta more and more into the national mainstream, thereby
reducing the potency of regional discontent.

In many respects this is a compelling argument, but assumptions
of inevitability have to be taken with some large grains of salt. When
Peter Lougheed became premier in 1971, this was heralded as a new
era for Alberta, one in which Alberta would abandon the isolationist
worldview of the former Social Credit governments. However,
Lougheed eventually became the point man for a more aggressive
Alberta presence on the national stage. Although he, along with
OPEC-induced increases in the price of oil, moved the province from
the Depression-induced margins of Canadian life to centre stage,
conflict with the national community increased as a consequence.
Albertans did indeed become more like the rest of Canada, but the
transformation left them even more restless within the status quo.

A second grain of salt comes from the Quebec experience during and in the wake of the Quiet Revolution of the 1960s. There is no question that the Quiet Revolution transformed Quebec in ways that made the province more similar to other parts of Canada—birth rates fell, the Catholic Church disengaged from political life, and both urbanization and industrialization proceeded with great energy. However, although Quebecers became "more like us" in so many respects, this transformation was accompanied by the dramatic growth of Quebec nationalism, and by the emergence of the Parti Québecois. While it would be wrong to assume that similarity breeds contempt, it would be equally wrong to assume that social and economic convergence necessarily breeds political convergence. It would therefore be a mistake to assume that Alberta's distinctive political culture will necessarily fade in the wake of social change within the province. Political cultures can have quite remarkable staying power, if they are able to assimilate newcomers and new social paradigms into existing cultural mores. Indeed, newcomers may be attracted to the province because they think like Albertans, and thus may reject political convergence.

Will Alberta attachments fade in the face of globalization? Perhaps, but this does not necessarily mean that they will be replaced by a stronger attachment to Canada. The very forces that challenge the utility of "thinking inside the Alberta box" also challenge the utility of the Canadian box. To simply assume that the "problem" will go away with the passage of time is a risky strategy.

The West Wants Out?

The potential threat of separation was spiked by Alberta's adherence to "the West wants in" strategy. So long as Albertans were wedded to institutional reform at the centre, to finding a more effective voice within the national political system, threats of separatism fell on largely deaf ears inside the province and on totally deaf ears outside the province. Now, with the strategy of national engagement in tatters, with any hopes of institutional reform abandoned and with western-led parties unable to win national office, the situation may change. The distance between an Alberta firewall and the advocacy of independence is much smaller than the distance between that advocacy and the desire for inclusion in the mainstream.

To date, however, polling data provides no evidence of any significant or growing public support for independence. Separatist parties exist, but they feed only at the fringe of the electorate, with no prospect of winning office. Nonetheless, we may still see a gradual disengagement from the national government, albeit stopping well short of support for an independent Alberta. In positive terms, this disengagement expresses the desire to get on with life, to look for home-grown public policies rather than relinquishing political leadership to Ottawa. At heart, though, it reflects a withdrawal from the national political community.

National Leadership by Example

In many respects, Albertans see themselves as national leaders. Alberta, for example, was able to rein in deficit spending long before most other provinces (the main exception being Saskatchewan) and, through the political threat provided by Reform, was able to give the Chrétien government the political muscle it needed to rein in federal deficits, and eventually tackle, in a modest way, the national debt. Now admittedly, many outside the province dismiss this claim to national leadership, arguing that any government with Alberta's oil wealth could eliminate the deficit and debt, and/or that on many social issues Alberta tends to lead from behind, fighting a rear-guard battle against social changes that mainstream Canada has long accepted. We would argue, however, that the opportunity for national leadership by example is real, and in fact offers the best go-forward strategy for the province.

Sitting as it does outside the tent of the national government, Alberta can be the squeaky wheel that draws attention to new ways of public policy thought and action. Albertans can afford to take the initiative, to take risks, to be the North American laboratory for creative public policy. Rather than trying to change the national government from the inside, we can lead by example from the outside.

Alberta's centennial provides the opportunity for Albertans to shift gears, to shed the outsider costume, and to define their province on their own terms. It provides an opportunity to turn inwards, not in order to turn our backs on the rest of the country, but in order to address things right at home. If Albertans can be as good as they can possibly be on their own turf, if they can harness their province's truly awesome potential, they can exercise national leadership by example. By thinking outside the box in this way, Alberta can come in from the cold as a national leader on its own terms, no longer a supplicant.

"I think western Canada very much wants to be part of the national debate. Western Canada is growing, it's strong, it's vigorous, it has solutions and ideas to bring to the table. And it wants to do that. I think its frustration is that the central government, the West believes, is utterly indifferent to the ideas and aspirations that western Canada wants to put on the table in the national debate." Diane Ablonczy, Conservative MP for Calgary Nose Hill.

3

Who are the Albertans?
The Peoples of Alberta

James H. Marsh

Head-Smashed-In Buffalo Jump, one of the richest archaeological sites on the North American plains, was declared a World Heritage site in 1981 (Glenbow Archives/NA-4035-10).

While part of the story of Alberta's peoples is a story of conflict and antipathy, the longer narrative is one of forging social harmony. The change from a time when almost everyone viewed ethnic and religious difference with suspicion to a time of far greater, if not perfect, harmony has been almost imperceptible. The keys to this change are not completely obvious, but certainly a growing respect for individual rights, and the shedding of discriminatory laws and immigration policies, as well as economic growth, have played their part. These days there is a different ambivalence. While many Albertans laud their diverse origins and multicultural nature, they are not always sure how to regard it, especially at a time when the assimilation of many groups is almost complete and when even our educational policies encourage our youth to regard themselves as "global" citizens.

Original Peoples

Alberta was a cultural mosaic even before the European settlers arrived. Nine different tribes, speaking three different languages (Dene, Algonkian and Siouan) occupied the plains, woodlands and mountains of what is now Alberta. The First Nations have been in Western Canada for at least 50 generations, the beginning of time in any estimation. More than a million ancient stone circles, or teepee rings, are scattered about the province. Head-Smashed-In Buffalo Jump (near Fort Macleod), where First Nations hunters stampeded herds over the edges of high cliffs, was in use at least 6000 years ago.

The history of the First Nations is often portrayed as static, with a snapshot from the time of contact with Europeans taken to represent the whole story, but like all cultures it evolved. The extensive trade networks, which later made the fur trade possible, were established long before the Europeans arrived.

By the time the Hudson's Bay Company began to keep records in the eighteenth century, it appears that a great displacement of the Plains people had begun. Anxious to acquire European goods, the First Nations near Hudson Bay had begun intruding into one another's hunting territories. The Cree and Assiniboine rapidly became middlemen of the fur trade. They entered into Blackfoot country, pushing interior tribes north and south. The Cree soon established their control over a wide area north of the North Saskatchewan River. The Chippewa (a Dene speaking group) also expanded their territory westward.

European fur traders reached the Athabasca and Peace River country in the first two decades of the eighteenth century. Their arrival marked the emergence of the Métis, as the traders took First Nations wives, on whom they relied for their survival: to make pemmican, fish, gather berries, repair canoes, guide, translate and carry provisions.

The Métis borrowed from both the First Nations and European cultures. Being bilingual, they became indispensable to the fur trade, acting as interpreters, traders, clerks, canoemen, packers and labourers. They used leather and furs to make their clothes in the European style and their wives learned to make the round, flat Scottish loaves of bread, or bannock. Most important, they developed a new means of transportation, the Red River cart. These

Crowfoot

Crowfoot was born a Blood in 1830 along the Belly River. He earned his prestigious name *Isapo-muxika* (Crow Indians' Big Foot) from an act of bravery during an attack on a Crow camp. Crowfoot had a keen intelligence and his awareness of the bleak future his people faced, with the disappearance of the buffalo, led him to treaty negotiations. Despite his tragic life, he remained a man of great dignity and compassion.

Peacemaker, orator and warrior, Chief Crowfoot (Glenbow Archives/ ND-8-390).

two-wheeled ox-drawn vehicles moved furs and trade goods from Red River to Fort Edmonton, on routes followed today by modern highways.

As the Hudson's Bay Company's need for pemmican declined in the mid-nineteenth century, many Métis migrated west into Alberta, most notably to Lac la Biche, Lake Athabasca, Lac Ste. Anne and St. Albert.

While the fur trade brought an equal partnership between First Nations and Europeans, the physical contact brought devastating diseases, such as pneumonia, influenza, smallpox, measles and tuberculosis, against which the First Nations had no immunity. In the epidemic of 1837–38 alone, smallpox wiped out up to 75% of the Blackfoot, Blood, Peigan, Sarcee and Assiniboine. Traders from Montana brought an almost equally lethal plague with them: alcohol. The international market for buffalo hides seemed inexhaustible and hunters decimated the herds while stripping the Blackfoot of their possessions for a few cups of degraded alcohol. Whole First Nations were almost destroyed by this combination of alcohol and disease until the North West Mounted Police finally ended the whisky trade in 1874.

The process of settlement by Euro-Canadians, which accelerated through the latter half of the nineteenth century, led to the dispossession and economic marginalization of the aboriginal peoples. These developments forced the First Nations to enter into treaty agreements in the 1870s and 1880s. In 1876 the commissioners negotiated a treaty with the Cree of central Alberta and in 1877 they approached the Blackfoot tribes, the Sarcee and the Stoney. These were inauspicious times for the western tribes, seriously depleted by disease and facing the extinction of their livelihood with the slaughter of the buffalo. By Treaty Six the government acquired an area of Alberta and Saskatchewan as large as the entire British Isles. In 1877 at Blackfoot Crossing in southwest Alberta, the Blackfoot, Blood and Peigan, Sarcee and Stoney signed Treaty Seven. The year 1883 marks the end of the Plains Indians' independent existence. With the completion of the prairie section of the CPR, the First Nations' isolation ended, as hundreds and then thousands of whites arrived.

By the early twentieth century both the status Indians and the Métis faced difficult conditions. The mortality rate remained high. The aboriginal population of Alberta fell in a generation by two-thirds, from about 18,000 in the 1870s to less than 6000 by the 1920s. Finally, in the 1920s, health services for Aboriginals improved with additional hospitals, nursing homes and improved living conditions. The educational system took much longer to improve. The regrettable system of residential schools, in place from the early 1900s to the 1970s, separated aboriginal children from their families, forbade them to speak their tribal languages or to practice their traditional religion.

Despite their exclusion from Canadian society, the First Nations supported Canada's war effort from 1914–18, serving in the military and contributing disproportionately to organizations such as the Red Cross. Nevertheless, conditions continued to decline, many living at little more than a bare subsistence. At least the aboriginal population made progress politically between the wars. In 1929 prairie First Nations formed the League of Indians in Western Canada, which challenged the arbitrary power of the Indian Affairs Branch. To protect their rights, Joe Dion and Adrian Hope organized the Alberta Métis Association. In the early 1940s Malcolm Norris contributed to the founding of the first modern political organization in the province, the Indian Association of Alberta.

Conditions improved considerably for many status Indians after the war. Thousands served in Canada's Armed Forces. The close contact between whites and aboriginals led to increasing awareness of native issues. Gradually the federal government extended the entire social welfare system to the aboriginal population. Thanks to improved medical attention, the aboriginal population continued to grow. Since 1944 the number of status Indians in Alberta has increased nearly sevenfold from 12,441 to 80,775 in 2001 (statistics gathered by Statistics Canada for DIAND). Education has improved as Native bands have taken over control of their own school systems. After 1951 the Indian administration somewhat relaxed their paternalistic and authoritarian policies. Status Indians obtained the vote in federal elections in 1960 and in provincial elections in Alberta in 1965. In 1958 James Gladstone, a Blood rancher, became the first Canadian aboriginal appointed to the Canadian Senate. Since 1945 the greatest economic news for many Alberta First Nations has been the discovery of oil and gas on their reserves. As the Constitution of 1982 gave explicit recognition to aboriginal rights, there have been dramatic signs of restored pride and community across the province.

Like his brother Clifford, Arthur Sifton was an instrumental figure in Alberta's early history. Elected in 1899 to the Legislative Assembly of the North-West Territories, he worked tirelessly to have Alberta and Saskatchewan made into provinces (Glenbow Archives/ NA-448-1).

Who are the Albertans?
The Peoples of Alberta

Missionary and colonizer Father Albert Lacombe was called Ars-Okitsiparpi ("man of the good heart") by the Blackfoot (Provincial Archives of Alberta/B-9527).

Intrepid fur traders such as Alexander Mackenzie were responsible for mapping much of Alberta (Library and Archives Canada/C-2146).

French-speaking Albertans

French was the first European language spoken on the prairies: the word *prairie* itself comes from French. French explorers, fur traders and voyageurs arrived in the West in the early eighteenth century. At Fort Edmonton, so many of the Hudson's Bay Company employees spoke French that French was the *lingua franca* of the fur trade until the mid-nineteenth century.

The arrival of French missionaries at Fort Edmonton in 1842 strengthened the French presence. Father Thibault began the Catholic mission at Fort Edmonton and the following year he established a mission at Lac Ste. Anne. In 1861 Albert Lacombe founded a new mission near Edmonton to be named St. Albert. By the late 1880s St. Albert had developed into a successful agricultural community with a population of about 1000. Of the total non-native population in the Edmonton area in 1885, roughly 60% were of French origin.

The Northwest Territories Act of 1875 allowed the use of French in the legislative council and the courts, but the peaceful co-existence of French and English did not survive the influx of Ontario Protestants in the 1880s. Obsessed with making English supreme, the majority succeeded in making English the sole language in the legislature in 1892 and the sole language of instruction in the schools. The French population resisted and efforts were made to increase the number of French settlers. Abbé Morin began a farming community north of Saint Albert, at Morinville, and he and Father Lacombe brought in thousands of other francophones, more than half of them from the United States.

In their efforts to survive, the French-speaking community was reinforced by the arrival of immigrants from France and Belgium in the early twentieth century.

Through much of the twentieth century Franco-Albertans had little legal support in their attempt to survive as a distinct community. The situation changed after the findings of the Royal Commission on Bilingualism and Biculturalism in the mid-1960s. In its wake, Alberta belatedly recognized a number of long-standing demands. In 1964 the provincial government altered the School Act to allow the use of French. Under the new Canadian Constitution (1982) the rights of francophones to attend publicly funded schools when numbers warranted were guaranteed and the first all-French schools opened in Edmonton and Calgary in 1984.

Anglo-Celtic Foundation (Ontarians)

The first English speakers to arrive in Alberta were Scots. Men such as Alexander Mackenzie and Simon Fraser came as fur traders and explorers over 200 years ago. The Hudson's Bay Company's permanent fur-trading posts at Fort Chipewyan and Fort Edmonton were often manned by Scottish clerks and factors recruited in the Orkney Islands or from the Scottish mainland. Perhaps the best-known Scot who actually lived in Alberta was George Simpson, who played a leading role in administering the fur trade.

Confederation in 1867 and the transfer of the Northwest to Canada in 1870 brought the largest and most influential group of English-speaking newcomers. The tens of thousands of Ontarians who migrated to Alberta in the 1880s and 1890s brought with them the preconditions of an established Anglo Canada. A number of the early Ontarians became prominent politicians and journalists. Among them was Frank Oliver, the first Alberta newspaper editor, who played a very important role in the province's political life.

A Brampton classmate of Frank Oliver's, James Lougheed, also proved a success in Alberta politics. He came to Calgary in 1883 and at the age of 35 became a Conservative senator. He had a strong sense of nationalism as well as an Anglo-Saxon elitist attitude towards new immigrants. The first premier of Alberta, Alexander Rutherford, was raised on an Ontario farm in the Ottawa Valley. His successor, Arthur L. Sifton, was born in St. John's, Ontario, and the third premier, Charles Stewart, came from Trabane, Ontario.

Ontario women also came west and took up positions of leadership in the reform organizations: the Women's Christian Temperance Union, Women's Canadian Club and the female suffrage movement. Three of the five leading Alberta suffragettes came from Ontario: Emily Murphy, Louise McKinney and Nellie McClung.

The Liberal Oliver and the Conservative Lougheed joined forces with fellow Ontarian Frederick W.G. Haultain to fight for provincial status for the Northwest Territories. The peak period of Ontario migration to Alberta occurred at the turn of the twentieth century. The population of Alberta rose from about 25,000 to 375,000; the number of Ontario-born in the province rose proportionally from 4500 to 57,500.

By the late 1880s, English-speaking and mainly Protestant set-

Frank Oliver moved from Brampton, Ontario, to Winnipeg, and then in 1876 he joined an oxcart brigade bound for Fort Edmonton. For four years he worked as an itinerant trader before buying his own newspaper. He never pretended that his newspaper was impartial. He had an uncompromising antipathy to John A. Macdonald and was a vigorous supporter for western rights. He had a boundless confidence in the potential of the new territories. He ran as a Liberal and won, serving as Minister of the Interior for the Laurier government. He made sure that Edmonton, and not Calgary, became the capital of the province.

Newspaperman and politician Frank Oliver, a member of the powerful expatriate Ontario elite, played an integral role in Alberta's early political life (Archives of Manitoba/N20911).

63

**Who are the Albertans?
The Peoples of Alberta**

Louise McKinney was raised on a farm near Ottawa in a family with a strong social conscience. She kept that social commitment on her travels through the American Midwest before coming to Claresholm. In Alberta she became involved in the temperance movement and in 1917 ran as a Non-Partisan League candidate. She won the election and became one of the first two women to take a seat in a Legislature in the British Empire (shared with Roberta MacAdams, another Ontarian).

Louise McKinney was one of the appellants in the Persons Case and one of the first women elected to a legislature in Canada (Provincial Archives of Alberta/A-3718).

tlers from Eastern Canada, Britain, and the United States controlled the political, educational, and cultural life of what is now Alberta. If we were to take an image of the Alberta "state of mind" one hundred years ago, it would be distinctly Anglo-Protestant and tightly wound to the ideals of the British Empire.

An Ethnic Pecking Order

In 1896, Clifford Sifton, the federal minister responsible for immigration 1896–1905, began an aggressive immigration campaign that not only increased Alberta's population but also altered forever its ethnic complexion. Because Anglo-Canadian Albertans associated population growth with prosperity, they initially applauded the new arrivals. As non-Anglo-Saxon newcomers began flooding into the region at the turn of the century, however, the initial enthusiasm was replaced with hostility. Most politicians, the press, and the Anglo-Celtic public measured the "quality" of the new immigrants through the nationalistic prism of God, king, empire, and the supposed superiority of the Anglo-Saxon "race." They perceived the acceptability of newcomers according to their resemblance to their own British norm.

At the top of the "pecking order" came settlers from Northern Europe, who were considered both ethnically suitable and easy to assimilate. In contrast, the Anglo elite regarded Central, Eastern and Southern European settlers as a serious threat to the values and mores of mainstream society. Both before and after World War I, politicians debated the advisability of allowing such ethnically "inferior" people into the region, and argued about how best to speed their assimilation. There was no doubt about non-European immigrants. Nativists of all political persuasions considered Asians and Blacks utterly unacceptable.

The visible minorities were the easiest targets for public discrimination. Japanese residents, small in number, economically useful, and hidden in scattered farm settlements, received relatively tolerant treatment. Black residents, however, suffered much informal discrimination, as did Alberta's resident Chinese. In small southern Alberta towns, Euro-Canadians excluded Chinese residents from community life. In Calgary, this undercurrent of animosity erupted in 1892 into a violent attack on residents of the town's highly visible Chinatown.

Broadening Diversity

At the turn of the twentieth century, many of the rural areas of the province were settled predominantly by a single ethnic group, which left a permanent imprint on the region. The Mormons settled in southwestern Alberta, Germans in the southeast and central Alberta, Scandinavians in the centre and eastern Europeans in north-central Alberta.

Between 1904 and 1912 Dutch immigrants, who comprised the fifth largest group, established several rural settlements in scattered parts of Alberta. The first and largest was in the southern Alberta area of Granum, Nobleford and Monarch. The second was founded by Dutch Catholics in 1908 near Strathmore, east of Calgary. The settlements around Monarch combined two streams of immigration, one directly from the Netherlands and the other from the Dutch American settlements.

By 1931 the number of people of Dutch origin in the province was 13,665. This number rose to 20,429 prior to the massive postwar influx. By 1961 this number had increased to 55,530. Virtually all parts of the province felt the impact of the post-World War II wave of Dutch immigration. Of the many postwar groups of immigrants to Alberta, the Dutch gave up their language and folk culture with the greatest speed. However the Reformed immigrants made strenuous efforts to erect a complete institutional structure based on their church, which is their main expression of cultural identity.

The Icelanders have a fascinating history in Canada and Alberta. Insular and poor, they were nevertheless devoted to education and literature. They came to Canada in a single wave of immigration in the 1880s and 1890s. They established only one major area of settlement in Alberta, at Markerville, the home of their most famous son, Stephan Stephansson, considered by many to be the greatest Icelandic poet of the twentieth century.

The Icelandic community remained small, never exceeding 3000 or so, but despite their small numbers they have been tenacious in preserving a sense of ethnic identity.

Eastern Europeans

"I think a stalwart peasant in a sheep-skin coat, born on the soil, whose forefathers have been farmers for ten generations, with a stout wife and a half a dozen children, is good quality," Clifford

Stephan Stephansson was a pacifist and political radical, though he never joined a political party. He bitterly criticized Canada's participation in the Boer War and later in the First World War. "In Europe's reeking slaughter pen," he wrote, "They mince the flesh of murdered men/While swinish merchants, snout in trough/Drink all the bloody profits off." Stephansson was a prolific poet whose philosophical wisdom gave him an assured place in modern Scandinavian literature. He managed all this while at the same time raising a family of eight children.

The great Icelandic poet Stephan Stephansson, photographed here in 1925, came to Alberta in 1889 and homesteaded north of Markerville. His homestead remains and is one of Alberta's Historic Sites (Glenbow Archives/NA-2613-1).

Who are the Albertans?
The Peoples of Alberta

Ukrainian settlers such as the Zahara family, who settled in Rycroft in 1925, left their overpopulated, war-torn homelands to find prosperity in the West. Prosperity came, but only with patience and hard work (Glenbow Archives/NA-3237-3).

Sifton famously said. His policy of valuing farming skills over the ethnic sensitivities of the Anglo-Celtic elite opened the door to immigration from Eastern Europe. The Ukrainians were among the most numerous of these "stalwart peasants." Most of them left the poverty and overpopulation of the provinces of Galicia and Bukovina in the former Austro-Hungarian Empire.

Interest in Canada was aroused by two Galician peasants, Ivan Pylypiw and Vasyl Eleniak, who visited Canada in 1891. About 170,000 Ukrainians immigrated to Canada before World War I, most of them settling in the West.

The first Ukrainian settlement in Alberta was founded at Edna-Star, east of Edmonton, between 1892 and 1894. The Vegreville settlement, as it became known for its largest village, flourished. A physical Ukrainian imprint was made on the landscape in north-central Alberta. Traditional Ukrainian cottages, plastered, whitewashed, thatch-roofed, became a common sight on the prairies. The cohesiveness of the settlement bloc has deteriorated over time with advanced education, upward social mobility and the rise of a professional class. The move to the cities began at an early stage as early immigrants, without ready cash, became low-paid unskilled labourers. Edmonton absorbed some of these workers, while others went to the mining towns in the Crow's Nest, Drumheller and Lethbridge.

The Ukrainians emerged from the war scarred by the enemy alien stigma, an image bolstered after the war by their association in the public mind with labour unrest and radicalism. These stereotypes gradually modified as Anglo-Canadians became more familiar with the Ukrainians and their history. This happened as the Ukrainians themselves enjoyed greater economic prosperity and adopted mainstream lifestyles.

The Ukrainian community was a major force behind the federal policy of multiculturalism. In the early 1970s the Edmonton Ukrainian Professional and Business Federation was instrumental in persuading the Alberta government to permit bilingual instruction in the province's schools.

With the ever-growing numbers of Canadian-born, allegiance to the traditional Ukrainian churches has dropped and intermarriage has risen. The use of Ukrainian at home had dropped to less than 18% by 1981. Nevertheless, as Ukrainians increasingly identify

themselves as unhyphenated Canadians, there is still widespread interest in the community and among other Albertans in traditional Ukrainian art forms and folk culture. There remains also a strong identification with the travails and hopes of the homeland among the older generation.

The history of the Romanians in Alberta is closely associated with that of the Ukrainians, for most of them and nearly half of the Ukrainians came from the same province in the Austro-Hungarian Empire: Bukovina. Both groups settled in the same east-central region of the province and both faced the same trials of pioneering. Both were agrarian, peasant people who lived close to the land. Their customs and folklore were similar and they shared a common Orthodox faith.

The experience was similar but not identical. Unlike most of the other inhabitants of eastern Europe, the Romanians are not a Slavic people. They are descendants of the Dacians and the Romans and their language grew out of Latin.

The first Romanians to settle in Alberta chose land in the Ukrainian bloc in east central Alberta, having heard about the area from their neighbours in Bukovina. As the Romanian community has prospered economically, it has experienced a gradual erosion of cultural ties and an increasing assimilation of the third and fourth generations.

A group of American immigrants from Colorado arrive in Bassano. By 1911 immigrants from the United States comprised 22% of Alberta's population (Glenbow Archives/NA 984-2).

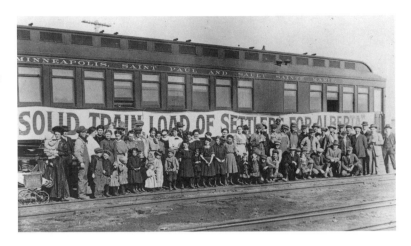

Poles and Hungarians

The large number of Poles who came to Canada from the 1890s to 1914 originated in the Russian and Austrian parts of partitioned Poland, impelled to leave by overpopulation. Though the government discouraged it, fearing that it would prevent assimilation, the Poles formed small, coherent communities, often clustered among larger Ukrainian settlements.

The Poles who came to Alberta prior to World War I were of peasant background and an overwhelming majority of them settled in rural Alberta. Free land was a magical attraction for all the immigrants from central and Eastern Europe. The foreign culture that the Poles brought with them and their lack of knowledge of English prevented their immediate involvement in Canadian society.

Mining is a centuries-old occupation in Poland; hence it is not surprising that Polish settlers also established several mining communities. Some worked in the Crow's Nest Pass. Other groups settled near Banff, in Canmore, Bankhead and Exshaw. The most active of these communities was in Coleman.

The Polish ethnic group in Alberta grew dramatically after World War I but immigration dropped after 1936. After the World War II 4500 Polish veterans arrived in Canada. Most of them were dispatched by the Labour Department from Lethbridge to farms all over Alberta.

The Hungarians' presence in Alberta dates back to the earliest establishment of coal mining in the south of the province. Hungarian miners came to Alberta from Saskatchewan and

Crofters on their way to the Canadian West in 1920 (CPR Archives/NS8454).

Pennsylvania in 1886. The first Hungarians to settle in Alberta arrived as part of a plan by Count Paul O. Esterhazy, who wanted to remove Hungarian immigrants from the exploitative environment of Pennsylvania. In 1886, 130 men arrived to work in a coal mine near Medicine Hat, but they were just as badly treated as they had been in the United States and a few moved on to work in the mines near Lethbridge.

The largest movement of Hungarians occurred between 1925 and 1930. It was composed primarily of farmers and workers. Virtually all were young men, both single and married. About 4000 of the 34,000 Hungarians who came to Canada at this time came to Alberta. Most were farmers, but many found work in the coal mines near Lethbridge and Drumheller, as well as the Crow's Nest and Edmonton.

During World War II the Canadian government treated the Hungarians as "enemy aliens"; they were fingerprinted and subjected to police surveillance. However, unlike the Japanese and Germans, most Hungarians emerged from the war unscathed, at least by internment or loss of property. A large wave of political refugees from the 1956 Hungarian Revolution arrived in Canada. Approximately 3000 of these refugees landed in Alberta. Most settled as labourers in the major cities until their education and skills were welcomed in a booming economy.

Relations among these different waves of immigrants have been marked by both co-operation and conflict. The old-timers did as much as they could to help the refugees, but a feeling of distrust developed among some of the postwar refugees, who tended to look down on the earlier wave as "peasants." The newcomers were disdainful of the low economic status of the old-timers and were baffled by their leftist orientation. The old-timers in turn felt that their struggles were misunderstood and unappreciated by the newcomers, who arrived during economic prosperity and who received aid from the government.

Jewish Heritage

Jack Switzer

Alberta's Jews have balanced the conflicting demands of maintaining their religious and cultural identity while very successfully integrating themselves into Canadian society.

Despite their small numbers, their isolation from major centres of Jewish life, and the presence of frequent, albeit muted, hostility, they have emerged as what may be the province's most successful minority group.

The Jacob Diamond family settled in Calgary in 1888. Abraham and Rebecca Cristall were in Lethbridge in 1891, and became Edmonton's first Jewish residents in 1893. The 1901 census counted only a handful of Jews, 31, in the area that would become Alberta.

Tsarist repression of the failed 1905 Russian revolution sparked a major exodus of Jews from eastern Europe, and Jewish numbers grew across Canada. Philanthropists aided the settlement of Jews on prairie homesteads; Jewish farm "colonies" were established near Trochu and Rumsey in 1906, and near Sibbald, the Montefiore Colony, in 1910.

In 1911 Alberta had about 1500 Jews; over half were in Calgary and Edmonton. The remainder were in Lethbridge, Medicine Hat, Vegreville, on farms, and in numerous small towns, where Jewish merchants were common.

The Calgary and Edmonton Jewish communities shared similar growth patterns: the purchase of cemetery land, then the building of traditional synagogues (1911), the establishment of Hebrew schools and rival Yiddish-based schools, and the explosive growth of organizational life. Clubs of every sort marked Jewish life in the cities: women's

A large percentage of Jewish immigrants settled in cities. Julius Erlinger, Henry Goldberg, Max Rosenbloom, William Diamond, and John Sternberg, pictured here, settled in Edmonton at the turn of the century (Glenbow Archives/NA-3368-4).

groups, refugee and immigrant aid organizations, Zionist societies, athletic and social clubs, men's lodges, and mutual aid societies, as well as literary, drama, and music groups.

Most immigrants during both the pre- and post-Great War immigration periods were relatively poor, spoke Yiddish and were in many ways both foreign and alien to the Anglo-Albertan majority. Alberta cities did not have garment factories offering "sweat shop" jobs to immigrants, so Calgary and Edmonton Jews became petty merchants: peddlers, second-hand dealers, and grocers. Geography played a role; Edmonton had Jewish fur and hide dealers while some Jewish men in Calgary became cattle dealers.

Not all the early Jewish Albertans fit the penniless immigrant mould. Austrian-born brothers Henry and Alexander Sereth came to Calgary in 1904 and established a building-materials empire—the Riverside Lumber companies. A Sereth daughter, Cecyle, married Harry Bell, whose family ran what was then Canada's largest theatre chain out of Calgary.

Another Sereth girl, Emily, married Edmonton's first Jewish lawyer, Morris (Moe) Lieberman, who was also a football player and went on to head the Edmonton Eskimos and become a high-ranking provincial judge.

Minnesota-raised Henry and Marcia Goldberg came to Edmonton in 1907; he was a grain trader. (They moved to Calgary in 1921.) Other second-generation Edmonton Jews, such as John Dower, and brothers-in-law Joshua Newhouse and Joseph Shaw, established sizeable wholesale and retail business groups.

The 1920s saw more Jewish immigration from Europe. By 1931 Alberta had about 3700 Jews. Calgary had 1600 Jews, Edmonton just over 1000. Some Jewish farm families stayed on the land for another decade, but most left for the economic opportunities, urban amenities, and communal life available in the cities.

The Depression curtailed immigration. Jews in Alberta faced the same hardships as their neighbours, but were also concerned about the rise of Nazism and the vicious anti-Semitism in Germany. The "none is too many" sentiment of federal bureaucrats was echoed by some Albertans.

There was also apprehension about Alberta's Social Credit government, elected in 1935. Despite premier William Aberhart's cordial relationships with many Jews, his party was perceived by the province's Jewish population as being inherently anti-Semitic.

Jews were active in Canada's armed forces during World War II, with most enlisting in the Air Force. About one in 10 of Alberta's Jews, about 400 men (and a few women), joined up. Twenty died, mainly bomber crewmen.

The veterans became community leaders and led the post-war Jewish building boom. Edmonton put up three major Jewish buildings in the 1950s, two synagogues and a new Hebrew School building. Calgary Jews erected five buildings in just three years, 1959 through 1961, two synagogues, two day schools, and a funeral chapel.

A Jewish summer camp, still active, opened near Pine Lake in 1955. The Medicine Hat Jewish community built a new synagogue in 1955; Lethbridge Jews opened their new centre in 1962.

Holocaust survivors began to reach Alberta in the late 1940s; several hundred came to join both major Jewish communities.

The Jewish immigrants and their children shared in Alberta's post-war prosperity. The rags-to-riches dream became reality for many. Self-confidence and optimism characterized the community. Alberta Jews have been elected to the legislature (Abe Miller, Sheldon Chumir, Ron Ghitter), appointed to the Senate (Ron Ghitter), and elected mayor (Harry Veiner in Medicine Hat, Stephen Mandel in Edmonton).

Jews joined the professions in disproportionate numbers. Jewish academics have filled many university positions. About 30 Alberta Jews have been presented with the Order of Canada.

In the 1970s, the Keegstra affair again sent waves of apprehension through the Jewish communities of Alberta, but the government's anti-hate response was more comforting than in previous encounters.

A third wave of new building took place in later decades; essentially the communal institutions followed their members to new and more distant suburbs.

Jews from Quebec and Ontario provided a major growth spurt for the Alberta Jewish community in the 1970s. They were joined in the next decade by Russian Jews, who by then were able to leave the Soviet Union. In recent decades a cosmopolitan group of newcomers—Americans, South Africans, Iranians, Israelis, Argentinians, and others—have added depth and texture to the Jewish milieu.

Alberta now has about 15,000 Jews. The 2001 census counted about 8000 Jews in Calgary, and close to 5000 in Edmonton. The smaller centres have lost most of their Jewish residents, and only a few Jews still farm or live in small towns.

Jews comprise less than one percent of the people of Alberta, but in terms of personal achievement and maintenance of their community identity they are an admirable, remarkable group.

Religious Minorities

The first Jews came to Alberta in the 1880s, when the Canadian government decided to promote Jewish settlement in the West. Jacob Diamond came to Canada from Lithuania, via the United States, in 1888, setting up in the liquor trade in Calgary. His brother William joined him in 1892, setting up a tailor shop. Jews were not immune to the anti-foreign sentiment in the province and while their numbers remained small, local newspapers evoked the image of Shylock when referring to them.

While most Jews settled in the cities, there were two significant farm colonies, one at Trochu and another at Sibbald in east-central Alberta. By 1931 Alberta had about 3700 Jews, of whom only 8% were rural. Most lived in Calgary, Edmonton and Lethbridge. During the late 1920s and 1930s Alberta experienced an upsurge in nativism. While Jews were not the only Albertans to experience prejudice, anti-Semitism left a legacy that lasted well into the Social Credit years.

The Hutterites have their origin in the Anabaptist movement, which took root in Germany, Holland and Austria in the sixteenth

Two Hutterite women contemplate a duck pond at the Standoff Hutterite Colony near Fort Macleod in 1963. Established in 1918, the colony was one of the first founded in Alberta (Glenbow Archives/NA-1752-44).

Who are the Albertans?
The Peoples of Alberta

century. The movement's beliefs include adult baptism, the priest-
hood of all believers, pacifism and non-conformity with the outside
world. Descendants of this movement include the Mennonites, the
Amish and the Hutterites, whose fundamental characteristic rests
on the basis of communal living. The Hutterites have kept their
Tyrolese dialect and their historic patterns of dress and organization.

In 1899 the Hutterites received assurances from the Canadian
government that their pacifism would be respected and that they
would be accorded full religious freedom, and between 1918 and
1920 most of the South Dakota colonies moved north. Four colonies
settled in Alberta near Cardston.

In the beginning the Hutterites suffered hostility from veteran's
groups and newspapers, not only for their pacifism but for their
communal living style. During the Depression attitudes changed.
The Hutterites' diverse agriculture and self-sufficiency enabled
them to survive price declines and poor crops.

Despite their relatively small population, making up less than
0.3% of the province, the Hutterites have made an important contribution to the province, through their beliefs, assistance to
neighbours, and in the diversification of Alberta's agriculture.

Good Works and Good Business: Alberta's Jews in the Community
Jack Switzer

Alberta's Jewish immigrants, with some exceptions, largely kept to
themselves in the pre-war decades. Limited English skills combined
with limited acceptance by the greater community meant that few Jews
joined the economic and social mainstream. Their charity was also
devoted to Jewish causes, only sometimes reaching beyond Jewish
circles.

This changed after World War II when Jewish philanthropic resources
and business development skills expanded into non-Jewish spheres.
Alberta's academic and cultural scene has also seen a major infusion of
Jewish-origin resources.

The University of Alberta, for example, has had two Jewish presidents, Max Wyman and Myer Horowitz. Tevie Miller, a senior provincial
judge, was Chancellor of the University from 1986 to 1990. The
Edmonton campus has seen scores of Jewish faculty, many of them

deans. Muriel Kovitz served as an early Chancellor of the University of Calgary, where Harvey Weingarten is currently President.

Mel Hurtig, publisher of *The Canadian Encyclopedia* and an influential economic nationalist, grew up in Edmonton's Jewish community, as did filmmaker Arthur Hiller. Lawyer and businessman Joseph Schoctor, a scrap-dealer's son, founded the Citadel theatre.

Edmonton's sports community has many Jewish roots. Moe Lieberman, as noted previously, was active in Canadian Football League management. Henry Singer and Joe Schoctor were founders of the modern Edmonton Eskimos, and Zane Feldman was an owner of the original Edmonton Oilers. Tiger Goldstick, son of Edmonton's first rabbi, was a noted broadcaster and sports booster.

We can note only a few influential Jewish businessmen. Daryl Katz runs the Rexall pharmacy chain from Edmonton. The Ghermezian family, of West Edmonton Mall fame, first came to the city in the 1960s.

Calgary's Jewish philanthropy includes the work of three major private foundations. The Kahanoff Foundation, founded by oilman Sydney Kahanoff in 1979, devotes most of its Canadian funding to the general community. The same is true of the Harry and Martha Cohen Foundation, noted for cultural patronage. The Al and Mona Libin Foundation is best known for its funding of innovative projects at Foothills Hospital and the University of Calgary medical school.

The Calgary-born Belzberg brothers, Sam, Hy, and William, are major philanthropists. Calgarians Hy and Jennie Belzberg both have honourary doctorates and Order of Canada decorations to mark their contributions to the community.

Blacks

While many have heard of the famous cowboy John Ware, few are aware that Black fur traders preceded him to Alberta. Businessmen, farmers and other cowboys followed him. The white response followed the American pattern of racism and discrimination. Albertans were the major force behind the federal government's restrictions on Black immigration introduced in 1911, and residents of Calgary and Edmonton erected a wide range of discriminatory barriers.

The nature of the Black community in Alberta changed dramatically between 1908 and 1911 with the arrival of 1000 Blacks fleeing

John Ware was born a slave on a plantation in South Carolina. After the Civil War his strength and skills with a horse qualified him to join a cattle drive that eventually led him across the border. His willingness to endure long hours in the saddle under severe conditions impressed the local cattlemen. Eventually he acquired his own land near Millarville. In 1902 he moved to the Brooks district. Here his luck turned when his wife died in the spring of 1905. That autumn he fell from his horse and was fatally injured.

Cowboy John Ware, his wife Mildred and their two children Robert and Nettie in 1896 (Glenbow Archives/NA-263-1).

a rising tide of racism in Oklahoma. It led to the founding of one all-Black community at Amber Valley and of several other settlements near Edmonton. The most vociferous denunciations came from groups in Edmonton. In 1911, when the public outcry became most intense, Frank Oliver drafted an Order in Council to bar Black immigration, but it failed to pass.

During World War I younger Blacks went to Edmonton to find work or to join the army. The Black pioneers of Amber Valley faced all the same hardships faced by other pioneers. Many of the Blacks who could not make a living there moved to Calgary and became railway porters, virtually the only job open to them. In Edmonton there was more opportunity in construction and business. While Blacks found most doors closed to them, they could excel in the less rigidly guarded, informal worlds of entertainment and sports. The musical tradition continued later with Clarence "Big" Miller, and Blacks achieved recognition in numerous sports.

In some ways the experience of Blacks in Alberta has been similar to that of other ethnic groups in the province. The rural pioneering struggles, the establishment of familiar institutions to help cope with a new life, the shift from refugee consciousness to a strong identification with Canada, all are a part of a pattern that has been followed repeatedly. But Alberta's Blacks have also faced problems that affected few others. Some of the stereotypes were brought by immigrants from Ontario and Britain, but most came directly from American culture, which had a growing impact on Alberta throughout the twentieth century. The record reveals that Blacks encountered considerable prejudice, but fortunately that prejudice was never formalized into law.

Asians

When Kumataro Inamasu stepped off the train in Calgary on New Year's Day 1906, he headed to the Alberta Hotel. He was not a transient worker, but was the hotel's new pastry chef and the first Japanese to settle in Alberta. That same year Takemoni Nagatani, a recent graduate of the Ontario College of Agriculture, hired several Japanese farmers to work land near Cheadle, east of Calgary. Many of the first Japanese were brought in by labour contractors Bueimon Nakayama and Ichiro Hayakawa, who brought 1000 labourers to work in the sugar beet industry and to help build irrigation systems and railways. They came to earn money so that they could buy farms back on their overcrowded home islands.

The arrival of the Japanese did not go unnoticed. Any anti-Japanese rhetoric faded quickly, however, for the sugar beet industry was in desperate need of labour. Very few of the migrant workers stayed in Alberta. Most moved on to the coast or to the United States. Only a few moved to Edmonton and Calgary to set up small businesses. By 1911 only 244 were left in the province.

At the outbreak of war in 1939 there were 540 Japanese in Alberta. Most of them were farmers in southern Alberta. Their lives changed with the bombing of Pearl Harbor on December 7, 1941. Fortunately, fears that they would be mistreated proved groundless. Newspapers and politicians reminded Albertans of the contributions to the life of the community and their public declaration of loyalty. Japanese in British Columbia were less fortunate as politicians and the public there demanded the removal of the Japanese "menace." Alberta's beet farmers saw an opportunity and requested that the displaced Japanese be sent to work on their labour-depleted farms.

At the end of the war a continuing labour shortage determined the fate of the displaced Japanese. Premier Ernest Manning reluctantly agreed to allow them to remain. Only in March 1948 did Manning publicly announce that the Japanese were entitled to the same rights as any other resident. Today the Japanese community is less cohesive and the intermarriage rate exceeds 80%. The community has gone from field hand and coal miner to urbanite and professional.

The first Chinese pioneers in Alberta arrived in 1885, but during the 1880s and 1890s there were relatively few Chinese in the area. By 1910 there were Chinatowns in Calgary, Edmonton, Medicine Hat and Lethbridge. These communities faced determined prejudice and shameful exploitation. Legislative action at all levels created much misery, frustration, and consternation, culminating in Canada's extortionate federal head taxes imposed on Chinese immigrants.

By about 1910, the garrison mentality of Alberta's urban centres began to ease. In 1910, the Chinese in Calgary successfully

Chinese students study on the steps of a school in Lethbridge early in the 20th century. In 1910 a city bylaw banned Chinese businesses from certain neighborhoods, creating what amounted to a ghetto (Galt Museum Archives/P-19851002000).

relocated Chinatown in an area of their own choosing, despite minor opposition.

The Chinese had to work very hard to make a living, and few opportunities were open to them outside restaurants, groceries and laundries, which had to open early in the morning and close late in the evening in order to make a profit. For most early Chinese immigrants, the daily routine was almost solely working, eating and sleeping.

Recent Chinese immigrants are not a uniform group. In 1984 China and the U.K. reached an agreement for Hong Kong to be returned to Chinese sovereignty in 1997. This spurred a large exodus from Hong Kong, many of whom chose Canada. After the 1989 student uprising in China, Canada changed its humanitarian policy, allowing thousands of Chinese in Canada to obtain landed immigrant status. In the 1990s, the Mainland Chinese government eliminated most of the remaining restrictions on the exit of citizens. As a result, a steady flow of Mainland Chinese began arriving in Canada.

The Chinese: How this City has Changed
Stephanie Ho Lem

I remember in my childhood days my friends and I, when I got my allowance, would look forward to a bowl of won ton soup at Linda Mae

Calgary's Chinatown, shown here in 1967, was relocated to this area in 1910 after successful lobbying by Chinese immigrants (Glenbow Archives/NA-2645-52).

restaurant on the northwest corner of Centre Street and 3rd Avenue, heart of Calgary's Chinatown. Mr. Poon, who owned Linda Mae's, had a thriving restaurant and continually brought in cooks from Hong Kong and they became known as the Linda Mae graduates. Jack Wong, who is the owner of the Silver Dragon, is one of those graduates. The Chinese population was very small then and the families knew each other. The Ho Lems, Poons, Kwongs, Mah Yets, Luey Yings, Wong Wahs, and High Wos were a few of the oldest families in Calgary. I always wondered why there were double surnames but I was told the name included the village in China.

I remember walking along Centre Street and peering into shop windows muddied by dust and rain. You would find some nice porcelain ware, but it was stacked clumsily and unattractively displayed behind the dirty windows. Having experienced San Francisco's Chinatown, I felt the urge to open up a porcelain store to display Chinese collectibles the way Bowrings does. I saw the potential to help make Calgary's Chinatown more attractive. Full of ambition, I opened Stephanie Ho Oriental Imports and had great reviews as one of the most attractive stores in Chinatown in 1979. High interest rates hit all of us in the early 80s and we had to close.

I remember travelling to New York in the mid-80s and a taxi driver asked where I was from. When I told him, he asked "Oh, is it near Montreal?" Even the Calgary Stampede wasn't known to a lot of Americans. After the Calgary Flames won the Stanley Cup, and we hosted the 88 Olympics and the G8 Summit, finally it wasn't necessary to explain where Calgary is in Canada.

As you'll learn from reading about history, the early Chinese in Calgary were not always accepted as equals. Chinese immigration was limited because of the $500 head tax imposed in 1903. Additional legislation virtually halted immigration from 1923 to 1946. Calgary's Chinatown was the largest in the province with about 1000, one-quarter of the province's Chinese population, in 1931. Today's Chinese population in Calgary is about 80,000 and is still growing. Alberta has come a long way in recognizing the Chinese in the province, with Normie Kwong appointed as the Lieutenant Governor in 2004.

Chinatown hasn't changed dramatically over the past 40 years. There a few new buildings but very little has changed compared to the rest of downtown. Chinese businesses are moving out to the city's communities, and the question is, how will Chinatown survive in the next century?

What is my vision for the province in the next century? The city has to conserve land and should concentrate the population in the inner core, thus reducing the need to build more roads. We should reduce the price of public transportation and make it more readily available so people will leave their cars at home. Alberta should stop catering to the oil and gas industries and get on the bandwagon to reduce carbon emissions, and welcome the ethanol industry in this province by creating incentives as Manitoba and Ontario have done.

From 1980 to 2000 nearly 800,000 Chinese immigrants were admitted to Canada. Of these 45.6% came from Hong Kong, 27.7% from Mainland China, 11.8% from Taiwan and 5.2% from Vietnam.

The Chinese highly favour large urban centres, and 4.4% of the total came to Calgary and 4% to Edmonton.

The first known Korean contact with Canada came in 1898 as the result of the Canadian mission movement and its pastoral, medical and educational work in the historic Hamgyong Province and neighbouring China (Manchuria). There was little Korean immigration to Canada before World War II, although a small group of students and Christian converts, deeply influenced by Canadian missionaries, had come during the prewar period. Canada's first permanent Korean settler was Tae-yon Hwang, a mission-sponsored medical intern who came to Alberta in 1948. He chose to remain after his training and he was soon joined by other students.

When Canada adopted a more liberal immigration policy in 1967, whereby applicants would be officially judged on the basis of individual skills and the needs of the Canadian economy, and formal diplomatic relations were established, Koreans began to arrive in greater numbers. In the 1996 census of Canada, a total of 66,655 persons claimed Korean ancestry, of whom 4845 resided in Alberta.

Most of Alberta's Koreans are highly skilled workers or professionals, including physicians, nurses, dentists, accountants, and college and university teachers. A number of Koreans have also climbed into the entrepreneurial class, opening small businesses.

Koreans who have come to Canada have shown remarkable initiative in creating community associations. These associations in Toronto, Winnipeg, Edmonton and Vancouver organize and administer a wide range of social and cultural activities. They also participate in numerous multicultural and municipal events, including the Heritage Festival in Edmonton. Korean Canadians also organize around common or shared interests and kinship ties.

The changing demographic of Alberta can be predicted by regarding the origins of immigrants in 2003: China 2131, Philippines 1946, India 1815, Pakistan 905, U.K. 691, Korea 587, United States 533, Afghanistan 444, Colombia 425 and Sudan 358. By destination in that year, 57% settled in Calgary and 28.8% in Edmonton. It is a mark of the contemporary state of mind that this trend would be viewed by most Albertans (if they knew it at all) with optimism and acceptance.

Fort Edmonton. Edmonton owes its origins to the fur trade. When Paul Kane made this painting in the 1850s traders had been plying the North Saskatchewan for well over 50 years (Oil on canvas, 1850s, Royal Ontario Museum).

Métis Hunters Running Buffalo by Paul Kane. The Métis were a new people with aspects of both their Aboriginal and European origins (Oil on canvas, 1850s, Royal Ontario Museum).

Indian Encampment on the Prairies. Watercolour, 1911, by William Armstrong (Library and Archives Canada/C-010513).

Dunvegan was founded in 1805 by Archibald Norman McLeod, who was inspired to travel to the area by Sir Alexander Mackenzie's account of his adventures there in 1793 (Travel Alberta).

Prosperity Follows Settlement in Western Canada. The Canadian government undertook a massive campaign to attract immigrants from all over Europe. This poster was issued under direction of Hon. Frank Oliver, Minister of the Interior (Provincial Archives of Alberta/A7536).

Canada West. Western Canada was the "Last Best West". Those who came on the basis of these advertisements were in for a shock if they thought they would find such a welcoming landscape (Canadian Museum of Civilization).

Constructed during the height of the Beaux-Arts fashion, Alberta's legislature building in Edmonton (1908–12) was designed in the grand classical manner, with a monumental portico and a massive central domes (Travel Alberta).

The Ukrainian Cultural Heritage Village east of Edmonton educates thousands of visitors each year on the history of Ukrainian settlement in east-central Alberta from 1892 to 1930. Visitors can take part in traditional activities (Travel Alberta).

The tranquility of the Japanese gardening tradition is conveyed at the Nikka Yuko Japanese Gardens in Lethbridge (Travel Alberta).

Vegreville's pysanka, constructed in 1974, is a giant jigsaw puzzle consisting of 524 star patterns, 1,108 equilateral triangles, 3,512 visible facets and 6,978 nuts and bolts (Travel Alberta).

For over 5000 years the Plains Indians used buffalo jumps as hunting tools by directing bison over the edge. UNESCO designated Head-Smashed-In Buffalo Jump as a World Heritage Site in 1981 (Photograph by James H. Marsh).

Established in 1869, Fort Whoop-Up was one of the original American whiskey posts where trading was carried out in un-policed territory, until the RNWMP's arrival in 1874. This interpretive centre is located in Lethbridge (Photograph by James H. Marsh).

Writing-on-Stone Provincial Park near Milk River houses the largest concentration of rock art created by the Plains People (Travel Alberta).

The Northern Shadow Dancers began as a dance troupe in 1990 that helped native youth realize their potential through artistic mediums. Here they are seen performing at Peace River (Travel Alberta).

The Brooks Aqueduct National and Provincial Historic Site is a monument to the early irrigation engineers whose novel idea helped to transform Alberta's southern plains into productive farmland (Travel Alberta).

These Grain Elevators at Hussar combine new technology with the old-style elevators that helped to establish Alberta as part of Canada's breadbasket (Travel Alberta).

South Asians

The people commonly referred to as South Asians have been relative newcomers to Alberta. Like Europeans, the South Asians originate from many places with diverse histories and they exhibit an enormous range of cultural, linguistic and religious identities. They are best defined as people who derive ultimately from the Indian subcontinent, from countries with their own identities, including India, Pakistan, Sri Lanka, Bangladesh, Afghanistan, Nepal and Bhutan. The cultural range in these countries is enormous, but they do share some commonalities, such as a relative isolation, the dominant religion of Hinduism and a shared colonial experience.

Very few South Asians lived outside British Columbia until the 1960s. Just after World War I a handful of Sikhs began farming in southern Alberta, but immigration was only a trickle until Canadian immigration policy was changed in the 1960s, when racial restrictions were removed. By 1971 the number of South Asians in Alberta had grown to about 4400, most of them from India and Pakistan. During the 1970s immigration to Alberta increased dramatically. By the end of 1984 there were 20,000 South Asians in Alberta, about 1% of the population. Only about one-third to one-half of these came directly from India, 10% from Pakistan and the rest from Sri Lanka, East Africa, Britain, Fiji, Guyana and Trinidad.

South Asians are easily the most diverse ethnic group in Alberta. Many had certain advantages when they arrived, since they already spoke English and were familiar with Western institutions. That is not to say that they have not had settlement problems, especially when their cultural values clash with Canadian customs. This has been particularly evident in the family, as South Asian children identify with their Canadian friends and take on their values. The smaller groups, such as those from Fiji or Trinidad, tend to assimilate quickly, while others, especially those who retain their religious beliefs, as the Sikhs and Muslim Pakistanis do, change less.

Alberta: A New State of Mind

Who are Albertans? It is a question no easier to answer than "Who are Canadians?" We are obviously a collection of diverse origins and perhaps equally obviously a people of indeterminate identity. History helps us here because it is easy to see the differences in Alberta society between today and 100 years ago, or 50 years ago or

A group of South Asians at the Canadian Pacific Railway station in Frank, Alta, 1903 (Library and Archives Canada/PA-125113).

even 20 years ago. In 1906, as we have seen, an Anglo-Celtic elite dominated the political and economic life of the province, and looked with suspicion or worse on the growing diversity. But the need to populate the rural areas of the province helped to put aside objections and, as it always seems to do, economic opportunity tended to bring social progress as well.

The interesting question that remains is to what extent the official, almost clichéd, portrait of Alberta as primarily a "multicultural" society is based in reality. Most literature on multiculturalism, particularly that written by social scientists, sees the maintenance of previous ethnic identity as positive and treats "assimilation" as a failure of the ideal. Much of this ideology was set in stone by the official multicultural policies of the federal and provincial governments, but it has played out unevenly in the ethnic groups themselves. Whatever the motivations of older generations to preserve fragments of their previous lives, the younger generations seem to make their own decisions and, given the freedom, often choose the mainstream. In today's world, that mainstream seems increasingly global. As in the past, when certain groups, such as the Scandinavians and Germans, assimilated faster than others, such as the Ukrainians, today's immigrant groups continue to adjust to Alberta society in their own ways and at their own pace, according to their religious, cultural, linguistic or economic imperatives. Whether something is lost or gained in this process is a matter of interpretation. What is sure, again in the perspective of history, is that Alberta is a far more tolerant, accepting and flexible society than it was in 1905. But these dates are artificial markers and overlook the fact that Alberta's history is still in the making and that outstanding challenges, notably determining the place of the aboriginal peoples, still remain.

The Aboriginal People of Alberta

4

GERALD T. CONATY AND MIKE ROBINSON

Human beings have lived in the place we now call Alberta for a very long time. First Nations oral traditions tell us that this has been the homeland and heartland for many cultures for thousands and thousands of years. By the early eighteenth century, this world began to include Europeans seeking pelts for a burgeoning fur trade. Before long a new people appeared—the Métis—with a unique culture that blended the ways of the newcomers with those of the indigenous people. By the time Alberta became a province in 1905, aboriginal and non-aboriginal cultures had been interacting for over 200 years. These relationships shaped the way the territory developed and they continue to influence our lives.

A Métis Heritage

Colleen Klein

When I think of how best to define Alberta, I think of the word heart. There are so many dedicated and compassionate people in this province who put their hearts and souls into everything they do.

I'm particularly inspired by those who have dedicated themselves to making our province the best place in the world to raise our children, and by those who are working to honour and encourage Aboriginal people and culture. I've dedicated myself to helping with that work in any way I can.

My dedication grew out of my own life experiences. While I have many happy childhood memories, I also endured some very difficult times. I grew up unaware of my Métis heritage. I was also born with a large port wine birthmark across my face. That mark and my aboriginal features made me different, and those differences weren't very well

Colleen Klein (Office of the Premier, Government of Alberta).

tolerated by others. I suffered bullying and abuse and I often felt isolated and confused.

As an adult, I pieced together my heritage and began to understand
the difficult life my father and so many others like him had been forced
to lead. He was Aboriginal and trying to fit into a white world. Like me,
he was someone who didn't feel like he belonged.

Today, I am proud of my Métis heritage; I am Scottish and Cree. I
give back as much as I can to my Aboriginal sisters and brothers and I've
developed many lasting friendships. I believe the Creator had a reason
for my life experiences, and teaching me to give back to the community
is a very big part of that reason. I was honoured by the Blackfoot nation
by being given my name "Tanataakii," which means wonderful lady.

I also believe those early experiences gave me the understanding I
needed to become an advocate for children and youth. I am a survivor,
but not all children are. They need voices; today I try to be one of those
voices.

My vision of Alberta is one where young souls are never made to feel
shame, never know the pain of abuse, and where all children are
healthy, happy and loved. I also want Alberta to be a place where all
people can feel proud of who they are and where they came from—a
place where we are all encouraged to celebrate the things that make us
unique.

Many Albertans share that vision. People from across the province
are finding ways for Aboriginal people to honour, celebrate and preserve
their wonderful and unique heritage. They're also working to make sure
we do everything possible to nurture the bodies, minds, hearts and souls
of Alberta's children.

We still have work to do before we fully achieve our shared vision, but
I'm excited by what the future holds. The past 100 years have proven
that the people of this province have no shortage of energy, optimism and
ability. They've also shown that this is a province with true heart. I think
that heart will continue to shine through in the years ahead.

Who Was Here?

Long before the Canadian Pacific Railway brought immigrants from
throughout Europe to the Canadian prairies, Natives were coexist-
ing in the region we now call Alberta. The Blackfoot-speaking

people (Piikani, Siksika and Kainai) ranged across the plains, eastward from the foothills to central Saskatchewan and between the North Saskatchewan River and the Yellowstone River in southern Montana. Sometime within the last 1000 years they were joined by the Tsuu T'ina (a Dene-speaking people) who had moved southward from the forests of northern Alberta. Many of the Nakoda made their homes along the foothills of the mountains, from the Bow River northward to the North Saskatchewan River. Others lived along the North Saskatchewan River in the parkland of central Alberta. Plains Cree were encountered along the edges of the parkland and plains, between the North Saskatchewan and Red Deer rivers. Cree camps also moved as far south as the Cypress Hills. The boreal forest was home to both Cree and Dene Tha'.

The presence of other First Nations was also recorded. The Snake were reported to have lived south of the Bow River and frequently to have been at war with the Blackfoot-speakers. Historians generally believe that these were Shoshone-speaking people, although some have speculated that they may have been Siouan. The A'aninin (Fall or Gros Ventre) camped along the upper reaches of the South Saskatchewan River. Once allies with the Blackfoot, relations between the two groups became strained and by the mid-nineteenth century they were often hostile towards one another.

Others visited the regions on buffalo hunting or raiding excursions. Ktunaxa, Nez Percé and others came from the west, following

Starting a campfire, Blackfoot (Siksika), 1910 (Provincial Archives of Alberta/P138).

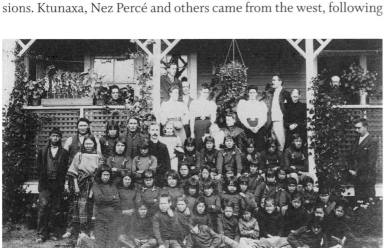

The Blackfoot North camp boarding school staff and children at Gleichen, 1890. The only names given are those of the priests and teachers, while the rest are marked simply "unknown" (Glenbow Archives/NA-1773-7).

Frank Tried to Flay and George Left Hand, Blackfoot, sowing seed by hand near Calgary, 1880s. The First Nations faced an almost impossible task, often imposed on them, of abandoning their traditional hunting economy and becoming farmers (Glenbow Archives/NA-127-1).

ancient trails across the continental divide to the open plains. Sometimes treaties were made and these visitors were allowed to hunt in peace. When treaties were not agreed upon, they were harassed and chased back across the mountains. Visitors from the south and east included Siouan-speaking Lakota and Assiniboine. Their incursions became more frequent as pressures from American settlers and the dwindling buffalo herds forced them to move further west during the late nineteenth century.

Sometime during the past 2000 years another people journeyed through southern Alberta. Siksika oral tradition recalls the presence of people who constructed dwellings of logs covered with earth.

The treaties signed in the late 19th century marked the decline of First Nations power in the face of settlement. This painting by A. Bruce Stapleton depicts Crowfoot speaking as he negotiates the terms of Treaty 7 with Colonel Macleod and Lieutenant Governor Laird, who are seated (Courtesy Glenbow Museum).

Remnants of earthworks at Blackfoot Crossing (near the town of Cluny) may have been made by these "earth dwellers," although the identification of these people remains an enigma. The Numakiki (Mandan), Minitari (Hidatsa) and Sahnish (Arikara), who lived along the middle Missouri River in present-day North Dakota, constructed such houses. The Apsaalooke (or Crow) split from the Minitari and travelled across the plains until they found a new home in the Big Horn Mountains of southern Montana and Northern Wyoming. The oral traditions of both the Apsaalooke and the Siksika recall meetings between the two people.

All of these people travelled vast distances each year. These were not aimless wanderings but, rather, reflected extensive knowledge of regional ecology. The distribution and availability of plants and animals were continually monitored and camps were moved in order to harvest these resources. People understood that they had a complex relationship with all facets of their world. Their spiritual beliefs recognized the importance of coexistence and the need to maintain a balance between human needs and the rights of Other Beings (e.g., plants, animals, rocks) to complete their own life cycles. Survival was contingent upon knowing not only where and when certain plants and animals were available and how to harvest them, but also how to make a connection with the spirit of the Other Beings in a way that would contribute to the balance and functioning of a complex world.

The principle of coexistence was also reflected in relationships between humans. When people from different cultures met, they ensured friendly relations by smoking a pipe and "making treaty." This concept entailed the right of each party to keep their own traditions while respecting those of others. Treaties were not only a promise to other people, they were a promise to the Creator that an effort would be made to maintain a sense of balance with other people.

The Newcomers

The French *coureurs de bois* Pierre-Ésprit Radisson and Médart Chouart, Sieur des Groseilliers, outlaw fur traders from New France, arrived in England in 1665 looking for financial backing to support their plans for a great fur trading venture in the New World. Through a combination of luck, good timing and well-placed connections, their proposal won the support of the English

King Charles II, who granted The Company of Adventurers Trading into Hudson Bay (the Hudson's Bay Company) exclusive trading rights in all the land that drained into Hudson Bay. Rupert's Land, as it was called, included all of northwestern Canada, except the southernmost parts of the prairie provinces, and encompassed an area six times the size of present-day Alberta.

This intrusion into what the French considered their hinterland was challenged from the first by the governor of New France, who sent armies overland to burn the English forts and attack the traders. In an effort to circumvent this harassment, the Hudson's Bay Company sent explorers overland to survey for suitable locations of inland posts and to entice the First Nations to travel downstream to trade at the posts along Hudson Bay.

These explorations had great effects on what was to become Alberta. From 1690 to 1692 Henry Kelsey journeyed southwest from York Fort as far as south-central Saskatchewan. While he failed to convince the A'aninin that they should make the journey to the Bay, his trek illustrated the possibility of inland travel and the potential for trade on the plains. In 1754 Anthony Henday was sent southwestward from York Fort toward the homeland of the Archithinues (probably Blackfoot-speaking people) with the intention of convincing them to travel to the Bay to trade. But the people he met had all they needed on the plains and, moreover, were unfamiliar with the use of watercraft. They declined his invitation and suggested that the traders should come to them.

While the French threat ended in 1763, when New France was ceded to England at the end of the Seven Years' War, by 1780 a new challenge emerged. Among the refugees who fled to Canada from the newly independent United States were fur traders of Scottish descent. Many of these individuals settled in Montreal, where they formed independent fur trading companies and turned their attention to the wilderness of northwestern North America. As they explored the lakes and rivers, routes were established for the shipment of supplies to the hinterland and furs to Montreal. The most successful of these was the North West Company.

By 1820, both companies had overextended themselves. Trading posts dotted the landscape from the Great Lakes and James Bay, across the prairies and parklands, to the Arctic and Pacific Oceans. At the same time, the market for furs in Europe had reached its limit and fur prices fell. The two companies merged in 1821 to form a restructured Hudson's Bay Company.

A New People

Many of the newcomers found companionship with women from the First Nations. These partnerships were formed for business and practical, as well as romantic, reasons. Successful trade depended upon one's knowledge of what was being said, of how to act, and of whom one was meeting. The women acted as linguistic and cultural translators who offered advice to the traders. Moreover, European food and clothes were not always well suited for life in this "new" land. Native wives provided important sewing, cooking, and hide-tanning skills. The women also provided a privileged avenue of access to trade goods for their relations.

William Pearce built his sandstone estate, "Bow Bend Shack," in 1889. Originally encompassing 197 acres, it was torn down in 1957 to make way for a Simpson Sears store on Calgary's city limits (Glenbow Archives/NA-2289-6)

These liaisons, themselves, were multicultural. The newcomers were from the English middle class, the working class of the Orkney Islands, Scots from Montreal, French Canadian voyageurs from Quebec, and Americans from Montana. There were also Iroquois and Anishinabe men who had been hired by the Montreal traders. The women were from nearly every First Nation in northern North America. As their children grew, they chose a variety of lifestyles. Some were sent to England to be educated and then returned as clerks of the fur trade companies. Others lived with their First Nations relatives. Some settled on farms near Fort Gary (present-day Winnipeg); others spent much of their time hunting buffalo to supply meat to the fur traders.

Whatever their background or lifestyle, these people all understood their identity in terms of their role within the fur trade. When Rupert's Land was sold to the government of Canada, these people were concerned that their right to self-determination and their tenure on the land would not be recognized. They joined together in a provisional government and petitioned the Canadian officials for recognition. Some of these rights were recognized in the Manitoba Act, 1870. However, the Constitution Act, 1871, obscured the differences among the mixed-ancestry cultures. Henceforth, the legislators assumed that all were Métis, a blend of French-Canadian and First Nations (usually Cree).

Government Relations and the Native Peoples

After purchasing Rupert's Land from the Hudson's Bay Company in 1870, the Canadian government began negotiating with any other people who might claim rights to the land. Beginning in 1871, a series of eleven numbered treaties were made with First Nations people of the prairies and forests of western Canada. These treaties declared that the First Nations "ceded" and "surrendered" all claims to the land. In exchange, each First Nation was given a land base, the size of which was in accordance with the population of the Nation. Oral traditions also recall verbal promises of medical assistance, education, and food supplies in times of distress.

The physical presence of the Métis, and their right to occupy the land, was also recognized. At the time of treaty making, the Métis who were "following a Native lifestyle" were presented with the choice of taking treaty as a First Nations person or receiving scrip. Scrip, a certificate that distributed Crown land to individuals, was issued for either land or money, that could be used to purchase land. If the money was not spent to purchase real estate, the people lost any chance of acquiring a land base. People taking treaty surrendered many individual rights and became subject to the provisions of the Indian Act. A person taking scrip gave up any rights he might have as a Treaty Indian. As most of these negotiations took place in areas that were very far removed from the centres of development, it was hard for people to understand what these rights entailed; it was impossible to foresee the consequences of making a choice.

Oral traditions from throughout Western Canada affirm that the First Nations did not understand the government's intentions. By the early 1870s the people on the Plains were aware that their traditional way of life was facing a great change. Disease had ravaged them for over a century. Buffalo were becoming scarce. Immigrants were arriving from the east, forcing other First Nations from their homes and creating pressure and friction across western North America, while the decline of the fur trade meant that a new economy was on the horizon. The Hudson's Bay Company had always demonstrated a willingness to assist the First Nations in times of need. If the government was to replace the HBC, it was assumed that they would continue in this role. For their part, the First Nations were willing to help any newcomers learn how to live in this land, just as they had helped the traders. The treaties were understood to be a formal agreement to continue a relationship that was nearly two centuries old.

The pattern of treaty-making illustrates the government's intentions. The numbered treaties follow the route of settlement and development through Western Canada. The earlier treaties (Numbers 1 to 7) included land along the route of the Canadian Pacific Railway, in the region that Sir John A. Macdonald saw as the new homeland for immigrants to a new country. Treaties in the more northerly regions were negotiated only after the value of the resources in the region was recognized and their development became feasible. Moreover, the government became very concerned about the costs incurred by treaty obligations and aggressively encouraged Reserves to become self-sufficient and adopt Western social, political and education systems. Residential schools were established in the early 1900s to teach new ways to the children and to discourage traditional language and culture. Sometimes, Reserve land was sold to pay for rations.

Native People in the Province of Alberta

While the proclamation in 1905 of Alberta as a province brought many advantages, few of these benefits found their way to the Native people. Land continued to be appropriated for use by newcomers. Rations were scarce. In the south, expensive agricultural implements were beyond the means of most Native farmers and ranchers. The Natural Resources Transfer Act of 1930 identified hunting, trapping and fishing as provincial responsibilities. In the north, this meant that new provincial regulations limited these traditional subsistence activities.

The situation had become desperate by the 1930s. The Métis organized L'Association des Métis d'Alberta et des Territoires du Nord Ouest (the Métis Association of Alberta) in 1932 to draw attention to their concerns. The province responded by forming the Ewing Commission to investigate the poor social and economic conditions of the Métis. The Métis Betterment Act, 1938, arose from the Commission's recommendation and identified Métis Settlements as a land base. In 1943 a trust fund was established for the benefit of the settlements. However, Métis were still left in limbo within the province's administrative structure. After prolonged negotiations, the Métis Settlement Accord, 1989, defined the nature of the settlements, how they are to be administered, who may have membership, and how they are to be funded.

The Indian Association of Alberta (IAA) was also formed in the 1930s. The IAA's initial goals were to lobby for reforms to the Indian Act, effect changes in the education and health systems, create awareness among non-Aboriginals of living conditions on Reserves, and educate the public about treaty rights. Throughout the 1940s and 1950s, the IAA was a national force in the preservation of aboriginal rights. In the late 1960s, the focus shifted to more contemporary issues as the leaders began to address economic development. Today individual Reserves have taken the lead in settling land disputes and resource allocation. The issues of a century ago have not been mitigated; they are being argued in different arenas.

The Future

As we look out on Alberta's next hundred years, we need to conceptualize how aboriginal people will continue to affect the history and the destiny of the province. To begin with, we need to consider how the original spirit and intent of the Albertan numbered treaties (6, 7, and 8), can be honoured in a world vastly changed from that of their creation in the 1870s. As the 1996 *Report of the Royal Commission on Aboriginal People* notes:

The Aboriginal view of the treaties was very different. They believed what the King's (sic) men told them, that the marks scratched on parchment captured the essence of their talks. They were angered and dismayed to discover later that what had been pledged in words, leader to leader, was not recorded accurately. They accepted the monarch, but only as a kind of kin figure, a distant "protector" who could be called upon to safeguard their interests and enforce treaty agreement. They had no notion of giving up their land, a concept foreign to Aboriginal cultures.

Today, descendants of those who made treaty seek a modern reinterpretation of what their elders thought they were creating when they agreed to sign the documents that codified their oral negotiations. Fundamental to this rethinking, however, remains their original spirit and intent. To the Dene, Cree, Nakoda, Tsuu T'ina, and Blackfoot of Alberta the treaties were about peace, safe travel and protection. Aboriginal Albertans now seek a fair share of the resource royalties in their traditional territories, which encompass vastly larger areas than the allocated reserves and Métis settlements. They also want much more comprehensive consultation on the next phases of resource development (including forestry, oil and gas, mines, wind farms and tourism), predicated on what they hold as the Crown's duty to consult. Recent judgements of the Supreme Court of Canada are giving new life to these hopes, and if current judicial trends hold, more royalty sharing and much broader consultation, including the occasional power to say no to development, will occur. From the aboriginal perspective this is respect consistent with the original spirit and intent of the treaties; it is also a respect that flows from aboriginal title, something they never intended to surrender at the time of treaty making.

Indian Association of Alberta meeting at Saddle Lake in 1948 (Glenbow Archives/NA-4212-156).

The expression of new treaty rights may greatly influence economic development in Alberta in the next century. The aboriginal population in Alberta (and across Canada) is growing rapidly, and now is 10 times what it was in the 1870s. Over one million aboriginal people now are included in the Canadian population. In Alberta, the rapid growth rate of the aboriginal population guarantees that many young people will continue to move from isolated reserves into the larger towns and cities, and rural reserve economies will continue to be stressed. In the north of the province this stress will be due to a high demand for skilled labour; in the south much economic stress will be linked with depopulation and lost opportunity.

In northern Alberta economic opportunities in forestry and oil and gas will continue to grow. The Dene Tha' (which means in the Dene language People Common to the Territory or Common Peoples) who live in three separate northwestern Alberta communities—Bushe River, Meander River and Chateh—will continue to develop their uniquely mixed economy. They struggle to maintain hunting and trapping in the face of today's explosion of clear cuts, well sites and pipeline development. Their *Dene Tha' Traditional Land Use and Occupancy Study* (1997), demonstrates a pattern of broad ranging land use tied to the bush economy. If you asked a Dene Tha' elder today "Where did you used to live on the land?" he would reply without hesitation, "Everywhere." Their community goal is to try to keep this bush economy option viable for the next generation.

The Honourable Ralph Steinhauer, who served as Lieutenant Governor of Alberta from 1974 to 1979, was the first Aboriginal to hold vice-regal office in Canada (Provincial Archives of Alberta/J1953).

The same attitude is also reflected in other northern Alberta aboriginal communities. Elders across the provincial North hope that the bush economy lifestyle can be maintained. Fort McKay elder Julian Powder noted this in his community's traditional land use and occupancy study in 1994, "There is Still Survival Out There." What he envisaged was the opportunity to survive on the bounty of the land if the industrial economy crashes sometime in the future. Alberta elders still alive today have strong memories of the Depression in the 1930s, and distrust an excessive reliance on cash, city life and modern amenities. They passionately desire that today's youth grow up with the skills to succeed in both worlds: the bush and the corporation. We must ask: "Is this really possible?"

"We have to believe that it is!" argue many aboriginal Albertans who still have a foot in both worlds. Fred MacDonald of Fort McKay stresses the duty of elders to document the bush lifestyle, and leave information for the youth, "so they know there is a living to be made out there." Like Julian Powder, Fred lived through the Great Depression, and he is still instinctively distrustful of government and corporate promises. Jacqueline Auger of Desmarais echoes Fred's sentiments and hopes that young people will develop more respect for their elders and the lives they lived. "I've never seen anything like what goes on today. There is so much alcohol and drugs in our community today." Clearly the bush economy cannot compete with the cash available to workers in the oil sands or big pulp mills, but it does offer an alternative lifestyle, and as Sophie Noskiye says, "Life back then was harder, but people were healthy and happy."

Key to maintaining the bush economy option is stewarding the land base. Pat Auger, another Desmarais elder, notes:

Back in the old days you would shoot, hunt, fish, trap anywhere or anytime you saw anything. Today you have to have licences for everything. You can't even shoot a duck or go fishing without some type of officer there to tell you what you can or cannot do. We used to have a lot of wildlife and fish. Today you are lucky if you can kill a moose within one hundred miles of here.

Clearly there must be strong regulations to protect the land, water and air resources, but they must also factor in the role and importance of traditional ecological knowledge (or TEK). The combination of traditional ecological knowledge and western scientific knowledge to take resource management decisions is called co-management in Canada, and Alberta is just beginning to acknowledge its importance to resource conservation regimes. If we are going to preserve our future options in the quest of sustainability, co-management is going to have to be vigorously pursued.

Ironically, the ability to hunt, fish and trap is greatly influenced today by the availability of cash. Skidoos, gas-powered tricycles and quads, boats, motors, fishing tackle, guns, and ammunition are all necessary tools for success in the modern version of the bush economy. Getting them requires success in the corporate world, in the industrial economy. As a consequence, the people with the greatest access to bush economy resources are workers in oil and gas, forestry, mining or government. Given more aboriginal participation in these sectors, there should be at least enough money to get back into the bush in the next 100 years!

My Life as a First Nations Person in Alberta

Sandra Crazy Bull

I wonder what Mi'k ai'stowa (Red Crow) would think? Our people acknowledged Mi'k ai'stowa as a leader and looked to him for wise decisions. He spoke on behalf of my people (the Kainai) when we made treaty with the representatives of the Queen. Our oral traditions recall that Mi'k ai'stowa believed he was offering help to the new settlers who did not know how to live in our land. In exchange, we were to receive education, health care, and food that would help us adjust to a time when the buffalo were no longer around. When asked if he would give up the land, Mi'k ai'stowa held up a handful of earth and said he could never give away that which belonged to Creator. He then plucked a tuft of grass and told the officials his people would willingly share that with the newcomers.

If he were to come back today, I wonder if Mi'k ai'stowa would be satisfied with how the treaty has been honoured?

At the start of the 1900s, the government provided education to us by giving the responsibility to religious organizations (most often the Anglican, Roman Catholic and Methodist churches). Residential schools were built throughout Canada and Aboriginal children were compelled to

Sandra Crazy Bull
(Sandra Crazy Bull).

live away from their families for most of the year. We could not use our own language or practice our traditional ceremonies. We were taught only the rudimentary skills. There was no attempt to teach us the ways our people had contributed to the development and prosperity of Alberta. We were given no opportunity to find pride in our people. Instead, we were encouraged to adopt Euro-Canadian lifestyles. Instead of education, we got assimilation. Some people resisted; others lost touch with their cultural roots. For most, it has left a lasting feeling of loss and cultural disorientation.

The residential school system lasted from the early 1900s until the 1970s. It will take many generations for Native society to recover.

Our people had been ravaged by epidemics since the 1600s. By the time we made treaty with the Queen, we had seen the effects of small-pox, measles, whooping cough, tuberculosis, and alcohol. We knew that European medicine could help us and our leaders asked that government provide health care. Although a provision for health care was not written in the Treaty, we expected to be treated well, as we would treat our own relatives. But, from the start, health care had strings attached.

During our first days on the Reserve, health care was often denied to those who did not give up their traditional lifestyle. The treatment of the ill was tied to assimilation.

Today, the cost of health care has grown. We must continually press the government to pay for new kinds of treatment and new, more effective drugs. Most often, we get reimbursed only for "generic" prescription drugs. If we are allergic to these drugs, we must pay for other brands that we can use.

We have endured these hardships and, recently, have begun to take control of our own destiny. The Kainai (Blood Tribe) is the owner and operator of several successful businesses. Kainai Agri-Business coordinates the agricultural industry on the Reserve. Its professional management provides a profitable return to the Kainai on investment from all of the agricultural assets. Our diverse crops provide feed for the livestock industry and raw materials for the food sector and export markets.

Our Kainaiwa Resources Inc. has overseen vast improvements in responsible resource management on the Reserve. This tribally owned entity allows members to take back internal management of natural resources on the Reserve and move beyond being passive royalty recipients while a third party (the federal government) manages our resources.

We have always had our own ways of law enforcement. We have adapted these to the Western ways of law enforcement and the Blood Tribe Police represents a blend of these approaches. We also maintain our own Emergency Medical Services and Fire Department.

Our health and education continue to be a significant part of our lives. The revenues generated through our involvement in agriculture and natural resource development have helped us take control of these. We now manage our own extended care facility. Schools have begun integrating Blackfoot immersion programs within the curriculum. Students in these classes excel in all areas of study and are confident and excited about learning.

When Red Crow College opened its doors as a post-secondary and technical training institute in 1995, it signalled the governance of our own education system. Over the past 18 years, the college has evolved and now offers diploma and degree programs. This empowers our people to continue their education within a comfortable, welcoming atmosphere and without having to confront the feelings of isolation and discrimination that pervade off-reserve institutions. Hence, our students have a greater chance of success.

We have also reclaimed responsibility for our social welfare system. We have negotiated with federal and provincial governments to assume responsibility for our own child welfare system. Children who are at risk will now be placed in Kainai foster homes, assuring that assimilation and loss of culture will be minimized.

All this has been achieved through constant negotiation with governments. The struggle to retrieve our aboriginal and treaty rights has been on the political agenda for my entire life. Throughout history, our perspectives have been misunderstood and neglected. Now, we seem to be moving in a more positive direction.

I wonder what Mi'k ai'stowa will think if he comes back when my children are grown?

Continued rights of access will also be important for sustaining the bush economy option. The law of Aboriginal title will be helpful in this cause. As more and more litigation is pursued by First Nations and Métis Albertans, more precision on Aboriginal land rights will emerge. At present the Canadian common law establishes three things:

Aboriginal people have rights of occupancy or use of portions of Canada that far exceed their current land base. These rights are based on their history of having lived in or used those lands since time immemorial.

Agreements between the Crown and an Aboriginal nation (such as treaties) must be worked out before non-Aboriginal people can occupy or use that nation's traditional lands; and

The Crown of Canada is the guardian of Aboriginal titles to their traditional lands and is obliged to support and protect their interests in those lands.

As Alberta heads into the next century, it will be wise to acknowledge proactively the above in negotiations where the affected parties talk face-to-face. More time spent in court will only build on existing aggravations in many cases, and not provide the human solutions necessary for co-management and revenue sharing from Crown lands to succeed in practice. One thing seems to be certain: Aboriginal claimants are succeeding in court more often than they are failing, and court resolutions generally lack the creativity inherent in negotiations. In the words of Chief Edward John:

It has never been the role of the Courts to define the detailed terms of the accommodation between the Crown and the First [Peoples]. We have gone to the Courts in our own defence.

Beyond the Courts and the assertion of Aboriginal rights and participation in decision-making related to traditional lands and their contemporary use, Aboriginal Albertans, north and south, seek economic development close to home. This desire will increase in Alberta's second century because of demographics. Higher birth rates and life expectancy will continue to provide sharp increases in the rural and urban Aboriginal population. As local job opportunities are exhausted, young Aboriginal workers will move in search of a decent living. Institutes of technology, colleges, and universities will all welcome growing numbers of Aboriginal students. The decisions they take about their education and training will be diverse. Back in their home reserves and settlements, simplistic, cookie cutter economic development programs will fail to excite new graduates with cutting edge skills. And there will still be the dilemma of creating balanced development that meets the needs of both the bush and industrial economies, and offers the hope of sustainability.

Didi Umperville of Syncrude, which has worked hard to form partnerships with the First Nations (Syncrude Canada Ltd).

Aboriginal Partnerships and Development
Eric Newell

The partnerships between First Nations, Métis settlements and the energy industry were critical to the success of the oil sands development in the Fort McMurray and Wood Buffalo regions. Developing successful partnerships was not easy. We needed to find opportunities for Aboriginals, to aid industry but also because it was the right thing to do. As we proceeded, we made every mistake in the book. We thought we were in a hiring program. If you've grown up in a small community, being thrown into a huge industrial complex is not a formula for success, whether you're Aboriginal or not.

Our fundamental mistake was that we were not in a hiring program. We were in a huge *development* program. We met with the Chiefs and worked with them to identify role models. Successful ventures are so important and we wanted this to be a positive experience for the Aboriginal communities. For partnerships to be effective, there must be shared interests, mutual goals and responsibilities for all parties. Industry, First Nations and Métis shared strong common areas of interest. Aboriginal peoples have a deep attachment to the land and industry learned to respect and adopt that interest. At hearings, it was important not just to talk, but to understand the issues and be proactive about the environment. Environmental issues require ongoing consultation among regional stakeholders and not just at hearings to gain operating approvals.

Everyone needed education; those working for Syncrude managers and supervisors in the area took cross-cultural training so they understood the peoples and their history.

Education was key for the Aboriginals who would be working with Syncrude. We needed to raise the educational levels of the community, especially with the youth.

This would allow Syncrude to achieve its stated goal within the local communities—that they would benefit equally from oil sands development. First Nations and Métis want to become self-sufficient and industry worked with them to develop native-owned companies.

All benefited from employment opportunities. We worked with leaders in five First Nations and six Métis settlements to foster entrepreneurial skills and independent company ownership. We also focused on community development in the social arena.

When only Syncrude and Suncor were operating in the area, we were able to work with the Aboriginal communities without much formal structure. Once the oil sands started to boom, attracting other energy companies, we formed the Athabasca Tribal Council Industry Partnership with the five First Nations and industry players. It has a formal structure with signed agreements and roles and responsibilities. The industry is required to pay for consultants that the First Nations hire to ensure environmental sensitivities are respected.

The results of Aboriginal education and employment now speak for themselves. Syncrude is one of the largest employers of Aboriginals in Canada, with over 700 employees and contractors. That's 13% of Syncrude's total work force and that is also consistent with the population of Aboriginals in the area.

We have a mutual obligation with the Athabasca Tribal Council to encourage young people to share in the education and opportunities.

We identify and work with the Tribal Council on entrepreneurship as well as develop business plans for prospective companies. Syncrude does over $90 million in annual business with Aboriginal companies. Aboriginal businesses are very effective and provide important and worthy competitive services, and have helped us to achieve triple our original target.

We still have many challenges in the area of community development. As oil sands development grows, Aboriginal partnerships need to expand and to be formalized, particularly long-term benefit agreements with all governments—municipal, provincial and federal. We need to focus on benefit sharing and benefits that flow back to the First Nations. Such agreements would also provide more certainty for industry, as operating permits would be clearly outlined.

I believe that there is no place in the world where the partnerships and relationships with Aboriginal peoples equal those of Syncrude and the other industry players in northeast Alberta. Our local Aboriginal communities are key stakeholders, owner-operators and employees. Have we reached the ultimate goal? No, they are still disadvantaged groups when it comes to social and economic opportunities. We as a society and province need to become more inclusive so Aboriginal peoples can take a more active part in the Alberta economy. We need to help them to improve their educational outcomes.

Now we face either a big opportunity or a big challenge. The fastest growing segment of our population, by far, is Aboriginal youth. We need to create 400,000 new jobs for Aboriginals in Canada by 2020 if we are to match employment levels with non-Aboriginals. At the same time, we will have a national shortage of one million skilled workers, according to the Conference Board of Canada.

That's where we have a tremendous opportunity to close the skills gap. Aboriginal youth across the country, and especially in Alberta, can help make that happen. Taking this opportunity will also have an enormous social benefit to Aboriginals and the larger society.

Establishing successful partnerships will generate innovative and creative solutions. The will is there. But, as Will Rogers said, "Even if you're on the right track, you'll get run over if you aren't moving fast enough."

In grappling with this set of special economic development news, the Royal Commission on Aboriginal Peoples made four proposals:

A special 10-year program to train Aboriginal people for work that has to be done in newly self-governing nations.

A new approach to employment equity, in which employees work with Aboriginal organizations to forecast vacancies and train Aboriginal people to fill them.

Measures to increase the number of Aboriginal employment service agencies and their capacity to place Aboriginal people in the labour force.

Provision of culturally appropriate and affordable child care, so that more Aboriginal parents can join the labour force.

All of these recommendations would benefit Alberta right now.

Perhaps the best way to move in the quest for a more sustainable and accepting path in Alberta's second century is to follow more properly the road map established by Treaties 6, 7 and 8 in the 1870s. To Aboriginal Albertans the Treaties are sacred documents that have created bonds that cannot be broken. They have created between the First Nations and the newcomers an alliance akin to the highest form of marriage between two families. We must not forget that they are also Constitutional documents, recognized and affirmed by section 35 of the Constitution Act, 1982. By that Act they are binding upon us all as Canadians. Why not enter the next era of provincehood by honouring the provisions of existing treaties and interpreting their original spirit and intent in modern terms? This implies appropriate sharing of resource revenues and co-management of natural resources. Why not establish a treaty revitalization process to achieve these ends? Why not start right here in Alberta by taking steps to reallocate some land and resource ownership rights to those First Nations and Métis communities most in need? Such acts of grace could set the stage for a new millennium of cooperation and sustainability, and be a truly "made in Alberta" solution.

Albertans on the Land

5

ROGER GIBBINS AND KAREN WILKIE

Canadian communities are invariably shaped and moulded by their natural and physical environment. Indeed, it is difficult, if not impossible, to think of communities apart from their environments. For example, Vancouver, British Columbia and St. John's, Newfoundland, are not just any two cities; they are cities perched respectively on the edges of the Pacific and Atlantic oceans, and must be understood in terms of those locations. In a similar fashion, prairie communities cannot be separated from the "miles and miles of miles and miles," and from the endless skies that frame prairie society. Moreover, the Alberta landscape provides iconic images that are used to communicate the essence of the province to Albertans themselves, and to the world. Think, for example, of the Rocky Mountains, of the ancient river valleys around Dinosaur Provincial Park, of the prairie grasslands running up against the Cypress Hills

At the very depth of the Great Depression of the 1930s, this dust storm blew into Lethbridge (Glenbow Archives/NA-2308-1).

in the southeastern corner of the province, or the North Saskatchewan River valley cutting through Edmonton.

But this, of course, is only half the picture, for the relationship between people and the land is interactive. Not only are we shaped by the land; we shape it in turn, as patterns of settlement are imposed on the natural landscape. Just as we adapt to the natural environment, we try to adapt that environment to our social and economic needs. Thus the native grasslands are broken by plows, ranchland is fenced, and urban communities spill across the land. Many of our most powerful images depict human activity *embedded within* a breathtaking natural environment—the chateaus at Banff and Lake Louise, canoes on Maligne Lake, ranchers working in the foothills of the Rockies, immense fields of wheat and canola sweeping towards the mountains in the west.

It is not surprising, therefore, that the character of Alberta—our "state of mind"—cannot be understood without understanding Albertans' reciprocal relationship with the land. The emblematic images of that relationship are not ones of a remote physical landscape, or of one that has been conquered and subdued, but rather a physical landscape woven into the very essence of the province.

Somewhat more surprising, the relationship with the land will become even more important in the province's next century. Urbanization and patterns of agriculture and industrial development have so thoroughly transformed the original habitat that Albertans are beginning to encounter very real limits to land and water resources. Therefore, managing the land base of the province—its wild, working and urban landscapes, its watersheds and water—will be one of the most important but also most difficult challenges Albertans will face as they move into their second century as a provincial community.

The history of Albertans' relationship with the land can be broken into three very rough and overlapping periods. In simple, perhaps even simplistic, terms, they are 1) the period of early agrarian settlement, running from the turn of the twentieth century through the Great Depression of the 1930s, 2) the period of oil and gas development, running from the late 1940s through today, and 3) the period of rapid urbanization and overall population growth, running from the early 1970s through today. Taken together, these three periods also constitute movement from a frontier of seemingly limitless bounty and possibilities to a new reality where limits on land and water are rising to the top of the public policy agenda.

Agrarian Frontier

The original Aboriginal communities left little mark on the natural landscape of Alberta; First Nations worked within the constraints and opportunities of that environment without transforming the land in any significant way. Today, their early footprint can hardly be detected—inscriptions at Writing on Stone Provincial Park, stones from tipi circles found across the province, all but buried in the prairie grass. The prairie remained little changed, in fact, through the first contacts with non-Aboriginals who came in pursuit of the fur trade. Part of the natural bounty was harvested for distant markets, but man's footprint on the natural environment was still faint.

Workmen at the entrance to one of the many coal mines in the Edmonton area, photographed at the turn of the 20th century (Provincial Archives of Alberta/B-1544).

This relationship with the natural environment changed dramatically, and forever, with the arrival of settlers from other parts of Canada, the United States and Europe. They came in pursuit of open land that could be farmed and ranched, and thus the agrarian frontier brought a time of irrevocable physical transformation. Large parts of the prairie grassland were literally broken, plowed and cultivated for crops. Other parts of the province were cleared of trees or, in the southern half, fenced and used for raising cattle. Irrigation systems brought water and crops to formerly semi-arid land. The footprint of agricultural settlement, including the railroads, roads, section lines, power lines and phone lines is unmistakable. To fly over Alberta today is to fly over a radically transformed physical environment. While the Rockies and the far north may appear to be largely untouched, the massive grid of agricultural settlement dominates the landscape as seen from the air.

None of this, it should be stressed, is to bemoan or lament agricultural settlement. Rather, the point is that the agrarian frontier was just that, a frontier of seemingly limitless space and opportunity. The natural environment was there to be moulded and adapted for human use; it existed in such abundance that little thought was given to conservation. Indeed, the first generation of settlers could not have imagined that Alberta's small, albeit growing, population

The "dirty thirties" destroyed nearly 14,000 prairie farms and devastated the livelihood of thousands of Alberta's farmers and their families (Provincial Archives of Alberta/A3742).

could ever fill the vast land base of the province. Nonetheless, the province's wild beauty was not completely overlooked, particularly in the mountains where agricultural settlement would never penetrate. Thus we saw the establishment of Canada's first national park at Banff in 1885, and then the parks at Jasper (est. 1907), Waterton Lakes (est. 1895) and Wood Buffalo (est. 1922). Even here, however, lodges provided an outpost for human settlement, and the rawness of the natural environment was airbrushed to a considerable degree in the paintings of the national parks that were used to attract the first European tourists.

In many ways, the pioneer ethos shaped Alberta's emerging political culture, and thereby the attitudinal relationship between Albertans and the land. The land was there to be settled and tamed, and thus the expanding human imprint on the land was a sign of progress, even of civilization. While the beauty of the natural landscape was undoubtedly appreciated then as it is now, it was not seen as a necessary constraint on settlement. There was, or so it seemed, lots of land, and lots of natural beauty, to go around.

Although agricultural settlement was dealt a staggering blow by the Great Depression of the 1930s, when international markets for Alberta's crops collapsed, drought baked the land, and grasshoppers ate what little that did emerge, agricultural development in the province never stopped. Even in the Depression years, agricultural settlement pushed north into the Peace country. Irrigation opened up new lands for cultivation, settlement pushed further north, crops diversified, and intensive livestock operations began. Farms got larger, and productivity increased. Nonetheless, the open frontier is no more, and agriculture now increasingly butts up against oil and gas exploration, and against a rapidly expanding urban population. Suddenly, and in a way that could not have been foreseen in 1905, the province is crowded.

The Oil and Gas Frontier

Even during the early days of the agrarian frontier, Albertans did not ignore the resources found under the rich soil. The Athabasca oil sands were used by Aboriginal communities in a variety of ways, including for caulking their canoes. Vast reserves of coal were tapped at Drumheller, the Crowsnest Pass and north along the foothills of the Rockies. In the 1920s and 1930s, after oil was found in Turner Valley (1914), the flares of burning natural gas from the wells lit the sky in Calgary, 80 kilometres to the north. However, the primary attention of Albertans did not shift from the land to the resources under the land until the oil strike at Leduc in 1947. By then the ownership of natural resources had been transferred from the federal to the provincial Crown, and thus the foundation was in place for public revenues to be realized from the nascent oil and natural gas industries. National policies created a captive Canadian market for Alberta oil from the Ottawa valley west, and a growing network of pipelines began to move both oil and gas into American markets. Then in the 1970s OPEC escalated the price of oil, and the boom times arrived in Alberta.

There is no question that energy resources have had a huge impact on the province. In 2004–05, for example, non-renewable resource revenues for the provincial treasury were estimated to be $9.63 billion, with the total provincial budget being just under $23 billion. The impact, moreover, has been far more than financial—it has fueled both urban and rural growth, fostered a highly technological provincial economy, and stamped the image of Alberta for those inside and outside the province.

Within a week of the discovery of oil at Turner Valley on May 14, 1914, forty oil companies opened their doors in Calgary, giving rise to rampant stock speculation (Provincial Archives of Alberta/P-1238).

Not surprisingly, Albertans came to define themselves, and to be defined by others, in terms of the oil and natural gas industry. Admittedly, this definition carried with it some negative connotations for Canadians living outside the province who came to see Albertans as blue-eyed sheiks. Within Alberta, the definition was overwhelmingly positive, speaking as it did to wealth, entrepreneurship, and industrial development. Today, however, the primacy of the energy industry is no longer uncontested, as it too begins to run up against limits on land and water, and up against the growing edge of the urban frontier. Like the agricultural producers, the energy industry must now jostle for space in a finite landscape.

The Urban Frontier

At first blush it may be difficult to believe that Albertans are beginning to confront limits when it comes to land. The province, after all, constitutes a vast area and, with a population of just over three million, it cannot be considered densely populated by even the loosest standards. And to be fair, there is not a general problem of too many people, too little land. Rather, there are beginning to be significant pinch points in some regions of the province, most notably surrounding metropolitan Calgary and Edmonton, the Queen Elizabeth Highway 2 corridor linking the two metropolitan areas, and the Calgary–Banff corridor. Just as the agrarian frontier spread across the province at the beginning of the last century, today the demographic, economic and environmental footprint of urban communities is steadily expanding.

Although Alberta's total population is still relatively small compared to Ontario's and Quebec's, and for that matter to British Columbia's, its urban population is growing at a tremendous rate. Between 1996 and 2003, Calgary's population increased by 20%, faster than Vancouver's or Toronto's. Edmonton also showed impressive growth during the same period, with a 12% increase in population. In the face of such growth, urban areas are experiencing a boom in housing and real estate markets. Housing construction, new communities, and expanding infrastructure are common sights throughout Alberta, and are transforming the landscape. Population growth and concomitant housing demand are significantly altering the natural environment and the land base in Alberta. These changes are highly visible and are particularly evident at the interface between the urban and rural landscapes as the urban frontier continues to expand, thereby consuming agricultural land.

Alberta is as highly urbanized as any province in Canada, and the trend towards even greater urbanization will continue unabated. Urbanization in turn can be expected to transform how Albertans see the land and their relationship to it. Working relationships on the land—agriculture, ranching, oil and gas exploration—are increasingly remote to an urban population. The land will be seen more and more through an environmental lens, and as the growing legions of urbanites begin to impose their policy preferences on the political process, land management issues could become more contentious.

Challenges to Come

Alberta's future will be determined in large part by how well we manage our relationship with the land, how well we handle our physical landscapes, and how well we manage water resources. As Alberta seeks to attract and retain human capital in what will undoubtedly be a more competitive global environment for such capital, the quality of the natural environment could be one of our greatest assets if we manage our relationship with that environment well. However, the management issues go well beyond the conservation of natural areas. Although there is no doubt that natural areas are important elements in the environment, they do not function in isolation. They are interconnected and dependent on broader wild, working and urban landscapes that cannot be ignored.

What, then, are the challenges that lie ahead?

The rock slide that levelled the town of Frank on April 29, 1903 was one of Alberta's worst natural disasters (Glenbow Archives/NA-411-9).

Making the Environmental Connection

Alberta is a prosperous province with a bright future; economic and population forecasts are strong and show no signs of slowing down. This prosperity has been and will likely continue to be based in large part on the province's natural resource base—on oil, natural gas, the oil sands and coal. But as Alberta moves into its second century, the challenge will be to recognize the importance of the land base to both economic prosperity and a quality environment. The natural environment can no longer be viewed separately from economic goals, and it can no longer be thought of after the fact, as an add-on.

The new economic reality is that the effective management of natural capital will be indispensable to the attainment of economic goals, and therefore the challenge will be to manage the land in a way that balances environmental interests and economic goals— that achieves environmental prosperity. Certainly there is little question that Alberta's natural capital will be an essential asset in the competition for highly mobile human resources. We will compete successfully or not on the basis of our quality of life, and in that respect natural capital will be increasingly important.

Managing Nature Naturally

Throughout the past 100 years, Albertans have managed their land base by dividing it up into different jurisdictions and management units based on arbitrarily placed human boundaries. Meanwhile water, wildlife, and ecosystems cover large areas and cross through different cities, towns and counties, and sometimes even cross provincial boundaries. The decisions made in one area directly affect the larger system as a whole, and by slicing up and managing the land base in isolated units we could undermine the overall quality of the natural environment.

We need a different approach that moves towards a decision-making system that recognizes and manages the natural environment in a way that makes sense naturally—by following the natural boundaries that are already defined for us. In this respect, Albertans are beginning to use watershed boundaries as natural containers for public policy frameworks. As we move forward, this will become more and more the norm.

Managing Cumulative Effects

Oil and gas exploration, forestry, mining, agriculture, and residential development do not occur in isolation. In fact, many of these activities are taking place at the same time in the same areas. When you consider these activities individually, the effects on the natural environment may seem to be relatively minor. How significant is one more well, another access road, or another 50 homes? But when you consider them together, when you take into account, for example, that close to 20,000 wells might be drilled in a single year, the effects quickly add up. To maintain and enhance the quality of the natural environment, the challenge will be to add up the effects of individual land use decisions and manage them collectively. Although finding policy frameworks that can handle such cumulative effects will be difficult, it will be essential.

Managing Urban Growth

The current pattern of urban growth resembles an ever-expanding balloon that continues to get bigger and bigger, with the prairie urban footprint expanding without the constraints imposed by oceanfronts or mountains. New development is dominated by suburban growth at the edge of cities where houses are encroaching upon agricultural land, and where infrastructure costs increase as development moves further from the city centre. Although this is the dominant pattern, there are alternatives. The challenge will be for urban areas to use land more efficiently. One way to increase efficiency is to look inward and to redevelop under-utilized areas in the inner city and increase density in already serviced areas. Another way is to look at different patterns of development to incorporate the natural environment when building new suburbs on agricultural or natural lands. It is unlikely that we will see the end of new suburbs in the next century, so it will be important to look for alternative designs that better integrate the natural environment.

Urban areas are home to the majority of Albertans. The urban environment is the landscape that most of us interact with daily. The quality of this environment and the diversity of natural capital within urban centres will be key to maintaining and enhancing the competitiveness of our cities. The quality of the environment is not a frill.

New York actress Georgina Engelbard with CPR guide E. Feuz in the movie *She Climbs to Conquer*, filmed on Mount Victoria (Glenbow NA 4868-197).

Conserving and Protecting Water Resources

Water is key to Alberta's current and future economic success, quality of life, and the quality of the natural environment. Water provides the lifeblood for agriculture, manufacturing, energy production, resource extraction, and urban and rural livelihoods. The importance of water in Alberta's second century cannot be overstated.

On a global scale, Alberta is relatively rich in water resources. However, water is a finite resource and the concerns over future water availability are mounting. This is particularly the case in the relatively arid south of the province, where existing water supplies are largely committed to irrigation. Recent times of drought and water shortages highlight the importance of water, and the need to conserve and protect water resources. Water conservation is a priority issue and will need to become an integral component of water management to allow for future economic growth and diversification, and to support the health and quality of aquatic environments.

Water is a connected resource shared between rural and urban municipalities, between pulp and paper industries and oil sands projects, and between intensive livestock operations and recreational users. The quality and the amount of water flowing through one area directly affects the next user downstream. Alberta needs to establish a capacity to coordinate and manage upstream and downstream decisions relating to water use, quality and conservation.

When we think of water resources, lakes, rivers and streams most often come to mind. However, the land surrounding these visible sources of water is equally important in the management of water resources. Land use decisions not only affect the land, but directly and indirectly affect the quality and quantity of water resources. Recognizing and managing the relationship between land and water will be critical, and devising a way to manage the two together will be a challenge that needs to be overcome. It is in terms of finite and increasingly scarce water resources that the contrast between the earlier agrarian frontier and Alberta's second century is brought into bold relief.

Protecting the Natural Environment—Grasslands to Grizzlies

Alberta's natural environment is rich and diverse. Across the badlands, native prairie, the Rocky Mountains, and the lush boreal region, the natural environment is an important part of our provincial heritage. These landscapes have also become major drawing cards for attracting both domestic and international visitors to Alberta. Banff National Park is by far the biggest natural attraction, but other places, such as Dinosaur Provincial Park for its collection of dinosaur bones, the boreal forest for its bird watching opportunities, and Jasper for its diversity of outdoor adventure activities, are attracting new visitors each year.

However, these natural landscapes are not only important to humans; they are also important for the thousands of species that depend on the habitat they provide. Alberta supports a diversity of wildflowers, grasses, butterflies, songbirds, and large mammals, including caribou, wolves and grizzly bears. Alberta's list of native species is both lengthy and diverse. This means in turn that meeting the needs of the natural landscape and the species that depend on that landscape will need to be a key component of future land management. Taking these needs into consideration and proactively planning for a future that continues to support a diverse, abundant and high quality natural environment will be critical to ensuring that the quality of our natural heritage continues for years to come.

Protecting our Landscapes

In many ways, landscapes are intangible and elusive; they are literally in the eyes of the beholder. And yet intuitively we know the value of landscapes, and recognize when they are degraded. For example, drive west from Calgary on the Trans-Canada highway towards Banff and the mountains, and note the jarring impact of billboards and roadside developments. Drive south from Edmonton on Highway 2, and witness how strip commercial development is beginning to encroach on the vistas of agricultural land. Think of the loss that would happen if the river valleys in Edmonton were developed. The point is a simple one, albeit a difficult one to embed in public policy—landscapes matter to our quality of life. They speak to our souls; they reflect the beauty of our environment. If population growth is allowed to despoil our wild, working and urban landscapes, the province will suffer irrevocable harm.

Planning Ahead

Albertans have a strong connection to the land. We value the land for the livelihoods it provides, the aesthetics it offers, the recreational opportunities that we enjoy, and the overall quality of life it produces. To ensure that we will continue to have these opportunities and potentially more, we need a long-term vision of where Alberta is heading over the next 100 years and the quality of environment that we want to pass on to future generations. This vision and long-term plan will help guide the decisions that we make today, to make sure they do not compromise the desired quality of the natural environment in the future.

None of these management tasks seem easy even when considered individually, and when they are all taken together, the task may seem difficult in the extreme. In fact, the task is even more difficult, as it must be handled in a way that still permits natural resource development, tourism and continued urbanization. There should be no suggestion in any of the above discussion that the production of oil and natural gas will cease, that the oil sands will not be developed, or that new energy resources, including coal bed methane and the resurgence of coal, not be pursued. We simply have to do both— preserve natural capital while retaining access to the natural resource wealth that lies beneath the soil (or on the soil, for that matter, when it comes to forestry resources and agriculture itself).

Yet, despite the magnitude of the task, there is every reason to hope that it is within our reach. Resource development today encroaches less on the natural environment than it did in the past, and will encroach still less in the years to come, as firms adopt ever more environmentally sensitive forms of development. Urban planning is increasingly attentive to the value of natural lands and landscapes. And, perhaps most important, the frontier ethic that shaped Alberta's first century is giving way to a new ethic within which environmental values are embedded, a new ethic that recognizes the limits that the province now faces. Nothing will be easy, but neither is anything impossible. We just need a new frontier ethos that takes into full account Alberta's natural capital.

The Alberta Economy

6

Deborah Yedlin

If there is one story that typifies the changing nature of Alberta's economy it is Eric Harvie's. The Ontario-born lawyer came to the province in 1911, set up a homestead and began practicing law. By all accounts he did just fine, but it was by no means a success on the scale encountered by James Lougheed or R.B. Bennett, who had close ties to big business in eastern Canada through their representation of companies like the Canadian Pacific Railway and the Hudson's Bay Company. But Harvie's fortune, like that of the province, changed forever on February 13, 1947.

Mr. Harvie's clients couldn't always afford to pay him in cash. Instead, they would pay him by signing over tracts of land. When Imperial Oil spudded Leduc #1 in February, 1947, it happened to be on one of the properties Mr. Harvie had received as payment for his services. He went on to become one of Canada's wealthiest entrepreneurs and a generous philanthropist, founding the Glenbow Museum in Calgary and funding the Banff School of Fine Arts (now the Banff Centre), the Calgary Zoo, and Heritage Park, which is dedicated to the preservation of the city's history.

The discovery of oil at Leduc, which was a long time coming after the Turner Valley oilfield was discovered some 35 miles southwest of Calgary in 1914, marked what the late Professor Henry Klassen defines as the fourth phase of Alberta's economic development.

But before examining how Leduc #1 changed Alberta from an economic standpoint, it's important to look at how the economy had developed up to that point.

A column of flame and a cloud of black smoke marked the beginning of Alberta's post-war oil boom when the Leduc #1 well came in on February 13, 1947 (Provincial Archives of Alberta/P2727).

Alberta's Economic Development: The First 50 Years

There are four essential commodities that played key roles in Alberta's economic development: fur, wheat, oil and natural gas, and the companies associated with each—The Hudson's Bay Company, the Canadian Pacific Railway and Imperial Oil.

The first stage of growth began with the fur trade, in which the Hudson's Bay Company and the North West Company organized their operations around a network of fur trading posts throughout the province. One of the biggest posts was Fort Edmonton, built in 1795. With Confederation in 1867 and the establishment of Fort Calgary by the North West Mounted Police, the government of Sir John A. MacDonald had embarked on a strategy based on the notion that for confederation to succeed the prairies had to be annexed and developed. This meant negotiating with the aboriginal peoples in order to gain control of the lands and pave the way for new settlement, establishing the NWMP as the legal authority, and building the railway in order to facilitate the transport of goods and services across the country. With all this in place when Alberta became a province in 1905, Alberta's economic base was characterized by the rise of enterprises that encompassed farming and ranching as well as the distribution and sale of dry goods. Alongside these larger operations grew a healthy number of small, specialized firms run by entrepreneurial types. This was a time of rapid growth and despite a few blips, including the century's first economic slowdown in 1912 and the outbreak of World War I in 1914, it continued apace until the Great Depression of 1929.

In that time, the provincial Liberal government passed the Farm Loan Act in 1917 in order to boost agricultural activity. This seemed to work because by 1920, agriculture accounted for 70.9 per cent of economic activity, while oil and gas was responsible for 12.4 per cent, with most of it coming from the Turner Valley area. The railway made it possible to export the province's agricultural output and until 1947 wheat was Alberta's number one export.

Critical to the province's economic development was the transfer of property from federal to provincial jurisdiction. In 1930, lands that were previously under the jurisdiction of the Federal Government—the so-called Dominion Lands—were transferred to the Province. This is a key event in Alberta's economic development because it gave the province control over its natural resources and in

The introduction of steam threshing machines in the 1880s helped to reduce the back-breaking work of bringing in the harvest (Provincial Archives of Alberta/B-274).

1931 the province began sharing in the benefits as it instituted a five per cent royalty on what was produced.

Another important development was the establishment of the Treasury Branches in 1938 by Premier Aberhart. Their mandate was to lend to Alberta-based businesses because the Eastern banks had essentially abandoned Alberta in the Dirty Thirties—137 branches disappeared from the landscape—leaving Albertans without banking facilities. To this day the ATB continues to be a key player in the provincial economic machine, growing from a loan portfolio of $1.6 million in 1944 to $12.1 billion by the end of 2004.

During this third phase of growth, which lasted until 1947, a shift took root in Alberta's economic landscape that saw the decline of the big enterprise that encompassed a wide variety of businesses, to one that was more specialized and in some respects marked the beginning of some of Alberta's bigger companies. It was during this time, for example, that the Burns family began buying up local butcher shops around the province, including the one run by the father of prominent Calgary businessman, Dick Haskayne, in the small town of Gleichen south of Calgary. In Edmonton, Gainers Ltd.—the meat packing plant established by John Gainer—had become one of the biggest employers in the city.

But it wasn't until 1947 and the discovery of big oil that Alberta's fortunes really changed. In the 20 years following the Depression, Alberta's economy didn't chalk up anything that could have been construed as impressive in terms of growth, with the majority of the province's gross domestic product coming from agriculture, construction, oil and gas, and manufacturing activities. In 1950, 44 per cent of Alberta's GDP was from agriculture, 16.3 per cent oil and mining and 19.7 per cent from construction. By 1978 more than half of GDP was attributable to the energy sector and only 7.7 per cent came from agriculture.

Birth of the Oil and Gas Industry: Turner Valley

Alberta's oil and gas industry grew in fits and starts, beginning with the accidental discovery of natural gas in 1883 near Medicine Hat by the Canadian Pacific Railway as it was drilling for water. In 1914 a rancher named William Stewart Herron, hauling coal between Black Diamond and Okotoks, noticed natural gas seeping through the coal. In May of that year the first well was drilled, marking the discovery of the Turner Valley oilfield, which produced 90 per cent of Canada's oil and gas production in 1935 and remained the biggest in the country until 1947.

Interestingly enough, Imperial Oil began life as a Canadian company based in Ontario in 1890. In 1898 it was bought by the Rockefeller-owned Standard Oil Trust. Now for the Alberta connection. When the Turner Valley Field was discovered, the company formed was called the Calgary Petroleum Products Company and one of its board members was James Lougheed, grandfather to former Alberta Premier Peter Lougheed. In 1921 a controlling interest in the company was sold to Imperial Oil and by 1929 Imperial Oil controlled 75 per cent of the production from Turner Valley.

In retrospect, the fact that Imperial Oil was successful in finding oil illustrates the old adage of hope conquering experience. According to Eric Hanson, in his book Dynamic Decade, seven of eight exploration wells drilled in the province before 1947 were dry and only one in 20 found oil. Before 1947 oil had been elusive and more often than not, exploratory efforts directed at finding oil yielded natural gas instead.

This caused other issues. If natural gas was found it was burned off—or flared—as happened in great quantities at Turner Valley. There are many stories about folks in the area being able to work at night by the light of the gas that was being burned. This practice had two outcomes: by blowing off the "gas cap" that lay above the reservoir containing the oil, the pressure in the reservoir itself was depleted to the point where it would never be possible to produce oil.

As a result of these types of events, the provincial government established the Petroleum and Natural Gas Conservation Board—the forerunner to today's Energy and Utilities Board—with the purpose of overseeing production practices. In 1959, following a royal commission studying supply development, the federal government created its own version, the National Energy Board.

In addition to dramatically changing the course of Alberta's economic history, the 1947 discovery did something else, too: it ratcheted up the rivalry between Edmonton and Calgary. When the province was established in 1905, most Calgarians thought their city would become the provincial capital. But, thanks to closer business ties to Ottawa, it was Edmonton that got the nod. But in 1951, the result of a scarcity of office space in Edmonton and Calgary and the tenacious nature of a man named Jack Barron, the first office tower went up in Calgary, called the Barron Building. At 11 stories, it was called home by Shell, Mobil and the Sun Company and effectively established Calgary as the headquarters for Alberta's oil patch. Edmonton had the political power but after 1951 Calgary was where the money was, and still is.

The success at Leduc cracked the elusive geological nut and in short order other discoveries were made, among them Woodbend (1947), Redwater (1948), Golden Spike, Stettler, Duhamel and Big Valley, all found in 1949, Wizard Lake (1951) and the big Pembina field, discovered in 1953. By 1954 total oil reserves in the Western Canadian Sedimentary Basin were estimated at 2.5 billion barrels. At year-end 2004, more than 19 billion barrels of oil, including 4 billion from the oil sands and 135 trillion cubic feet of natural gas had been produced. Current oil reserves are estimated at 175 billion barrels, with all but 1.75 billion barrels associated with the oil sands, while natural gas reserves are pegged at 140 trillion cubic feet.

Oil Sands

It might come as a surprise to many that the oil sands were first discovered in the early part of the eighteenth century by a Cree

A bucketwheel reclaimer at the Syncrude site on the oil sands, 1950s (Provincial Archives of Alberta/J4248/12).

traveller near Fort McMurray, who gave a sample of the tar-like substance to a representative from the Hudson's Bay Company. But it would take until 1929 before a viable extraction process was developed to separate the oil from the tar-like goo and another 48 years before the first oil sands operation was up and running. The Sun Co.'s Great Canadian Oil Sands, now known as Suncor Energy, began operating in 1967, producing 14,200 barrels of oil per day in its first year. In 1978, after coming close to not being built at all, the Syncrude facility—with an initial capacity of 45,000 barrels per day—started operations. By December 2004 oil sands production averaged just over 980,000 barrels per day. Today, with the decreasing number of big oil pools left to be discovered in the western Canadian Sedimentary Basin, much of Alberta's continued prosperity hinges on the continued development and exploitation of this resource. By March 2005, more than $60 billion worth of projects were on the boards, waiting for development.

The Oil Sands

Frank Dabbs

Alberta's oil sands give up their unimaginably vast treasure grudgingly. Nothing about this black hydrocarbon molasses has ever come easily, quickly or cheaply for the dreamers, schemers, scientists and nation builders who have joined the quest to convert the world's largest known petroleum deposit—an estimated 1.7 to 2.5 trillion barrels of gooey bitumen—into useable energy.

For the oil sands, men have gambled their capital to the last penny; they have staked and squandered their reputations; they have sojourned for mosquito-infested summers in the northwest hinterland and hibernated for oily-smelling winters in laboratories from Edmonton, Alberta to Kingston, Ontario to Chicago, Illinois.

For the oil sands, men have contrived a legion of odd-looking machines, built makeshift production lines in wilderness shanties, patented myriad processes, and launched a fleet of wishful or simply larcenous promotions. (The noun "men" is deliberately chosen; women, on the whole, have had more sense.)

All this has been done in response to the siren song that the oil sands sing beneath the hypnotic sway of the northland's aurora borealis, a song of wealth and power and—the most alluring of all—of public accolades and a place in history.

The oil sands have bred the bitterest of commercial rivalries. The oil sands have created despair and destitution. After 130 years of sustained endeavour, the oil sands have reluctantly surrendered just a small fraction of their cache of riches. Yet the same oil sands have engendered greatness in ordinary people, produced brilliant science and technology, yielded visionary public stewardship and corporate governance and earned the place as North America's most important strategic oil reserve for the twenty first century.

The oil sands have divided the nation in the dispute over their lavish patrimony and united a continent into a common crude oil market. The oil sands have delineated and elevated fundamental human qualities that make Alberta the extraordinary place it is. Its people are pragmatic, curious, smart, independent, self-confident, tenacious, experimental and drawn to the future with an almost myopic compulsion to make a mark in the world.

The tars sands deposits, as they were first inaccurately known, are tantalizingly impossible to miss. Yet for all their unavoidability, the chemical stew of carbon, hydrogen, oxygen, nitrogen, sulphur, methane, and hydrogen sulphide, with traces of nickel, iron and vanadium, has resisted commercial exploitation with an inhuman stubbornness.

Geologists reckon that the crude oil in the bitumen was squeezed out of conventional oil reservoirs in thick beds of sedimentary limestone and sandstone to the west by the powerful mountain-building forces that threw the Rocky Mountains into the sky between 70 and 40 million years ago. It forced the oil eastward, driving it into ancient sand beds of long-forgotten rivers over a 140,000–square kilometre triangle incorporating the Peace, Athabasca and Cold Lake regions. (The actual oil sands beds cover a combined area of 80,000 square kilometres—about 12 per cent of Alberta's area.)

The migrating oil stopped where it did because the toe of the impenetrable continental craton—the Canadian Shield—blocked its eastward path. There it waited, embedded in the sands, until the last glaciers of the last ice age landscaped the wild lands of the sub-Arctic boreal forests and muskegs. When it emerged, it was a paste of sand grains coated with a microscopic layer of water held together by the bitumen.

When the first peoples of North America arrived in a land blessed with rivers rich in fish and beaver, skies dark with geese and rolling hills abundant with bear, buffalo and elk, they found places in the muskeg coated with pastures of oily sheen. The sands oozed at a glacial pace out of high, steep riverbanks in thick wedges of sand that were inter-layered with limestone reefs and capped by peat and gravel and glacial detritus. The oil sands were soft and malleable beneath the summer sun and diamond-hard in the sub-Arctic winter.

Through prehistoric millennia, from the last ice age to first contact with Europeans exploring for fur, Aboriginal peoples collected the odifer-ous pitch and used it in mosquito smudge pots, for caulking bark canoes, and as a medicinal ingredient. Europeans came to the region before the Industrial Revolution had transformed Europe's wood- and coal-based energy economy and before modern geology had been fully developed and popularly accepted.

More important, their primary interest in the region was in the furs that the First Nations traded with them. The Hudson's Bay Company, which had tenure over most of the Canadian northwest from 1670 to 1870, had little interest in the other resources of the region at a time when the Russians were first producing oil from surface seeps on their taiga and refining it for sale in Moscow. Accordingly, it is of little sur-prise that for more than 150 years, from 1719 to 1875, accounts of the oil sands were merely diary entries made by curious and thorough explorers or scientists on reconnaissance.

Henry Kelsey, the early Hudson's Bay Company explorer who discov-ered the Canadian prairies for Europe in 1690 and extended his employer's expanded fur trade to the South Saskatchewan River, trav-elled through oil sands country in 1719 in search of gold and minerals. His Aboriginal hosts seem to have understood the purpose of his mis-sion better than he, for they offered to trade oil sands with him. Presciently, this first recorded attempt to commercialize the oil sands failed: Kelsey was not interested.

Sixty years later, Peter Pond of the rival North West Company win-tered over on the Athabasca River in 1778–79 while on a daring fur-trading raid deep in Hudson's Bay Company territory. He diarized the canoe-caulking given to him by his Cree and Chippewyan guides. To Alexander Mackenzie, traversing the area in 1790, the great curiosities were the 20-foot-deep "bituminous fountains."

In 1820, Sir John Richardson, a naturalist travelling to the Mackenzie Valley and Beaufort Sea with Arctic exploration icon Sir John Franklin, applied a simple scientific test to an oil sands sample—he poured a small amount of acid on it: it fizzled and he knew for the first time that this was an organic material. He knew too little of petroleum and its deposition to grasp the significance of his experiment.

It fell to the Geological Survey of Canada to ignite the oil sands passion. In 1869, the Hudson's Bay Company surrendered its charter over Prince Rupert's Land in exchange for seven million acres of land and cash, and in 1870 the new Dominion of Canada assumed jurisdiction. The Geological Survey was assigned to conduct an inventory of the natural resources of Canada's new North West.

As the Geological Survey explorers chased down leads to oil deposits, they were driven by two Canadian "firsts": the development in Nova Scotia of the refining process for kerosene by Abraham Gesner, patented in 1854; and the drilling of North America's first commercial oil well in 1858 by James Miller Williams in Petrolia, Ontario.

The Geological Survey had its first success with the Athabasca "tar sands." It began on the rainy night of September 7, 1875, with 44-year-old John Macoun, a self-taught botanist, the chair of natural history at Albert College in Belleville, Ontario and, later in life, Canada's first Dominion Botanist.

His passion for Canada's wild places—from Sable Island to the Yukon—had given Macoun a profound sense of vision and of discipline.

On this particular night, however, he was cold, tired and poorly-fed after four months' travel from the Pacific Coast through the interior of British Columbia, and across the Peace and Athabasca river systems. He had spent that day poking and prodding the oily-smelling beds of bitumen on the riverbanks near Fort McMurray. Macoun huddled under his overturned York boat; the air was thick with campfire and tobacco smoke. The men of the expedition were singing and laughing: the end of their summer journey was just a few weeks away.

"Long after the noises ceased," he wrote in his report of the journey, "I lay and thought of the not far-distant future when other sounds than those would wake up the forest; when the white man would be busy, with his ready instrument steam, raising the untold wealth which lies buried beneath the surface and converting the present desolation into a bustling mart of trade."

For the next ten years, the Geological Survey devoted an extraordinary number of visits to the oil sands deposits; in 1883 it conducted the first laboratory tests at the Royal Military College in Kingston that used hot water to separate crude oil from the bitumen. In 1888, the

Survey's director, George Mercier Dawson, presented the Senate's Select Committee on the Resources of the Great Mackenzie Basin with the first map of the Western Canadian sedimentary basin and an account of its petroleum potential, with the oil sands as the focal point and lynchpin of the future.

In their report, the Senators stated, "The evidence presented to (the) committee points to the existence in the Athabasca and Mackenzie Valleys of the most extensive petroleum field in America, if not the world. The uses of petroleum, and consequently the demand for it by all nations, are increasing at such a rapid rate that it is probable this great petroleum field will assume an enormous value in the near future and will rank among the chief assets comprised in the Crown domain of the Dominion." From those fateful words flowed the first phase of oil sands exploration: the unsuccessful attempt by the Geological Survey of Canada and three private companies, over nearly 20 years, to drill wells down to free-flowing conventional oil deposits erroneously thought to lie beneath the bitumen deposits.

From those fateful words also flowed the federal government's decision in 1905 not to give the newly-created provinces of Alberta and Saskatchewan jurisdiction over Crown lands and natural resources. And from those fateful words came the first and possibly most productive rivalry of the twentieth century—between Sydney Ells of the Dominion Mines Branch and Karl Clark of the Alberta Scientific and Industrial Research Council, to commercialize the oil sands.

Ells and Clark respected one another and were, for the most part, cordial in their relations. There was, however, always a tension between them and a mutually jealous concern that their contributions be recognized. Ells came to the Athabasca deposits in 1913 as the Geological Survey wound down its futile effort to drill for free-flowing oil. He was the more flamboyant of the two and initially had the more generous paymaster. The Canadian government sent him on a tour of heavy oil refineries in the United States. It funded the experimental use of bitumen for paving. His success gained Ells the support of the Pittsburg-based Mellon Institute of Industrial Research for development of a hot water process to extract oil from bitumen and he developed several promising research leads.

Ells remained a champion of oil sands development to the end of his career in 1954. However, the advent of World War I marked a hiatus in Ottawa's interest in and support of his work. In 1926, the federal government and Alberta began the long process to transfer jurisdiction over natural resources to the province. Clark, as Alberta's oil sands champion, gained the advantage in their competition. The creation of the Alberta Scientific and Industrial Research Council in 1921, in collaboration with the University of Alberta, with a mandate to develop oil sands, coal and mineral resources gave Clark the support he needed.

In 1924, he built a pilot plant in Edmonton to test his ideas. By 1928 he and his research associate—graduate student Sidney Blair— had patented the hot water process that, essentially, was the one used in the first commercial separation processes. Blair, meanwhile, in 1929, completed as his doctoral thesis the economic model that was used for the Great Canadian Oil Sands.

Why the 40-year gap between the core economic and technical work and the launch of commercialization? The advent of the Great Depression halted the flow of public research money. The Alberta government defaulted on its bonds and was technically bankrupt until 1945. The coming of World War II rejuvenated the governments' interest, but Alberta had no money and Ottawa procrastinated on oil policy until almost the third year of the war.

Private ventures continued through the Depression and World War II. There had been a great winnowing out of the most speculative enterprises and the absurd confidence schemes in the first two decades of the twentieth century. However, the 1920s brought serious and legitimate ventures to the fore, while Ells, Clark and Blair did their more patient work.

The McMurray Asphaltum & Oil Company launched with great promise in 1922 but was destroyed by fire in 1924. The Alcan Oil Company, formed by New York City policemen in 1921, drilled for oil at Bitumount. When the cops ran out of cash, one the great figures of oil sands history, farmer and businessman Robert Fitzsimmons, took the site over in 1923. With Blair and Ells sidelined by the fiscal politics of the Depression, Fitzsimmons and American oilman and industrialist Max Ball began the commercial rivalry that carried oil sands development along for the next 20 years.

Ball's project, Abasand Oil, was founded in 1930 as a surface mining and separation plant project. Work on the Abasand lease started in 1936 and by 1941 Ball was producing 200 barrels per day in the summer months. When a fire destroyed part of the plant, Ball rebuilt it with more capacity and an expanded pipeline to the railhead at Waterways.

In 1943, the federal government invoked the War Measures Act to take control of the operation. A second fire in 1945 destroyed the plant and ignited a forest fire; the federal government abandoned the site when the war ended.

Meanwhile, Fitzsimmons had given up on drilling for free-flowing oil and begun small-scale mining and hot water separation at the Bitumount plant. In 1930, he achieved the first commercial production in oil sands history—300 barrels per day in the summer. Within a year, the International Bitumen Company had a small but sustained flow of product and had developed a market with the Marshall-Wells hardware chain. To Fitzsimmons goes the credit for the first commercial oil sands mine, separation and upgrading operation.

His success was short-lived. His operation was capital intensive and he was caught in the throes of the Depression. He was forced to shut down in 1932, and although he reestablished production in 1937, he was never solvent and surrendered control of the plant to Montreal financier Lloyd Champion. Fitzsimmons and Champion had a difficult relationship and Fitzsimmons abandoned the game in 1944. After several more years of financial difficulty, the province took the site over in 1948.

For ten more years, a series of owners tried to make a go of the site. Eventually, the Bitumount leases came into the hands of UTS Energy, which had entered into a partnership with Petro-Canada to bring the leases into production—as one of the next generation of oil sands megaprojects. Sadly, Fitzsimmons died a poor and forgotten man in Edmonton in 1971, his life a cautionary tale for all who seek the riches of the oil sands.

In the end, it was the patient professor Karl Clark and Sid Blair, returned to Canada after serving in World War II as a civilian fuel comptroller with the Royal Air Force, who put the commercialization of oil sands back on track.

Collaborating with a circle that included Mines Minister Nathan Tanner, the future chairman of Oil and Gas Conservation Board George Govier, Sun Oil Company controlling shareholder J. Howard Pew, and *Oilweek* Editor Les Rowland, Blair and Clark convened an oil sands conference at the University of Alberta in 1951.

In a matter of days, the participants created the alliances and set the course for the long distance marathon to the first commercial plants: the first two commercial integrated mining, separation and upgrading megaprojects, Great Canadian Oil Sands (now Suncor), which began commercial production in 1967, and Syncrude, which went on stream in 1978.

These landmark projects were followed by the development and construction of a Shell Canada *in situ* oil sands recovery project on the Peace River deposits and the Esso Resources Cold Lake *in situ* project in east central Alberta.

In 1974, the Alberta government created the Alberta Oil Sands Technology Research Authority, and AOSTRA was responsible for the next oil sands breakthrough, the steam-assisted gravity drainage (SAG-D) method of *in situ* recovery. AOSTRA also developed a cold water separation process, a dry separation process that has been applied to oil shale development, and a catalogue of other technology improvements that have accelerated oil sands investment.

Combined with the renegotiation of federal and provincial tax and royalty regimes in the late 1990s, the new technologies triggered $24 billion in oil sands investments between 1996 and 2002, and announcements of $70 billion in commitments to be undertaken by 2020.

The development of a continental oil market anticipated by the Canada–U.S. Free Trade Agreement of 1988, advanced by NAFTA in 1992, and nurtured by the U.S. Energy Policy initiated by President George W. Bush in 2000, has been made a reality because of Canadian oil sands production.

In 2004, oil sands production reached one million barrels per day and the knowledge that there are 176 billion barrels of crude oil that can be recovered with present day technology and economics has made Canada the credible supplier of choice to the U.S. economy—which depends on other countries for most of its domestic oil consumption. Meanwhile, the oil sands can provide Canada with energy self-sufficiency for the long term.

And yet, after 130 years of modern development that followed on 130 years of European curiosity, the story has just begun. The vast oil sands deposits of Alberta contain ten times the staggering amount of crude oil that can be recovered now.

The likelihood is that the human race will lose interest in oil as a fuel, for practical reasons ranging from the environment to economic necessity. As former OPEC Chairman Sheik Zaki Yemeni has frequently said, "The Stone Age did not end because the human race ran out of stones; the same will be true of the oil age."

Realizing the potential of the oil sands will take another 130 years—or more. It will call upon the pragmatism, curiosity, braininess, independence, self-confidence, tenacity, thirst for exploration and experiment, and focus on the future that have carried oil sands development since the first Aboriginal ancestor, following the last receding glacier, came upon the oozing bitumen on some northern river bank and said, in some long-forgotten tongue: "What gift is this and how will I use it?"

Pipelines

Once it became apparent there was more than enough oil to satisfy regional needs, thoughts turned towards building a pipeline to transport oil from Edmonton to Central Canada and into the United States. This led Imperial Oil to organize the Interprovincial Pipe Line Corporation in 1949. The discovery of the Pembina field, with reserves of 1.7 billion barrels, acted as the catalyst for the building of another oil pipeline—the Trans Mountain Pipe Line (now known as Terasen) in 1953. But it didn't stop there.

In 1954, with natural gas production at 240 million cubic feet per day, the provincial government passed legislation creating the Alberta Gas Trunk Line, with a mandate to build a natural gas pipeline infrastructure that would take gas from the field and feed it into national and international lines. This was intended as a pre-emptive strike against the possibility that foreign companies would move in to control where the province's natural gas production went. The company was the forerunner to Nova Corporation and is now part of TransCanada PipeLines.

Not to be outdone by the Alberta government and its decision to establish the AGTL, the federal government forged ahead with a plan to have natural gas from the province shipped across the country to supply Eastern Canada as well as access the United States. This proved to be a contentious battle for Prime Minister Lester Pearson (but after a heated debate TransCanada Pipelines was created under a parliamentary charter and today is one of the biggest natural gas pipeline companies in North America. Interestingly enough, when it came to natural gas transportation, the federal government was intent that the gas pipelines were to pass within the country, but the

Products made from Alberta's main natural resource, oil, ranged from gasoline and heating fuel to plastics and commercial goods (City of Edmonton Archives/EA-275-1671).

same concern did not hold for the transport of crude oil. In 1961 another market opened for Alberta's natural gas production. With the completion of the Pacific Gas Transmission Line natural gas flowed from Alberta to California.

Two events happened to boost the profitability of the natural gas producers that also had an impact on the pipeline industry. In 1985, natural gas markets were deregulated, which brought new buyers and sellers into the marketplace. Up until then, contracts were in place for as long as 25 years and served as a basis for further exploration and development of new reserves as well as the construction of new pipelines. After 1985, contract length shortened significantly, as did the amount bought, with the net effect being natural gas markets became much more fluid, which facilitated the development of a robust futures market. Perhaps the final step in the development of Alberta's natural gas markets was the opening of the 3,713-kilometre-long Alliance Pipeline in 2000, shipping 1.325 billion cubic feet per day down into the U.S and effectively eliminating the "made in Alberta" price for natural gas. Instead of praying for the commodity to sell for more than $1 per thousand cubic feet, natural gas producers saw prices soar to as high as $10 per thousand cubic feet in December of 2000.

Side Effects of the Energy Industry

The growth of the energy industry had more than a few side effects. In the years following the Leduc discovery, Alberta's population, which had been in decline, reversed the trend, growing by 40 per cent in the 10 years following the success at Leduc. The influx caused a rapid rise in the rate of urbanization that was unparalleled in the country and increased the importance of the non-agricultural

The first successful protest party in Alberta was the United Farmers of Alberta, which formed in 1909. The UFA built community halls around the province. The party swept the scandal-ridden Liberals from office in 1921 (Provincial Archives of Alberta/A10762).

workforce. Businesses supporting the oil patch—transportation, distribution and other service industries, established themselves around the province. There was a twofold effect on the family farm: while the burgeoning energy sector provided a new source of income for farmers in the winter months, it also drew from the farm labour pool and acted as a catalyst for consolidation. As the number of farms declined from 82,954 in 1921 to 62,702 in 1977, the average size grew from 353 acres to 790 acres during the same period.

While the discovery at Leduc was a turning point in Alberta's economic fortunes, so too was the shift in world oil markets that began in the early 1970s as the Organization of Petroleum Exporting Countries (OPEC)—formed in 1960—gained market share at the expense of the traditional multinational oil producers. The 1969 emergence of Colonel Moamar Khaddafi in Libya as a result of a coup is often viewed as the turning point in the balance of power because he successfully imposed higher prices and taxes on a group of American companies operating in the region. The rest of OPEC followed suit. All this wouldn't have mattered much had the global economic expansion following World War II not been built on the flawed assumption that the world's hydrocarbon supply was inexhaustible. This perspective was accompanied by a shift from coal to oil as the primary source for energy. As an example, in 1940 oil and natural gas supplied 33 per cent of global energy needs, but by 1974 the number was 67 per cent while coal dropped from supplying 75 per cent of energy requirements to 31 per cent. And nowhere was this more apparent than in the United States, where oil consumption began to exceed supply in the 1960s; by 1973 the U.S. was importing 35 per cent of its daily needs. Of this, Alberta supplied 20 per cent, or 1.1 million barrels a day, or 60 per cent of the province's total daily production. This was, and still is, good news for Alberta. It meant that there would be no shortage of capital for either provincial coffers or further investment, nor any shortage of entrepreneurs eager to try their hands at exploiting what lay below the ground. Alberta's potential was not lost on American oil and gas companies and by 1971 the province had the highest level of U.S. ownership in Canada, with 55.8 per cent of corporate taxable income in foreign hands. That number rose to 67 per cent by 1976, compared with 49 per cent in the rest of the country.

The 1970s were golden in Alberta. In 1971 a new provincial government led by Peter Lougheed was elected on a platform that was all about industrialization and decidedly more progressive than the Social Credit regime that had been in power since 1935. Lougheed's Progressive Conservatives set about nurturing the province's entrepreneurial spirit, maximizing the value of the oil and gas resources while recognizing at the same time economic diversification was important because the energy reserves would not last forever. Some suggest that the lack of industrial diversification was the result of much of the early provincial wealth being accumulated in non-industrial businesses that were either commodity-dependent or service-oriented. This left Alberta vulnerable to external events that affected prices for raw materials and their associated businesses.

The Social Credit governed Alberta from 1935 to 1971, and during this time eliminated much of Alberta's debt by establishing institutions such as the Alberta Treasury Branches, like this one in Edmonton, which provided low-interest loans (Provincial Archives of Alberta/PA53/1).

Whereas Social Credit had eschewed government involvement and the notion of crown corporations, Lougheed took a different approach by creating joint venture agreements between the government and the private sector. Not only did this further the economic agenda, it allowed more direct participation on the part of Albertans. Perhaps one of the best examples of this was the creation of the Alberta Energy Company in 1973, which was half owned by the province. When the province decided to sell its 50 per cent interest it did so by offering its 7.5 million shares to Albertans instead of another oil and gas company. Shares were sold through brokerage firms and banking institutions, and for a time in November 1975, representatives from the brokerage firms planted themselves in shopping malls around the province in order to ensure that everyone had the opportunity to buy shares. With Calgary hosting the Grey Cup that year, share subscriptions could also be had at Grey Cup parties around the province. And it turned out to be a rather good investment. Anyone who had taken up the government's offer at $10 per share was looking at a value of $379 in March 2005. Another example was the 50 per cent stake in the Syncrude oil sands plant. The province ceased to be an owner of Syncrude in 1995, selling its remaining 11.74 per cent interest to Athabasca Oil Sands for $352.2 million. Athabasca later merged

The 1914 Turner Valley discovery sparked a stock promotion frenzy as every available space in downtown Calgary was taken up by brokers, agents and traders (Provincial Archives of Alberta/P-1127).

with Canadian Oil Sands to form the Canadian Oil Sands Trust, now the facility's biggest owner, with a 35.94 per cent stake in the operation that produced 87 million barrels of oil in 2004.

The best illustration of the effects on the province of external factors came in 1973 with the oil embargo by the Arab world and the resultant quadrupling of oil prices within three months. In 1973, Saudi Light averaged US $2.10: it jumped to $9.60 in 1974.

During this period, Alberta's coffers swelled dramatically and the province went from debtor to creditor. In 1976, solidly in the black, Premier Lougheed rose in the legislature to announce the creation of the Alberta Heritage Savings and Trust Fund, with an initial contribution of $1.5 billion and a commitment that 30 per cent of the royalties accruing from non-renewable resources would flow into the fund. While meant to act as the "rainy day fund" for the time when oil and natural gas production no longer supplied the lion's share of provincial revenues, it was also the tool that was going to be used to aid economic diversification. Moreover, by being funded from revenues that would one day dry up, Alberta was sending a message to the rest of the country that it was mindful that the windfall would not last forever.

Strong oil prices spawned myriad new players in the energy sector, with a few achieving legendary status in oil patch lore. The 1970s saw the incorporation of Petro-Canada, reviled in Calgary because it represented Ottawa's unwelcome meddling, and the creation of companies like Canadian Hunter Exploration, as well as the acquisition binge of Dome Petroleum that ultimately led to its collapse. Optimism abounded that oil prices had nowhere to go but up, fuelled by predictions that $100 a barrel was possible.

These were heady times in the oil patch. But the 1973 oil embargo, instability in the Middle East and fears that oil prices were headed into the stratosphere and would make Canada's energy resources unaffordable to Canadians were enough to catch the eye of the Federal Government. Its first step was to freeze domestic oil prices and impose a tax on what was being exported to the United States. This kicked off a battle between the producing provinces and Ottawa as the provinces boosted royalties charged for using Crown reserves while the Federal government retaliated by saying the royalty payments could not be used as deductions in the calculation of federal income tax. Over time, negotiations produced a situation where oil and natural gas prices were in line with what was being charged on an international level. In the meantime, hundreds of millions of dollars were thrown at megaprojects—most of which have yet to produce a drop of oil or natural gas. It was a failed experiment in economic nationalism

The relative harmony was shattered in 1979–80 when oil prices doubled to U.S. $26 per barrel. This time the Trudeau government came up with something far more onerous. In the budget tabled in October of 1980, the federal government unveiled its National Energy Program. "Among its various measures were ones to maintain Canadian oil and gas prices well below projected international values, to tax a significant portion of the economic rent through a variety of measures, to redirect exploration and development to the north and east coasts and to increase the degree of Canadian ownership in the sector." Alberta, along with British Columbia and Saskatchewan, reacted by decreasing shipments of oil to the east, holding up the construction of oil sands projects and launching a court challenge.

Things were sorted out, more or less, by 1981—just in time for oil prices to collapse, which kicked off a recession that persisted until 1987, when employment levels returned to pre-recession levels.

One of the side effects of the NEP was that it fostered the development of oil and gas companies that might not otherwise have been viable but existed because of the myriad of incentives. In addition, many chose to fund their activities using debt. In 1980 the

Bank of Canada interest rate was 12.89 per cent; in 1981 it reached 17.93 per cent. The dismantling of the NEP in 1985, at the same time oil prices were falling, caused the collapse of many of these companies and, as University of Alberta Professor and Dean of its Business School notes, destroyed a generation of entrepreneurs that only began to regenerate in the 1990s.

Petrochemicals

The rise of the petrochemical industry is another illustration of how the Lougheed government acted as the catalyst for the development of a huge industry. Despite a chorus of naysayers, Lougheed recognized that the province had a competitive advantage ready to be exploited in the petrochemical industry. There was, and is, big business in making the building blocks for plastic—ethylene and polyethylene—both of which are made from by-products of oil and natural gas. Even though Alberta was said to lack the infrastructure and skilled labour necessary to establish a viable petrochemical industry and was too far away from markets, Lougheed's government believed the huge cost advantage arising from the abundant supply of natural gas would more than offset the perceived obstacles. While it did not get involved from a financial standpoint, the government did play an active role in brokering a deal that ultimately led to the creation of the Joffre petrochemical plant near Red Deer. At the beginning it was a complicated affair involving Dow Chemical, Dome Petroleum and the AGTL. The plan was to strip enough ethane from the natural gas shipped by AGTL to annually manufacture 1.2 billion pounds of ethylene. Today, several expansions later, the Joffre facility produces 2.82 million tonnes of ethylene every year and ranks as the largest in the world. It is also the lowest cost producer of polyethylene, generating 914,000 tonnes annually from the Joffre plant.

Tourism: The Allure of Alberta

Laura Neilson Bonikowsky

Tourism is one of Alberta's largest and fastest-growing industries. And it's no wonder, with all that Alberta has to offer to visitors. Besides the abundant natural beauty of the place, Alberta offers an array of man-made sights to see, and enough events and activities to satisfy any eager holiday-maker.

A list of beautiful places includes, of course, the many national and provincial parks located in the province. They include three of the four national parks that comprise the Canadian Rocky Mountains UNESCO World Heritage Site, the largest protected area in the national parks and among the largest world heritage sites. Those parks are: Banff National Park, Canada's first and most-visited national park, established in 1885; Jasper National Park, located at Banff's northern boundary and site of the Columbia Icefields; and Kootenay National Park, on the western border of Banff. The fourth park, Yoho, is in British Columbia and borders Banff and Kootenay.

In the southern Canadian Rockies, straddling the Canadian/American border, Waterton Lakes National Park is a geological marvel; in less than a kilometre, the prairies' rolling hills become craggy peaks soaring nearly 3000 metres into the sky. The three Waterton Lakes, nestled between the mountain ranges, are the deepest in the Rockies, at over 150 metres deep. On the south side of the border lies Montana's Glacier National Park. The two together form the Waterton Glacier International Peace Park, the world's first such park and a World Heritage Site. At the extreme northern end of the province, spanning the Alberta/Northwest Territories border, lies Wood Buffalo National Park, the world's largest park, another World Heritage Site, and the site of a globally significant wetland. It is the last remaining natural nesting site of the endangered whooping crane.

Alberta is also home to Elk Island National Park, a mosaic of rolling woodlands, mixed-wood forests, meadows and wetlands that was established to conserve dwindling wildlife. It is home to elk, moose, mule deer and hundreds of plains bison and wood bison, as well as smaller mammals such as beaver and at least 230 species of birds, including trumpeter swans.

Alberta's national and provincial parks combine to make the province one of the world's best destinations for outdoor adventure. The provincial parks and protected areas include some of North America's most awe-inspiring landscapes. Within this single province, visitors can see the site of more dinosaur fossils than any other single place in the world; experience the awesome power of the Alberta Badlands; take in one of the world's few boreal forest songbird observatories; walk through a forest oasis untouched by glaciers during the last ice age; and examine the

Mount Temple with a Miss Priest in the foreground, Banff, July 6, 1905. Alberta's mountain splendour has always been its main tourist attraction (Glenbow Archives/NC-53-52).

Before chair lifts and groomed runs, skiers like these at Lake Louise in 1932 were guided through the terrain by mountain guides from Switzerland, Austria and Germany (Glenbow Archives/NA-4868-172)

largest collection of aboriginal rock art on the North American Plains. Activities cover an array of adventures and pastimes, year-round. One can laze on sunny beaches, take in rodeos and concerts, golf, participate in a sweet grass ceremony, or enjoy music and drama festivals, including the renowned Fringe Festival. Outdoor enthusiasts can hike, ski, hunt, fish, camp, cycle, whitewater raft, or try to scale a monster sand dune. Alberta contains half of Canada's sand dunes; one near Fort Chipewyan is seven kilometres wide, and 13 kilometres long, and is moving at a rate of one metre per year.

For those who like their vacations to be a little less adventurous, there are scenic drives and historic sites in abundance. The Cowboy Trail, one of Canada's best drives, runs for 640 kilometres from Mayerthorpe, northwest of Edmonton, to Cardston, near the American border. The Frank Slide Interpretive Centre, in the Crowsnest Pass, tells the remarkable story of how, on April 29, 1903, in a mere 90 seconds, 82 million tonnes of limestone roared down Turtle Mountain. Tiny Torrington, north of Calgary, is an agricultural community that turned a liability into an advantage, with the Torrington Gopher Hole Museum. Alberta offers an abundance of museums, art galleries, and heritage sites. And of course, for those to whom no vacation is complete without shopping for souvenirs, there is West Edmonton Mall, the world's largest entertainment and shopping centre, with more than 800 stores offering enough PST-free shopping to satisfy any shopaholic.

For the province, all this activity and sightseeing translates into 83,000 jobs and annual revenues exceeding $4.5 billion, 48 per cent of which comes from Alberta residents themselves. Revenue from downhill skiing alone amounts to nearly half a billion dollars annually. Visitors to Alberta come from across the country and around the world, lured by the majestic scenery, the unspoiled environment, the cowboy heritage, festivals, events and Albertans' reputation as open, friendly people.

Attempts at Diversification

Over the last 30 years, starting with Lougheed, there has been a growing movement to diversify Alberta's economic base beyond the traditional segments of energy and agriculture, with the biggest thrust being into the realm of petrochemicals. But the 1980s saw a few other experiments in diversification, most of which ultimately failed: an environmental company Bovar, a Magnesium company called MagCan that was supposed to produce magnesium chloride from a new process and, of course, Novatel, which has since managed to reinvent itself as a viable wireless company now headquartered in Texas, even though the government never recouped the $500 million invested in the enterprise.

Beginnings. In one year after the construction of its first building, Stettler had some 70 businesses, including this bank (Provincial Archives of Alberta/A5024).

Apart from these hiccups, Alberta boasts a healthy number of companies that are not purely focused on oil and gas. In 1920, Earnest Poole left Saskatchewan for Edmonton, establishing what is now known as PCL, now one of North America's largest construction companies. ATCO, which began as a trailer company in 1946 and is now involved in natural gas and electric distribution, power generation and a wide range of other businesses around the world, is a prime example. After oil was found in 1947, Sandy Mctaggart found his way to Edmonton from England and established his real estate and construction concern, McLab Enterprises. Alberta's business history would be incomplete without mention of Frederick C. Mannix, whose company, LORAM Enterprises, was active internationally in real estate, pipeline construction, oil and gas, coal, the manufacture of railway equipment in North America, and mining.

Another story is that of Edmonton-based Wardair, founded by bush pilot Max Ward in 1953. The company grew steadily and by 1970 was ferrying one million passengers a year and had become well-known for its charter service that spanned North America and extended to Europe. When the airline industry was deregulated in 1987 to allow more regularly scheduled airlines to compete, Wardair jumped in with both feet. But it couldn't compete against Air Canada and Calgary-based Canadian Airlines International (which had bought CP Air in 1986) and by 1988 was carrying a debt load of $300 million. In January of 1989 it was bought by Canadian, which had high hopes for its future as a Canadian-based airline spanning the globe, but that was not to be, either.

A small upstart called WestJet, founded by a group of Calgary entrepreneurs, that included Clive Beddoe, Donald Bell and Thomas Morgan, entered the western Canadian air space in 1996 as a low-cost carrier. It had three planes and served five cities. But WestJet had a low cost-structure because it wasn't a union shop, owned its planes and was debt-free. As such, it put significant pressure on Canadian Airlines, which had long dominated the western skies. By 1996, Canadian was in a fight for its life—the victim of a confluence of events, including a protracted global recession and the high price it paid to buy Wardair. In 1999, hobbled by debt of almost $1 billion, Canadian was bought by its archrival, Air Canada.

WestJet expanded across the country and by 2005 had 56 planes serving 33 cities in North America and more than 26 charter destinations. Less than 10 years after being established, it is widely viewed as the catalyst that brought about significant change in Canada's airline industry.

A Look Ahead

Alberta faces many challenges as it enters its second century. As the only province in confederation that has paid off its debt, it must view itself as a nation-builder and not as an outlier that is not included in Federal decision-making processes.

But it continues to be a province whose revenues are primarily derived from a declining asset base. The commonly held view is that conventional natural gas production peaked in 1973. The challenge today and going forward is to produce the more than 300 billion barrels of unconventional oil that lie in Alberta's oil sands. At the time this chapter is being written, more than $90 billion in projects targeted at developing the oil sands is on the books. And one of the biggest questions facing the companies looking to develop these vast resources is securing the labour to complete the projects. Instead of financing being the constraint to development, it is the scarcity of labour that is causing the greatest amount of uncertainty, this despite the continuous in-migration to Alberta from other provinces and beyond.

The other big question mark is natural gas. With conventional production on a treadmill where record drilling levels every year only keep reserves flat, the energy industry is being challenged to find new sources for natural gas to supply not just the U.S. market—to which 9.75 billion cubic feet is shipped every day—but also to meet the needs of the ever-expanding oil sands at Fort McMurray. As it stands now, the current operations of Syncrude and Suncor consume more than 800 million cubic feet of natural gas per day, but if all the projects currently in the process of being developed go ahead, that number could double or even triple.

In addition to the extraction of natural gas from coal bed methane and gas reservoirs that require more technical expertise than the conventional shallow gas wells, the Arctic and Alaska are being eyed as two new sources of supply. Of course, talk to anyone in the oil business in Calgary about what they think of the prospect of natural gas coming down from the north and the immediate response is that the same source of supply was "10 years away" when they first started in the business in the 1970s. A combination of increased demand and higher prices are making the development of resources previously deemed uneconomic very attractive. If these sources of supply are developed, the next issue is how the gas will get to the end users. Once again, just like during the 1970s, talk of two pipelines—one from Prudhoe Bay in Alaska and the other from the Mackenzie Delta—are foremost, but neither one has received the necessary approvals to proceed with construction.

As Albertans—and indeed the rest of Canada—anticipate years of prosperity because of the richness of the resource base that has accounted for more than 50 per cent of the country's trade surplus, there is one fly in the ointment—the Kyoto Protocol. The Liberal government of Prime Minister Jean Chrétien, in the fall of 2002, promised that Canada, between 2008 and 2012, would reduce its emissions of greenhouse gases to levels that are 5.2 per cent below 1990 levels. Albertans were frustrated by what they felt was a lack of meaningful consultation. Moreover, a clear path as to how the goals of the accord are to be achieved has not been determined. Some of the more cynical folk are worried that a carbon tax imposed on Alberta by Ottawa is the only way it can meet the commitment, while others are looking upon Kyoto as a huge wealth transfer between countries that signed onto the Protocol to other nations that refused.

Another big question is the health of Canada's beef industry. In May 2003 a cow with Bovine Spongiform Encephalopathy (BSE), or Mad Cow Disease, was discovered on a farm in northern Alberta. The event saw the United States shut its borders to Canadian cattle, with the result the industry that once contributed $4 billion annually to the Alberta economy lost $7 billion within two years. Alberta—indeed Canada—is challenged with developing its own processing infrastructure so that it no longer relies on the American markets to handle its cattle for processing.

The crisis facing the meat industry once again pulls forward an age-old concern about the character of the provincial economy and the propensity to ship raw materials to the highest bidder south of the border and let them add the value. There is much said by economists about the lack of growth in productivity in Canada and much of this has to do with the fact that we choose to produce the raw materials but don't take it any further, which is where the real value lies.

Historically, Alberta has succeeded, unlike other parts of the world rich in natural resources, because the money generated from the exploitation of the resources stayed within the province instead of being exported elsewhere. It is now on the cusp of a new phase where its infrastructure continues to be stressed as a result of the significant jump in the population base, most of it because of the employment opportunities offered by the oilpatch and associated industries.

The good news is that there is a new generation of entrepreneurs at work in Alberta, including those like Al Markin and Murray Edwards, who saw opportunities in the late 1980s to fund companies with potential but that had been badly pummelled by the oil price collapse in 1986; Keith McPhail and Don Gray who are ahead of the curve on the generation of new oil and gas royalty trusts; and John Brussa, the Burnet Duckworth and Palmer tax lawyer who developed the oil and gas royalty trust structure. Of note, when it comes to those outside the oil patch, is Daryl Katz, the Edmonton-born founder of the second largest pharmaceutical retailer in Canada who has played the role of consolidator of pharmacies from coast to coast. The list of creative, hardworking entrepreneurs in Alberta goes on and on. These are the people who are taking up the mantle from the first crop of entrepreneurs encountered tremendous success in the post-1947 period and are on the cusp of retirement.

In the last 100 years Alberta has attracted and nurtured the optimist. Whether the dogged pursuit of Leduc # 1, the insistence on the part of Peter Lougheed that Syncrude must go ahead in the oil sands or even the continued existence of a healthy farming community despite the challenges posed by the elements and external events such as the BSE crisis, it's hard to find someone who simply gave up. There has always been the sentiment that another discovery is just around the corner or that the weather will be better for farmers next year. This optimism, along with determination and a healthy dose of philanthropy, has put the province in a position where it is ready to take on the challenges of the next 100 years.

Watering the Garden of Eden 7

GERALD T. CONATY

The settlers and promoters of southern Alberta have always regarded water as the single most limiting factor to the region's development. Extraordinary measures have been taken to ensure a stable water supply that supports a variety of economic activities, including oil and gas extraction and refining, agriculture, and both light and heavy industries. In addition, burgeoning population growth raises concerns about the sustainability of the drinking water supply. As we manage our water to meet these demands, the rivers of southern Alberta have become among the most intensively used and radically engineered watercourses in Canada. This is especially true of the Bow River, downstream from Calgary.

Palliser's Triangle

Captain John Palliser was amazed at the desolate landscape that confronted his group of scientists and explorers as they trekked across the Canadian prairies. The vegetation was sparse, and the water, when any could be found, was barely drinkable. Palliser dismissed the entire region as a place that was unfit for "civilized" people.

The young Irishman had been enchanted by the American plains. In 1847 he travelled by boat from New Orleans to Independence (present-day Kansas City, Missouri). From there, he journeyed west with fur traders and spent the summer hunting bison and other plains animals, meeting the Native people, and, generally, becoming enthralled with this new, empty land. Palliser spent the winter at Fort Union, on the Missouri River, and returned home to Ireland early in the summer of 1848. The experience left a lasting impression.

No sooner was he home than Palliser began organizing his return to the North American plains. While the Americans had

John Palliser and his partner, James Hector (right), led an expedition to the West to assess its "capabilities" for settlement. They concluded that although some semi-arid country (which is now known as "Palliser's Triangle") stretched across the southern prairies, it was surrounded by a "fertile belt" well suited to stock raising and agriculture (Provincial Archives of Alberta/PA6186).

commissioned several exploratory expeditions to traverse the continent, the British government seemed uninterested in knowing more about their possession. The Hudson's Bay Company and the North West Company, in their competition for the fur trade, had sent men to the west, establishing trading relationships and searching for a route to the Pacific Ocean. There had been no scientific expedition to document the natural history of the region.

An Empire Built with Fur

Gerald T. Conaty

Fur was a valuable commodity in the late 17th century. Fashionable Europeans wore coats, capes and even hats fashioned from the pelts of animals. The best fur came from northern North America, where the cold winter encouraged thick pelts.

The Hudson's Bay Company (HBC) was created as a British competitor to the French traders who had been dominating access to the rivers of northern Quebec that led to the fur resources. The English strategy was to build large forts along the shores of Hudson Bay, in the heart of the best fur trading territory. The First Nations people would not have to travel so far to trade and the English could avoid confronting the French along the rivers.

Over the years, the HBC moved inland from the bay, building smaller posts as they went. In time, this network extended across most of northern North America. Travelling to and from the ocean ports required a great deal of manpower, and provisions for those men. The company looked to the vast herds of buffalo for supplies.

Each fall, the First Nations compiled vast stores of pemmican (a mixture of dry meat, crushed, dried berries and fat). This light-weight, highly nutritious food became an essential supply for the fur brigades and the HBC soon found that trading for pemmican was as important as trading for furs.

Much of the fur, especially the beaver pelts, was transformed into felt and made into hats. When fashions changed, in the mid-1800s, demand dropped and the Hudson's Bay Company began to lose its business.

In 1856, Palliser presented the Royal Geographic Society with his proposal to cross the plains from the Red River settlement (near present-day Winnipeg) to the mountains, along a line near the border with the United States. With the Society's endorsement, he readily secured financial backing from the British government. While Palliser initially planned to engage only Métis guides to accompany him, the government required that other scientists be brought along to collect specimens and record the natural history of the region. Eugene Bourgeau, a botanist; Thomas Blackiston, a magnetic observer; James Hector, a geologist, naturalist, and medical doctor; and John W. Sullivan, an astronomical observer, comprised the expedition's scientific members.

For three years, from 1857 to 1860, the men traversed the plains. Sometimes they travelled together; at other times they separated to cover more territory. In the end, they produced a detailed and scientifically reliable study of the British North American plains. One of the most significant aspects of Palliser's 1863 report was the characterization of a large part of the region as a northern extension of the Great American Desert. This area, which has come to be known as the Palliser Triangle, was described as dry, barren, and completely unsuited for agricultural settlement. It was a characterization that has sparked debate and controversy over the past 150 years.

Homeland of Niitsitapi

These plains were not a wasteland to the First Peoples. This was the homeland and heartland of Niitsitapi, the Blackfoot-speaking people. The drought-resistant plants withstood prolonged dry periods and flourished during wet spells. The animals were very mobile, moving away from the drought-stricken areas to places where sufficient moisture brought plants to life. Vast herds of bison, containing millions of animals, drifted across the landscape, grazing on the rich diversity of grasses.

While the plains people were also highly mobile, their movements were not random wanderings. The people knew their environment intimately—where the plants grew; where there was water; where the animals travelled. Niitsitapi trails crossed the countryside, connecting all the important places on their landscape.

The Bow River was a vital part of their world. Trails that paralleled the river intersected with others that led to crossing places. At "Ridge-Under-The-Water," later called Blackfoot Crossing by the Euro-Canadians, the raised riverbed linked two broad, low floodplains that were covered with stands of cottonwood trees. Long, wide coulees sloped gently to the north and south of this crossing place. These gentle slopes were important to the Blackfoot. They transported most of their possessions on travois, pulled by dogs or, later, horses. If a slope was too steep, the travois tipped, spilling the load. At Blackfoot Crossing, dogs could easily negotiate the grade to the river's edge. As well, these coulees provided shelter from the winter storms and a bountiful supply of firewood. This location became a favourite winter camping place for the Moccasin Clan of the Siksika. In 1877 their leader, Crowfoot, chose it as the place to meet government officials and discuss making a treaty between the Niitsitapi and the newcomers.

Opening the New Land

In 1670, Charles II, King of England, granted the Hudson's Bay Company (HBC) exclusive rights to trade in all lands that drained into Hudson Bay. This vast territory included much of the subarctic forest, barrenlands and plains of what was to become Canada. By 1869, however, the fur trade was becoming less profitable and the Hudson's Bay Company could no longer afford to administer such a large region. Sir John A. Macdonald, Prime Minister of the newly confederated Dominion of Canada, recognized the importance of acquiring this land to unite the country from coast to coast. He wasted little time in arranging for Canada to purchase the region.

Macdonald was anxious to forestall American hegemony by populating the land with settlers. In 1872 the government of Canada passed the Dominion Lands Act. Newcomers were offered a quarter-section of land for a fee of ten dollars and received full title to their property after maintaining residence for three years.

The lack of transportation presented a great obstacle to settlement. How were new farmers to reach their land? Once there, how could they ship their crops to market? As the Canadian Pacific Railway (CPR) progressed slowly across the country, construction costs rose dramatically. The sparsely populated prairies meant that there was no immediate return for the money invested in the railway. Financial backers became wary of the venture.

Syncrude's "Giants of Mining" display at Fort McMurray (Travel Alberta).

The powdery slopes of Lake Louise's ski runs make it a desired travel destination of skiers worldwide (Travel Alberta).

Camping at Dinosaur Provincial Park offers travelers a chance to explore where Alberta's largest dinosaurs once roamed (Travel Alberta).

Built in 1908, Lethbridge's High Level Bridge provided a link between the town site and its main industry, mining. The longest and highest of its kind, it is still used by CPR trains (Photograph by James H. Marsh).

Designer Arthur Erickson envisioned the University of Lethbridge as a building that would nestle into the folds of the rolling coulees and, in its long, flat roof, echo the flatness of the prairie (Photograph by James H. Marsh).

Hiking in Cypress Hills Provincial Park. The Cypress Hills are a unique ecosystem, untouched by glaciation (Photograph by James H. Marsh).

The serenity of Bow Lake at Banff National Park offers hikers a chance for peaceful reflection (Travel Alberta).

In 1890, the CPR's general Manager Cornelius Van Horne envisioned a simple hotel for the alpinist and adventurer on the shores of what was then called Emerald Lake and is now the world famous Lake Louise (Travel Alberta).

Nestled in the Valley of the Ten Peaks, Moraine Lake's beauty was once featured on the back of Canada's $20 bill (Travel Alberta).

West Edmonton Mall's World Waterpark attracts some of the Mall's 22 million annual visitors (Travel Alberta).

Edmonton's River Boat Queen recalls the days when the North Saskatchewan River was Edmonton's primary transportation route (Photograph by James H. Marsh).

"My dream is to have a place where the people of our region can make the most beautiful music they are capable of—and share it with each other" —Dr. Francis G. Winspear, founder of the Francis Winspear Centre for Music, 1997. The hall is world famous for its fine acoustics (Travel Alberta).

In 1965, Joseph Shoctor and his friends purchased the Old Salvation Army Citadel on 102 Street, and 300 people crowed inside for the first theatrical production on November 10, *Who's Afraid of Virginia Woolf?* Since that time, the Citadel Theatre has become Alberta's premier venue for mainstream live theatre (Travel Alberta).

In its 23-year existence, the Edmonton International Fringe Theatre Festival has become one of the largest fringe festivals worldwide, second only to Edinburgh, Scotland (Travel Alberta).

Joy Spring, Kananaskis View. Oil on panel, 1991, by Terry Fenton (Terry Fenton).

Concord. Acrylic on canvas, 1996, by Terrence Keller (Terrance Keller).

The arrival of railways on the prairies decimated Alberta's bison herds, and early irrigation techniques further exacerbated herd conditions. By the early 1880s there were only a few free-ranging bison left (Travel Alberta).

As an incentive to the railway, and as an assurance to their investors, the federal government granted the company the rights to all odd-numbered sections within a 39-kilometre distance from the rail right-of-way. Both the government and the Canadian Pacific expected the company to profit from the sale of this land to settlers. These settlers would, in turn, become a market for rail services that would carry manufactured goods to the new settlements and convey agricultural produce to markets in more densely populated regions of the country.

Opponents of this settlement plan drew attention to Palliser's description of the arid landscape, but were rebuked and referred to the reports of James Macoun. Macoun was a self-taught naturalist from southern Ontario. In 1872 he was encouraged by CPR Chief Surveyor Sir Sandford Fleming to take part in the railway survey. Macoun travelled west from 1872 to 1881, first as a railway employee and later as an "explorer" for the Geological Survey of Canada and as the Dominion Botanist. He disputed Palliser's assessment, finding the region an "Eden." By 1883 his ideas were being challenged by others such as Alexander Galt, a prominent politician and founder of the city of Lethbridge, George M. Dawson, the geologist who mapped most of western Canada, and former explorer Henry Youle Hinde.

Why were the conclusions of Palliser and Macoun so very different? The answer lies in the phenomenal variation in the climate of the prairies. For example, between 1885 and 1897, there were only four years in which more than 254 mm of precipitation was recorded; the average was 227 mm. The next seven years (1898–1905) averaged 495 mm each year, with a range from 404 mm to 579 mm. The drought of 1914 was followed by mammoth crops in 1915 and 1916. Unfortunately, during the 1880s there were insufficient records for a long-term analysis of rainfall patterns.

Macoun's enthusiasm prevailed and the Government of Canada and the Canadian Pacific Railway began promoting "The Last Best West."

Watering the Garden

As the great land rushes in the United States drew to a close in the mid-1880s and settlers looked to western Canada, they were encouraged by a government that was anxious to fill the empty spaces.

Drought conditions returned just as the land rush boomed. The new arrivals soon found their crops devastated and their dreams smothered in dust. The government realized that water was the key to successful settlement and developed measures to ensure that sufficient quantities of the resource were available to everyone. The Northwest Irrigation Act, passed in 1894, suppressed all individual rights in any stream that could be used for irrigation, and centralized the control and regulation of water use. In conjunction with this, the government undertook extensive surveys to determine the nature of the soil and the feasibility of constructing irrigation works.

The Canadian Pacific Railway Irrigation Blocks

The 1882 agreement that granted land to the Canadian Pacific Railway stipulated that the railway was required to accept only land that was fit for settlement. Engineering studies sponsored by the company found that much of the land in the Canadian dry belt was unfit for agriculture and, therefore, not suitable for settlement. By 1889, the railway still had not selected over two million hectares of its appropriation and the government was becoming anxious that the agreement might never be fulfilled.

William Pearce, the Inspector of Land Agencies for the federal Department of the Interior, was a friend of William Van Horne, the Canadian Pacific Railway president, and an important advisor to Sir John A. Macdonald. Pearce advocated that irrigation was necessary before any agriculture could occur on the plains. At the time, most irrigation works were constructed by large land development corporations or independent water companies. Farmers were then charged a rate for using the water supplied through the irrigation system. Pearce had seen many irrigation companies go bankrupt and understood that the high initial construction costs doomed these operations to failure. There were far too many expenses to be paid before any of the costs could be recovered through water sales.

William Pearce
Gerald T. Conaty

William Pearce had a vision—irrigation would turn the wasteland of the Canadian Plains into a land that would sustain a burgeoning population.

Land sales in the West boomed as the railway reached completion in 1881. The federal government established Land Offices throughout the region to control the growing mayhem. When Pearce was appointed Inspector of Lands Agencies, he became responsible for the allocation of land, water rights, and mineral deposits. His influence expanded in 1882, when he was appointed to the Dominion Lands Board. He grew to be close friends with CPR President William Van Horne and a key advisor to Prime Minister Sir John A. Macdonald.

During a rail trip from Winnipeg to Calgary, he was greatly impressed with the similarity between the Canadian West and Utah and Colorado. Those southern areas flourished under extensive irrigation schemes. Pearce became a vocal advocate of irrigation as a way to reclaim the land for large stock operations. Over the next decade his arguments gradually persuaded the politicians and in 1894 the Northwest Irrigation Act was passed by parliament.

Pearce's interest in experimenting with irrigation techniques led to the formation of the Calgary Irrigation Company. Although he was a silent partner in the venture, he could not always keep separate his work, the company, and his friendship with Van Horne. In 1895 the company was reorganized and Pearce removed himself from its board. Controversy persisted and in 1904 Pearce left the government and joined the CPR, where he worked on development projects for the next 26 years. The pattern of rail links between prairie hamlets is, largely, his plan.

Pearce had a deep love of the prairie and a firm belief in its agricultural potential. He devoted his estate, southeast of Calgary, to experimental agriculture. His irrigated land had crop yields 70 per cent higher than non-irrigated neighbouring land.

The Bow River at the foot of the Rocky Mountains was the inspiration for the Bow River Irrigation Project that began in 1905 (Travel Alberta).

Pearce proposed that, instead of many small irrigation operations, there should be regional development programs covering thousands of square kilometres. There could be flood control in the foothills; settlement and population density would be strictly controlled. He also realized that, in late nineteenth-century Canada, only the federal government and the CPR had the resources to fund these large developments. Moreover, the rail construction meant that earth-moving equipment was already owned by the rail company, alleviating at least some of the initial capital outlay.

The scattered sections allotted to the railway made irrigation prohibitively expensive. At Pearce's urging, the government and the company agreed to consolidate the land grant into a large block that could then be settled and irrigated. This land stretched for 235 kilometres eastward from Calgary and northward from the Bow River for 66 kilometres. Engineers determined that the best place to divert the water would be close to Calgary, where the railway crossed the river. Here, little dirt would have to be removed and the main channel would be close to ground level. This canal would feed water to over one million hectares. By connecting existing coulees and streambeds, canals could reach to Medicine Hat with no cuts deeper than 20 feet. It would be an engineering marvel!

The proposal was met with outrage by settlers and other businessmen who believed that the Canadian Pacific Railway was obtaining an unfair advantage just when the price of land was beginning to rise. In response, the railway offered to irrigate land and to keep the water prices low. The company was intent on demonstrating that it was not in the business of land speculation.

The block of land granted to the Canadian Pacific Railway is an open, prairie plateau. In the western area, heavy black loam soil lies over clay subsoil, undulating in a gentle rolling topography with an average elevation of 1,066 metres above sea level. At the eastern extreme the land is almost flat and the soil is more sandy, with a clay

The firms of Grant, Smith & Co. & McDonnell of Vancouver built the ambitious Brooks Aqueduct nearly 80 years ago, employing 300–600 men in 38 construction crews during the summer (Glenbow Archives NA-5616-5).

and hardpan base. The average elevation in the east is 762 metres above sea level. Between these, the central section is generally higher than the other two. The energy needed to pump water up to this higher ground, together with the need for more flumes to cross the dips and swales, led the engineers to conclude that irrigation in this part was not feasible.

Of 415,848 hectares in the Western Section of the CPR Block, engineers found that only 160,000 hectares could be irrigated. Water was diverted through a weir just east of Calgary (it is now well within the city limits), through a main canal to an earth-dammed reservoir at Chestermere Lake. Three canals emerged from this lake, carrying water into secondary canals and ditches that distributed the water to each parcel of land. The length of canals and ditches that were excavated is remarkable: 27 kilometres of main canals; 406 kilometres of secondary canals; 2,126 kilometres of distribution ditches; and several thousand more kilometres of small ditches dug by farmers to bring the water across the land. Ten million cubic metres of material were excavated to construct the canal system. Thousands of headgates, spillways, drops, flumes, bridges, and weirs completed the system.

The Western Irrigation Association (WIA) was formed in 1907 to promote improved irrigation practices. It brought together farmers, small and big businesses, interested clubs and associations, and

The Alberta government faced considerable pressure from ranchers and surrounding communities to build an irrigation dam that could alleviate the severe drought conditions of the late 1920s. The Oldman River Dam project near Pincher Creek was a contentious issue for many First Nations (Travel Alberta).

Botanist, explorer and naturalist, Professor John Macoun sets up camp in southern Alberta, 1913. Macoun believed that settlers could do well in this area, for the region was clearly not the arid desert it was reputed to be. (Glenbow Archives NA-3840-5).

some government agencies. By 1912, members of the WIA were raising concerns about the irrigation system. The farmers argued that the Canadian Pacific should not be allowed to charge for water in "wet" years when irrigation was not necessary. They also observed that the ditches could neither carry enough water when it was needed nor could they hold the water when it was in full flood. Farmers also believed that the water was too cold for the plants and noted that the water brought heavy salts to the surface, creating alkali flats. In response to this, some land was removed from the irrigable status. The railway also established experimental farms at Brooks, Strathmore, Tilley and Cassils to instruct farmers in proper irrigation techniques.

The irrigation system in the Western Section was completed in 1920 with an extensive rail network linking the 64 grain elevators in the area. Five million bushels of wheat were marketed that year. Still, the basic problems of farming marginal land remained. Rainfall patterns continued to by cyclical, with bumper crops in wet years and devastation in dry ones. Most of the farmers' income was used to pay off debts as more and more people turned to deficit financing. By 1940 the cost of maintenance for the irrigation system was three times its earnings and in 1944 the Canadian Pacific Railway turned over its assets in the Western Section to the Western Irrigation District, under the management of the provincial government.

Irrigation of the Eastern Section was more complex. Water was diverted from the Bow River at a southward turn in the river known as Horseshoe Bend. Here, the outer bank is high and massive while the inner riverbank slopes gradually. This low bank meant that the main canal could be constructed by removing a relatively small amount of earth. The Bassano Dam, located 133 kilometres east of Calgary, was completed in 1914. It served a dual purpose, diverting water into a canal while, at the same time, maintaining the river's course. A steel reinforced concrete spillway lined the riverbed and buttressed the riverbanks. A 210-metre-long earthen embankment extending from the south end of the spillway gradually merged with the sloping ground running down to the river. The spillway contained 40,000 cubic metres of concrete and 1.2 million kilograms of reinforcing steel. The embankment was made of one million cubic metres of earth. The power of Bow River water is a force to be reckoned with.

As the water leaves the river, it flows through headgates and into a main canal leading to Barkenhouse Lake tailpool, five miles away. Two main canals branch from this pool, a smaller North Branch and a larger East Branch. The North Branch serves the country to the north of Mat-Zhi-Win Creek, following the west side of Crawling Valley. Smaller branches spread across the land, irrigating farmland as far north as the Red Deer River.

The East Branch, with a 21-metre-wide bed, carries water southeastward. The Spring Hill Branch waters the area between the branches of Mat-Zhi-Win Creek while the main canal continues to the head of Antelope Creek, where it forks to serve the Bow River Slope to the southeast and the Brooks area to the east. The Rolling Hills, south of Brooks, create a rolling topography containing a natural kettle. By constructing numerous earth dams, the Lake Newell Reservoir was created, with a storage capacity of 185,000 acre feet of water. Lake Newell's outlet is a canal that, in turn, discharges into a flume that delivers water to the Bantry Canal, serving the area north and south of the Rolling Hills.

The eastern portion of the irrigation block had a main canal eight kilometres long, which fed 765 kilometres of secondary canals and 3,280 kilometres of distribution ditches. These ditches and canals were designed to deliver a supply of water to parcels of land of approximately 32 to 64 hectares at a rate of two feet (60 centimetres) per second for 96 hours. Smaller parcels were to receive water at this rate for 48 hours.

The Bow River Irrigation District

As the Canadian Pacific Railway proceeded with its irrigation plans, others began to see the new potential of the arid West. While the land north of the Bow River was developed by one company, the area to the south involved several organizations. Their interrelationships demonstrate the complex nature of developing irrigated agricultural land in the early years of western settlement.

The first large-scale development south of the Bow River took place in 1905 when J.D. McGregor of Brandon, Manitoba and A.E. Hitchcock, of Moose Jaw, Saskatchewan, formed the Grand Forks Cattle Company and were granted a 21-year grazing lease on 38,250 hectares east and north of the Bow River—Oldman River confluence. They then bought one-tenth of this area for $2.50 per hectare. Later that year, they joined with Major St. Aubyn to create the Robbins Irrigation Company.

The following year, Robbins Irrigation Company sold 154,000 hectares of land to the Canadian Agency Company, a land agency company based in London, England, as well as to the Grand Forks Cattle Company. The land purchased by the Canadian Agency Company was then re-sold to the Southern Alberta Land Company, another English land speculation organization. The Southern Alberta Land Company (SALC) expected irrigation to substantially raise the land value, easily covering the costs of construction and operation of the irrigation works. However, Robbins Irrigation Company did not develop the irrigation, although they did make preliminary surveys to determine the best places for canals and other structures.

When the Southern Alberta Land Company began to survey for their own irrigation system in 1907, they found that the rolling topography meant that much of the land could not be irrigated without extensive—and expensive—canal and ditch construction. With federal government approval, they exchanged some parcels of land and, by 1908, owned 189,000 hectares, of which 69,000 hectares were irrigated.

Southern Alberta Land Company land stretched from their diversion dam at Carseland, 64 kilometres eastward to a reservoir at Lake

McGregor. From there a canal carried water a further 64 kilometres eastward to their land. Secondary canals spread out from the main canal. The irrigation water was also extended under the Bow River by means of a siphon, feeding a second reservoir 24 kilometres east of the Bow River, which, in turn, supplied a system of subsidiary canals that watered the Suffield area.

The Southern Alberta Land Company's irrigation system became the lifeline of the region. In 1911, F.P. Alywin transferred 27,900 hectares to the Alberta Land Company. The new owners agreed to purchase irrigated water from the Southern Alberta Land Company, which also sold 48,690 hectares of land near Suffield to Canadian Wheatlands, an English land company that, once more, agreed to purchase water from SALC. The growing irrigation commitment led the Southern Alberta Land Company to seek government approval to extract a large amount of water from the Bow River at its Carseland diversion. Permission was granted for a rate of 2,000 cubic feet per second at high water and at flood stages. However, as the Canadian Pacific Railway already had the rights to draw water from diversions upstream at Calgary and downstream at Bassano, SALC enlarged their Lake McGregor reservoir to ensure that they could meet their commitments at the low-water stage.

Land speculation continued and in 1912 the Alberta Land Company bought 27,070 hectares from the Government of Alberta. This block was northeast of the Southern Alberta Land Company's holding and the Alberta Land Company agreed to purchase water from SALC if the latter built the canals and other components of the irrigation system.

By 1912, the Southern Alberta Land Company had spent nearly eight million dollars constructing diversion dams, canal intakes, reservoir dams and outtake works at the Lake McGregor reservoir, and five large wooden flumes. Eleven million cubic metres of earth and rock had been excavated, mostly by horse-drawn scrapers. All this, and no land had yet been irrigated. As the system approached completion, the intake structure and sluiceway at the Bow River failed and over two million dollars was needed for repairs. The expensive accident pushed the company to the brink of bankruptcy.

Times were against the company. The government required that one-quarter of the land be irrigated before any could be sold. Without land sales as an income source, the Southern Alberta Land

Company was forced to borrow money. While the Canadian government guaranteed a loan of $2.50 per acre, this left a balance of $800,000 to be raised in the marketplace. A global economic depression, followed by World War I, made it impossible to raise the capital. All work ground to a halt.

With the 1918 armistice came an optimism that better times had arrived. In 1917, the Southern Alberta Land Company, the Alberta Land Company and Canadian Wheatlands had merged to form the Canadian Land and Irrigation Company (CLIC). The new company was soon delivering water and in 1921 4,050 hectares were being irrigated. Crop yields rose to a value of $27.73 per acre and livestock operations became profitable with a dependable winter wheat feed and stock water supply.

In spite of these promising developments, the company began to fail. Land sales were slow and the rising provincial taxes on the improved land eroded any profit. As well, other companies, such as the New West Irrigation District and the Bow River Irrigation Development were creating a very competitive climate. When the Canadian Land and Irrigation Company tried to raise money in Great Britain, they found that new regulations enacted by the British government restricted their fund-raising activities. The Canadian Land and Irrigation Company went into receivership in 1924.

Water was critical and the people of southeastern Alberta had become dependent on irrigation. As the Canadian Land and Irrigation Company began to fail, the water users who held contracts with the company met with the New West Irrigation District contract holders and formed the Amalgamated Water Users Association. With financial support and professional advice from the federal government, the association began operating the irrigation system eastward from Lake McGregor.

The effects of irrigation reached beyond improved crop yields. A 1921 health survey conducted by the Red Cross compared children in dryland farming areas with those in irrigated regions. They used a ratio of height and weight to estimate the extent of malnutrition. In the dryland areas (Lomand and Retlaw in the west to Bow Island and Winnifred in the east) two-thirds of the students were malnourished. This dropped to one-third in the irrigated regions.

The mid-1920s were difficult years in southern Alberta, as severe drought enveloped the prairies. While farmers in irrigated

This image depicts irrigation head gates and the weir on the Bow River, Calgary, as they appeared in 1922 (Glenbow Archives/NA-2179-27).

areas struggled to keep their water supply intact, those in the dry belts were losing their livelihood. Between 1921 and 1926 between one-fifth and one-quarter of the townships in southeastern Alberta lost 55 per cent of their population. Palliser's assessment was proving true.

By 1927 the Canadian Land and Irrigation Company was operating once again. However, while they had managed to raise sufficient funds, continuing drought and slow land sales meant that their operations remained on the verge of bankruptcy. Three conditions emerged as being critical for the company's success. First, they needed to settle their tax debt with the Alberta government. Second, they needed to settle other debts with the province. Third, they needed to find sufficient financial backing to enlarge the project to a point of self-sufficiency. This meant they needed to acquire at least 20,000 hectares of irrigable land.

Plans to realize these goals were preempted by the global depression of the 1930s, which was exacerbated by continuing drought throughout the plains. Prices plummeted and the meager crops that were harvested brought very little money for the farmers. The Canadian Land and Irrigation Company was faced with a massive abandonment of their land and defaults on payments owed by the farmers. During the 1920s the Canadian Land and Irrigation Company had sold land at a rate of six per cent interest on unpaid principal and ten per cent per year interest on all arrears. A decade later, the company was forgiving debt and granting credit to farmers. In 1934 and 1935, the province provided low-interest loans to the

Canadian Land and Irrigation Company to enable operations to continue. Still, essential maintenance of the dams, ditches and canals could not be completed and the system fell into disrepair.

Conditions had reached a crisis by the mid-thirties. To address the growing agricultural disaster, the federal government created the Prairie Farm Rehabilitation Administration (PFRA) in 1935. Its role was to provide financial assistance, agricultural advice, and manpower to rehabilitate farming practices in the west. In 1936 the Canadian Land and Irrigation Company received grants of $20,000 to pay its current expenses and $60,000 to undertake major canal rehabilitation and to construct new ditches that would irrigate land onto which farmers from the dry belts could be resettled. Work progressed slowly and disputes arose between the Canadian Land and Irrigation Company, farmers and the governments of Alberta and Canada.

Resolutions to these issues came slowly and discussions were interrupted by World War II. In 1949, the federal government purchased all of the Canadian Land and Irrigation Company property and assets for $2.25 million and organized the land into western, central and eastern districts. In the western section, responsibility for water delivery was shared between the province and the federal governments. The federal authorities assumed full responsibility for the central portion where they hoped to resettle farmers from sub-marginal land in Saskatchewan and Alberta. Policy for the eastern district was deferred until the central section had been fully developed.

The infusion of new money and the government administration resulted in significant changes. The main canal was enlarged, the Traverse Dam was built on the Little Bow River and the neighbouring reservoir was enlarged, old structures were replaced, new works were constructed, and additional land was irrigated. Nearly 5,000 hectares were set aside for resettlement and between 1952 and 1958 over 180 farm families moved to new lands.

By 1979, 53,800 hectares were under irrigation in the Bow River Irrigation District. These were administered by the federal government until 1973, when the province assumed responsibility. This irrigation came at a great price. Between 1950 and 1979 the Canadian government spent $25 million on development and $23 million on operation and maintenance.

Irrigation Today

A century after the first canals were dug, irrigation has become an integral part of southern Alberta. Although only four per cent of Alberta's land is irrigated, it is responsible for 20 per cent of the province's gross agricultural production. People are looking back to the roots of the industry as they develop improved water management systems. We must all recognize that water is a critical resource for food production, commerce, wildlife, and communities.

Water issues are of immediate concern for food producers. Large food production corporations must consider the marketability of their products. As consumers become more aware of how food is produced, these corporations want to meet expectations that the food was grown in a healthy environment, including the judicious use of a safe water supply for irrigation. Irrigation has also become an expensive component of the farming infrastructure. With a single pivot costing as much as $100,000, the entire farm must be incorporated within a reliable irrigation system. Moreover, producers often live in small communities where everyone is involved with the running of treatment plants.

Irrigation farmers are finding new ways of working. Modern systems are more efficient, using 30 per cent less water than they did a decade ago. Lower sprinkler heads distribute larger droplets, reducing the amount of water lost to evaporation. Farmers and scientists are collaborating to develop computer simulations that help determine the optimum amount of water to use on different crops under different weather conditions.

Irrigation affects everyone in southern Alberta. The system of canals and reservoirs has created 33,000 hectares of critical, drought resistant wetlands for waterfowl and other wildlife. The reservoirs have been stocked with fish and support a popular sport fishery. The canals bring water to over 50 communities that otherwise would rely solely on groundwater.

Watershed maintenance and conservation is important if irrigation systems are to function well. Unfortunately, in Alberta water literacy is low and few people understand the complexity of water-based ecosystems. Successful watershed management requires many groups, with many different interests, working together to ensure the resource is sustainable for multiple uses.

8 A Tale of Two Cities

SYDNEY SHARPE AND ROGER GIBBINS

The battle of Alberta is fading into history, a relic that endures only on the sports fields. Edmonton and Calgary have become a thriving nexus of growth and ideas. Today these two key cities are a symbiotic unit of economic action that affects every facet of the province, as well as western Canada and the country beyond. Each city has carved its character on the Alberta psyche with persistence, inspiration and pride. There have been brawls in the past, but today the cities are like an old married couple, dependent on each other's strengths but quick to make an affectionate joke at the other's expense. They serve as role models for the smaller cities and unite when senior governments try to erode their powers.

Both cities look beyond provincial and federal borders as they compare their competitive advantages. The smart civic politician realizes that Alberta's major cities are complementary, not combative, the dual engines of Alberta's future. Take out one and the other engine would cough and die. Edmonton is the government centre and the staging ground for the massive oil sands development to its

This image of Edmonton's Jasper Avenue in 1910 depicts the bustle of the new province's capital city (McCord Museum/MP-0000.1369.7).

St. Stephen Avenue, Calgary, in 1889. The city already had its sandstone elegance but was literally still "cowtown" (Glenbow Archives/NA-2864-13233).

north. Calgary is the corporate ground where multi-national companies plan growth for both the next quarter and the next quarter-century.

The Alberta that entered Confederation in 1905 was predominantly rural and agrarian, as indeed was the prairie West and for that matter most of Canada at the time. The immigrants who were flooding into Alberta were drawn by the province's rich agricultural land, and by what could only have seemed like a future of unbounded prosperity as Canada strove to become the breadbasket of the world. Yet even in the heyday of agrarian settlement, Calgary and Edmonton were already placing their stamp on the province. Although their primary roles were to service the burgeoning rural economy, right from the get-go they had their own unique personalities and contributions. In recent decades they have emerged as economic engines in their own right, motors of the knowledge-based economy. Alberta's heartland is now urban.

The story of the province's transformation, however, must be told against two important backdrops. The first is that Calgary and Edmonton are by no means alone on Alberta's urban stage; although Fort McMurray, Grand Prairie, Lethbridge, Medicine Hat, Red Deer and others are dwarfed by the two metropolitan regions, they are experiencing strong economic and population growth. Smaller they may be, but backwaters they are not. The second backdrop is the bi-polar nature of Alberta's urban development. Most Canadian

The early Canadian west was full of tall tales and idealistic reverie. At the bar (where else?) of the Queen's Hotel in Winnipeg on Sept.12, 1894, **Bob Edwards** was advised on his thirtieth birthday to travel to that land that would become Alberta, and sample the new cities.

"Tell you what—if you want to see good farmland, go along the new railroad between Calgary and Edmonton," he wrote. "Trains have been operating only three years, but that's the place for homesteading. Stuff grows so fast, well, you gotta jump out of the way when you put seed in the ground. A fellow at Red Deer didn't jump fast enough and he got hooked on a corn stalk—would've starved up where he was if the neighbours hadn't come and cut him down."

Edwards became the great Calgary humourist and *Eye Opener* editor whose story was told by the illustrious author and former Lieutenant Governor Grant MacEwan in his book, *Eye-Opener Bob*, published by the Institute of Applied Art in 1957.

provinces have a single, clearly dominant urban pole—Vancouver in British Columbia, Winnipeg in Manitoba, Toronto in Ontario, Montreal in Quebec, Halifax in Nova Scotia. Alberta, along with only Saskatchewan and perhaps New Brunswick, has two nearly equal urban regions, and it is not surprising that rivalry between the two has had a marked impact on the nature of the province, and on Alberta's "state of mind."

Nonetheless, this rivalry should not detract from the combined demographic and economic weight of Calgary and Edmonton. Together, the two metropolitan regions accounted for 63.5% of Alberta's population at the time of the 2001 census, a measure of dominance that compares to the 51% of British Columbia's population that lives in Vancouver's census metropolitan area, and the 41.0% of Ontario's population that lives in Toronto's census metropolitan area. There is every reason to expect that this dominance will only increase as Alberta moves into its second century.

The Early Years

In 1795, on the north bank of the North Saskatchewan River, the Hudson's Bay Company established Edmonton House, which the nostalgic company clerk named after his far-away London neighborhood. While the fur trade cemented Edmonton's early existence, the whisky business put Fort Calgary on the map in 1875. The bloody armed brawls of the whisky traders, often with native bands, created a chaotic maelstrom on the frontier until the North West Mounted Police entered the fray. Fort Calgary rose where the Bow and Elbow rivers meet, a longtime gathering place of the Blackfoot First Nations. While the hapless Inspector Ephram Brisbois wanted his name attached to the new fort, his commander, Colonel James Macleod decided on the name Fort Calgary, in honour of his mother's family castle in Scotland.

Even before Alberta's entry into Confederation, Calgary and Edmonton were raucous rivals for goods, services and favours. In 1883, Calgary grabbed the new Canadian Pacific Railway track, the first line to cross the country. The two most prominent settlements as the railway arrived from the east were Edmonton in the north and Fort Macleod (named after the illustrious colonel) in the south, but neither of them carried off the railway prize. Just as the whiskey trade had moved north from the southern United States border in

Montana, so had other supplies. The north–south route was a logical one forged by First Nations eons earlier, and one of the reasons Calgary won the CPR line was the need to supply Canadian settlements close to the American border with Canadian goods. Calgary's win wasn't supposed to happen, because Edmonton was a solid 80 years older than Calgary. But, happen it did, thereby dashing Edmonton's dreams of dominating the North West Territories. Edmontonians were furious, and the stage was set for a feud that would only begin to dissipate more than a century later.

Calgary again beat Edmonton to the punch by becoming the first official city in 1893, with a population that had grown nearly tenfold to 4000 in the span of a decade. Edmonton had stalled at 700 residents, in part because the CPR was not prepared to pay Edmonton land prices and put down rail. In 1891, on the south bank of the North Saskatchewan River, the CPR set up the competing town of South Edmonton, which was later renamed Strathcona. A rail line from Calgary to the town completed the north–south link.

When the lure of Klondike gold whisked dreamers and dilettantes through Edmonton in 1898, its population hit 2500, and in 1904 Edmonton also officially became a city. As the gateway to a vast agricultural region and resource cornucopia, Edmonton was uniquely positioned to serve both pioneers and prospectors. The city would boom, but not before Edmonton outwitted its rival Calgary to win the biggest prize of all. When the new province of Alberta was created in 1905, Edmonton was anointed the capital. Ottawa deemed its politics the right stuff (Liberal, after all), and named the Edmonton-Strathcona MP, Alexander Cameron Rutherford, as Alberta's first premier. Rutherford granted Strathcona the right to house the new University of Alberta in 1908. The slight to Calgary was palpable, especially when Strathcona joined Edmonton in 1912. The merger meant that formal political and intellectual power in the early years of the new province started and stopped in Edmonton. (The University of Calgary was not created until 1965.) Calgary, however, had other cards to play.

Turner Valley turned the tide Calgary's way when oil was struck in 1914, positioning the city for energy dominance in Alberta and Canada. Further strikes in 1924 and 1936 cemented its role as the province's business centre. What Calgary had lost through backroom dealing it gained through wildcatting. The grand Leduc oil strike in

1947 didn't dent Calgary's business prominence, even though the oil was now on Edmonton's doorstep. The energy headquarters in Calgary considered the entire province their claim, while Edmonton's role as the service centre to the oil and gas industry was reinforced. This bifurcation of the oil and gas industry, with white collar employees concentrating in Calgary and blue collar employees in Edmonton, helped create two distinctive urban styles.

Throughout the first 65 years of Alberta's history as a province, Calgary and Edmonton were vigorous and certainly competitive urban centres. At the same time, the heartland of the province remained rural; farming, ranching and resource exploitation dominated provincial life, with the two major cities acting as service centres by providing the rail connections, banks, lawyers, post-secondary education, medical specialists, and distribution networks. It was not until after Canada's centennial in 1967 that Calgary and Edmonton began to move to centre stage.

The Urban Boom

The 2001 Census marked a national watershed—80% of Canadians now lived in urban areas. Canada had become an emphatically urban country. Although this process of urbanization had been taking place gradually since Confederation, it accelerated appreciably in the last three decades of the twentieth century. Alberta not only reflected but led this urban trend. If Canada is now emphatically urban, Alberta is even more so.

Between 1966 and 2001, the percentage of the western Canadian population living in urban areas increased from 67.2% to 79.6%, an increase that far outstripped the rate of urbanization in the rest of Canada, where the urban population went from 75.8% in 1966 to 79.7% in 2001. For Alberta alone, the increase in the urban population went from 68.8% to 80.9%, or slightly above the national average. During this 25-year period, Calgary and Edmonton were the country's two most rapidly growing urban areas, posting population gains of 188% and 134% respectively (in comparison, Toronto posted an increase of 117%, and Montreal 41%).

To some degree, this period of rapid urbanization heightened the rivalry between Calgary and Edmonton. Growth threw new fuel on the fire as both cities attracted NHL teams and competed for migrants from other parts of Canada, international immigrants,

Alberta's Top 15 Populated Places

	Name	2001 Population	Area (km^2)	Pop Density/ Area
1	Calgary	878,866	701.79	1252.3
2	Edmonton	666,104	683.88	974.0
3	Red Deer	67,707	60.90	1111.8
4	Lethbridge	67,374	121.83	553.0
5	St. Albert	53,081	34.61	1533.7
6	Medicine Hat	51,249	111.99	457.6
7	Sherwood Park	47,645	70.98	671.3
8	Fort McMurray	38,920	56.61	687.5
9	Grande Prairie	36,983	60.42	612.1
10	Airdrie	20,382	21.48	949.0
11	Spruce Grove	15,983	26.40	605.3
12	Leduc	15,032	36.97	406.6
13	Camrose	14,854	25.85	574.6
14	Lloydminster (Part)	13,148	24.19	543.6
15	Fort Saskatchewan	13,121	45.30	289.6

investment, and university students. Neither community broke away from the pack; at the end of the century the two were virtually in a dead heat: in 2002, the population of Edmonton's metropolitan region was 967,166, compared to 993,182 for Calgary. At this point, however, the Edmonton-Calgary corridor was christened by Statistics Canada as the country's newest urban region, and indeed the urban region with the highest rate of growth and highest per-capita incomes. By ignoring longstanding rivalries, Statistics Canada created a singular urban region, at least conceptually. It now remains to be seen if Albertans can build the necessary interconnectivity to bring the corridor's potential to life.

While Calgary and Edmonton look to cities beyond the federal border for comparative identities, and often co-operate on economic matters, they love to poke fun at each other when it comes to their home teams in sports and politics. A hundred years ago, these two communities couldn't get enough of their communal fighting; today, an adrenaline-filled game of football or hockey between the two gets the blood flowing and the fans bellowing.

It is also interesting to note that Alberta's urban growth has not come at the expense of the rural population. Although 92.5% of Alberta's population growth from 1966 to 2001 was urban, there was still real growth in rural areas. Alberta's urban population grew by 139%, while the province's rural population grew by 25%. In Manitoba and Saskatchewan, by contrast, all of the net growth over the same period was urban; Saskatchewan's rural population fell by 34%, while Manitoba's rural population fell by just under 1%. Alberta's cities are not cannibalizing the rural countryside.

Rural Alberta

Lyle Oberg

One hundred years ago, the expression "rural Alberta" would have been considered redundant. With practically everyone living in or around villages and small towns, Alberta was rural. Today, four out of every five of us live in a city, myself included, and those who don't, often do their business there. It is easy to see why so many are so quick to concede the demise of rural life in the province. But is it true? Is small-town Alberta to be relegated to the history books, once and for all?

I grew up on a farm near Forestburg, population 700. Although small, it was a vibrant community, with two or three grocery stores, a hardware store and a clothing retailer. These stores were a focal point not only of commerce in the village, but also of social interaction, where neighbours met and visited with one another. The village hasn't shrunk any since I lived there, but the world has. These days, residents choose to do their shopping a hundred kilometres away at the Superstore or the Walmart in Camrose, where the selection is better and the prices low. With modern roads and cars, the distances seem shorter, and people think nothing of the hour-long trip. This has had a profound impact not only on the economy of this small town, but just as sadly, on its social fabric. So, too, has the migration of our young people to colleges, universities and jobs in the cities.

There is no question we should be concerned for the future of rural Alberta in the face of the growing urbanization of the province. But there is also cause for optimism because even while townsfolk continue to head to the cities in search of opportunity, I believe we are witnessing the rise of a reverse trend. Eager to escape the high crime rates, the

Hon. Lyle Oberg has fond memories of growing up in Forestburg, a small town of 700. Pictured here in 1957, it was typical of most, with a busy main street where the local community could shop and socialize (Provincial Archives of Alberta/PAA 113.1).

even higher housing prices, and the high-volume traffic of urban Alberta, more and more city dwellers are opting for the peace and quiet of the country. They're being lured by the spirit of small-town Alberta: open, honest and friendly people; safe neighbourhoods; a place where everybody knows your name and, for better or worse, your business. They're saying: "I want my child to grow up the way I did."

Meanwhile, modern technologies and conveniences are also helping make rural Alberta a more attractive place to stay or move into. The same roads that make it so easy for small-town residents to do their shopping in the city are making it equally easy for people who work in the city to live in the country. So even though their job is in downtown Calgary, for instance, they're choosing to live in Rockyford, a village with a good school, good roads and a shorter commute than the far-flung suburbs of the city.

Likewise, broadband Internet access is shrinking the distances and the differences between urban and rural Alberta. Through Alberta's SuperNet, rural communities will be able to offer high school electives and university and college courses through videoconferencing, effectively bringing big-city opportunities to the country. Rural students will be able to get a quality education, and even a university degree, without ever having to leave their hometown.

The rejuvenation of rural Alberta is not a given. It is an opportunity. With Alberta's second century, we are at a watershed. The Alberta Advantage should be shared by all, both urban and rural. Government cannot mandate people to stay in or move to rural communities, but it can help ensure rural communities have what it takes to make people want to live there—things like good, safe roads, top-notch schools, access to post-secondary educational opportunities. Indeed, it must ensure it, because while five or six new families in a city make little more than a dent in a neighbourhood, five or six new families in a town breathe new life into that town.

Ensuring the survival of rural Alberta is vital to our growth as a province and a people. That's because rural Alberta is more than a place: it is a spirit; it is a work ethic; it is a way of life. It is the root of what we are today. When someone calls Albertans rednecks, that doesn't offend me, because what they're really saying is that we do things and see things our own way. And that's what being Albertan means: expressing our individuality and knowing who we are, and taking pride in that. That doesn't mean we're all the same; it means that we are content with our own individuality. Just as strong as our sense of individuality is our sense of community. We look out for each other and, on a broader scale, for our neighbours across Canada. We have been blessed as a province and know that we have a responsibility to share that bounty as willing partners in Confederation. We still remember when Nova Scotia shipped us apples during the dark days of the Dirty Thirties, or more recently, when farmers in the east shipped us their hay for our cattle, and we are more than happy to be able to give back to the Canadian community.

All of this makes me fiercely proud to say I am an Albertan. It also makes me surer than ever that rural Alberta will not only survive, but will thrive again. It must if we are to continue to prosper in the century ahead.

The North American Free Trade Agreement, negotiated by Conservative Prime Minister Brian Mulroney and signed in 1992 by Canada, the United States and Mexico, was a great boon to both cities. With the free flow of energy assured, oil and bountiful natural gas have poured into the United States. Development of the Athabasca oil sands brought work and prosperity to Edmonton, while Calgary solidified its role as the main business centre, spawning several aggressive investment houses. Independents like Peters & Co. and FirstEnergy Capital Corp. have become dominant leaders respected across the country for their research and financing heft.

Four out of every five of the province's three million residents now live in a city, and nearly two out of three Albertans live in or near Calgary and Edmonton. Increasingly, Albertans are making the city their home and the countryside their playground.

The Contemporary Scene

Although urban growth in Alberta has been impressive, the transformation it has brought goes well beyond the rate of urbanization to the very character of the two metropolitan regions. Edmonton and Calgary have not only become two of Canada's most rapidly growing urban areas but also two of the most complex.

Take, for example, the impact of immigration. The Great Depression and the closing of the agrarian frontier brought immigration into Alberta to a virtual halt by 1930. When immigration began to resume in the latter part of the twentieth century, Calgary and Edmonton, not the countryside, provided the draw. Today the cities are, respectively, the fourth- and sixth-largest immigration magnets in Canada, albeit with both falling well below Toronto, Vancouver and Montreal.

Destination of Immigrants to Canada, 2001

Toronto	50.0%
Vancouver	13.7%
Montreal	12.9%
Calgary	4.1%
Ottawa	3.6%
Edmonton	1.8%
Winnipeg	1.5%
Hamilton	1.1%

The successful attraction of immigrants means that Calgary and Edmonton have now become complex, multi-cultural communities. To a degree, of course, this was always the case, for when immigrants from Eastern Europe poured into Alberta at the turn of the last century, the two cities benefited from substantial Ukrainian, Polish, Russian and Scandinavian communities. Today, new waves of immigration have brought immigrants from Asia, Africa and the Middle East, and the ethnic complexity of Calgary and Edmonton has increased in turn. While popular commentary often lauds the multicultural character of central Canadian cities and laments the supposed homogeneity of Alberta cities, Edmonton and Calgary better epitomize the new Canadian urban reality than do Ottawa or Montreal.

Visible Minority Population by Census Metropolitan Area, 2001

Vancouver	36.9%
Toronto	36.8%
Calgary	17.5%
Edmonton	14.6%
Ottawa	14.1%
Montreal	13.6%
Winnipeg	12.4%

The visible minority population as measured by Statistics Canada does not include Aboriginal peoples. It is worth stressing, therefore, that in addition to the ethnic complexity noted above, Aboriginal peoples constituted 4.4% of metropolitan Edmonton's 2001 population, and 2.3% of Calgary's. By way of comparison, only 0.4% of Toronto's population was comprised of Aboriginal peoples, and 0.3% of Montreal's. Aboriginal people provide an extra level of complexity and social vitality that is largely absent in cities outside western Canada.

Alberta's two major cities also have a relatively high proportion of foreign-born residents. Although they are in a different league from Toronto and Vancouver, they are still very much in the national mainstream.

Foreign-Born Population by Census Metropolitan Area, 2001

Toronto	43.7%
Vancouver	37.5%
Hamilton	23.6%
Windsor	22.3%
Calgary	20.9%
Montreal	18.4%
Edmonton	17.8%
Ottawa-Hull	17.5%
Winnipeg	16.5%
Halifax	6.9%
Quebec City	2.9%

In short, Alberta's two major cities fully reflect the new urban realities in Canada. They look a lot like other major Canadian centres that have been transformed by immigration and ethnic complexities. True, the two may be seen from outside the province as bastions of white, red-necked cowboys, but this perception no longer has any foundation. It is the pejorative stuff of mythology and stereotyping.

Municipal politicians in Edmonton and Calgary have been very active in driving the national debate on Canada's urban future. They argue, and we would agree, that Alberta's urban regions typify the tremendous opportunities and somewhat daunting challenges that will confront urban Canada in the decades to come. What remains to be seen is whether those same municipal leaders will begin to train their guns on the provincial government, arguing that the big cities need a new deal from the province just as they are creating a new deal with the federal government.

Edmonton's Place in the Next Century

Mayor Stephen Mandel

At the beginning of Alberta's second century, Edmonton is on the cusp of what could be the most significant period of economic growth in the city's history.

It's an exciting time to be in the Capital City—living, doing business, going to school, raising a family.

Edmonton is an active city, a multicultural city, a cosmopolitan and *confident* city.

Our region has just reached the one-million mark in population—a momentous psychological milestone in terms of how other cities and governments view us. And it will forever affect the way we view ourselves as Alberta's capital.

It makes us a little more self-assured when we stand up to tell the world that Edmonton is one of this country's leading cities.

We're a leader in the arts, supplying stages and galleries around the world with talent, and bringing the world's best to perform at our renowned festivals and our internationally revered concert halls and stages. Our commitment is to build that reputation through the coming century.

His Worship Mayor Stephen Mandel of Edmonton (City of Edmonton).

We're a leader in education, with post-secondary institutions rated among the best on the planet. Students and academics from all continents come here to study and teach. We want to solidify that status and develop it for generations to come.

Edmonton is a leader in research in health and industry. We've launched medical discoveries that have changed the lives of people around the world. Health professionals and researchers look to us for example and leadership. The next century will produce and attract even more brilliant people, who will provide the spark that will expand our economic opportunities, and that will ensure the world will continue to look to us for insight and innovation.

The world knows us as an international leader in biotechnology and biomedicine, nanotechnology and Microsystems, and information and communications technology—all areas virtually unknown just a few short years ago. Now we are leaders of the next-generation economy. We are moving ahead of the curve—fuelled by a workforce that has the energy and attitude needed to lead.

Whatever unimagined opportunities present themselves in the next decade, the next generation or the next century, Alberta's Capital City will be involved.

Building a great city means more than looking to the future economy. It means ensuring Edmonton continues to be a lively and liveable city—a city where people want to build their lives and raise their families for generations to come.

Edmonton has embraced this challenge and nurtured the quality of life here.

Professional and amateur sport, music, theatre, recreation and culture started developing a following here from our earliest days. Now, those pursuits provide a healthy living for thousands of practitioners—and they form some of the most influential factors that people consider when choosing to live in Edmonton. That quality of life will most certainly continue to define us in 2105.

The decisions we make as we enter Alberta's second century will have an impact on one of the most influential areas in Canada for generations to come. A hundred years from now, when the Mayor of Edmonton looks back at 2005, I'm confident that he or she will be just as proud of the city's contributions to Alberta as we are today, looking back over the *first* hundred years.

The Urban Future in Alberta

In 2005, Edmonton and Calgary were expanding at a pace hardly anyone had ever imagined or anticipated. Land values soared along with energy prices, and the cash-rich provincial government poured billions into new roads and infrastructure. The cities reached levels of growth, with nearly a million people in each urban area, that brought them to the threshold of big-city status. Calgary municipal expert David Jacobs described the big cities astutely, and hinted at coming challenges, when he said early in 2005: "Calgary and Edmonton aren't large small cities any longer—they're small large cities. That brings big differences in the psychology and in the challenges that have to be faced."

There is little question, moreover, that the demographic and economic weight of Calgary and Edmonton in Alberta will only increase in the years to come. It is not too much of an exaggeration to say that as Calgary and Edmonton go, so goes Alberta, for there is now a general consensus within the public policy communities that urban regions are the engines of growth in the knowledge-based economy. They are the homes to research-intensive post-secondary institutions, the magnets for immigration, and the cauldrons of creative talent. They also provide global connections through both commerce and their immigrant communities. Thus the health of the Alberta economy will depend to a considerable degree on how successful the two regions are in attracting migrants from the rest of Canada, and international immigrants, in how successful their business and academic communities are in attracting innovation, creative talent and investment. This in turn will depend on how well they manage growth.

Alberta's cities offer a quality of life unsurpassed in Canada. A study in 2004 revealed that Alberta cities have the overall lowest cost of living across the country. These cities boast all of the amenities of a technologically advanced society, yet they still display the old Alberta virtues of friendliness and freedom from snobbery. The test will be to see if these virtues can be maintained as growth continues in Alberta's second century, for growth inevitably comes at a price. The two mega-cities struggle with crime, badly stretched social and medical services, rush-hour gridlock and the need for improved rapid transportation.

His Worship Mayor Dave Bronconnier
of Calgary (City of Calgary).

Calgary: The Values That Define Our City
Mayor Dave Bronconnier

What will Calgary look like in a hundred years? I couldn't possibly tell you. Technology and accumulated human knowledge is changing our world at an enormous pace.

Imagine if you asked the same question of Mayor John Emerson in 1905. Do you think that he would have contemplated, or even believed for that matter, that in 100 years public trolley cars powered by wind would deliver Calgarians to work and home? Or that from their offices, homes or even a public park, Calgarians could turn on an electric box and read a newspaper, complete with photographs, from the other side of the world? Or that Calgarians could travel a short distance to a station called an airport, which could transport them in the air to any part of the world in a matter of hours?

Perspective is everything, and painting a picture of what our city will look like in 2105 is an exercise best left to futurists or science fiction writers. But if you ask, "What will Calgary *be like* in a hundred years?" that's a question that can be answered with greater certainty. The essence of a city is not determined by technological change; rather it is established by the enduring values that have built and sustained a community.

Calgary is a pioneer spirit. With the exception of our First Nations people, we are all relative newcomers here. We are a city built by immigrants, who left the safety and security of their homelands to come here and start a new life. The same is true today. Calgary remains a preferred destination for migration from other parts of Canada and the world, people who come here to live and work, put down roots and adopt their new home. Calgary is a city that welcomes newcomers and embraces their traditions and cultures.

Calgary is an entrepreneurial spirit. Calgarians have an inherent trust in the marketplace; we believe in the free market and the value of competition. We also have a healthy skepticism about, or rather impatience with, government. Building a world-class city from a tiny frontier outpost required hard work and a willingness to try new things. A strong work ethic, fortitude and courage are values strongly woven into the fabric of our city. We remain Canada's frontier, but now it is because of our attitude and deeds, rather than geography.

Calgary is born of the land. Calgarians are environmentalists. We understand our connection to the land, and the importance of a sustainable relationship with it. Our roots as a city have taught, and continue to teach, us that this is paramount. Most early settlers to our city arrived on the back of a horse or by the new railway—their only connections to the rest of the world. They endured enormous hardships: harsh winters, hail, prairie fires, drought and seclusion, all with only the barest of necessities for life. But they persisted. They turned the sod and tended their herds, and the land returned its bounty. Our farming and ranching industries now feed the world, and these traditions have taught us that we are the stewards of the land—it's important to our survival. These lessons have been passed down through generations of Calgarians, and are instilled in new generations through the annual cultural showcase of the Calgary Stampede and Exhibition. This is more than just a ten-day festival every July; it is an annual expression and affirmation of our heritage.

Calgary is pride and hospitality. We're proud of our city. You hear that pride when ordinary Calgarians tell distant friends, family (or complete strangers, for that matter) about their community. They talk about the Calgary Stampede, the Rocky Mountains, and our spectacular outdoors. They talk about our cultural amenities, our restaurants, and our nightlife. And they talk about a big friendly city that likes to play host to the world, and likes to greet our guests with a warm smile and a white Smithbuilt hat. They represent a corps of nearly a million "good-will ambassadors" for our city, with links throughout the world. Calgary's hospitality is one of our most precious commodities.

I really don't know what Calgary will look like in 2105. But I do know this: we will still be a city that welcomes newcomers, values hard work, and doesn't shy away from doing things differently. I am certain that Calgary will still be an entrepreneurial capital, where bureaucracies are scorned and fortunes are won and lost and won again. I am confident that we will be a city that values our environment, and identifies with the land that gives us life. And I am assured, without a shadow of a doubt, that Calgary will still be a city that loves to host and enjoys making new friends.

These are the values that define our city—past, present and future.

The question that arises from this urban growth is: who will pick up the tab to ensure that cities are sustainable and that the quality of urban life is sustained and improved? Because cities will be so important for Alberta's second century economy and quality of life, they necessarily engage the attention and interest of the provincial and federal governments. After years of lobbying by big city mayors, the senior governments are acknowledging the need for cities to have a steady flow of tax revenue outside the limited base of property tax. The province of Alberta broke the ice by signing an historic agreement to share gasoline tax revenue with Calgary and Edmonton, passing on five cents for each litre of fuel sold in the cities. The federal government began with GST rebates to cities and now is starting to share its own excise tax on fuel. These are major and positive steps that will make cities less dependent on grants, and eventually more autonomous.

By American standards, however, our cities are still severely constrained by provincial laws that prohibit them from creating new taxes of their own. Canadian cities have always been creations of the provinces and hence very junior partners on the provincial and national scenes. They have no legislative representation provincially or federally. (In some European countries, cities have separate representation in federal governing bodies.) Yet with increasing urban populations, this junior status no longer fits political and economic realities. Senior governments have no option but to open the traditional bases of funding and power. When the group known as the Big City Mayors hold their meetings, they often raise issues just as important to Canadians as the premiers do at their traditional annual gatherings. This signals a gradual but pronounced seepage of authority toward the cities. Revenue sharing is surely just the first of an array of new arrangements that will hasten this trend.

At the same time, history teaches us, if it teaches us anything, that urban communities must be prepared to cope with not only the booms but also the busts of a resource-based provincial economy. Edmonton and Calgary have been through rough economic cycles before. High prices brought booming prosperity to the province in the 1970s, but the combination of the federal National Energy Program in 1980, followed by sharply lower energy prices in the mid-1980s, sparked one of the sharpest economic tumbles since the Great Depression of the 1930s. In Calgary, hundreds of people walked away from homes that were suddenly worth far less than the mortgages they carried. We can only hope that Edmonton and Calgary now rest on such broad, solid launch pads that they are largely self-sustaining. They can afford to pause for a while to refuel before taking off again.

Nonetheless, the smart money suggests that Edmonton and Calgary will continue to grow and prosper. But what kinds of cities will they become—prosperous ones with extensive natural capital, creative urban design and bustling artistic life, or just two more vast tracts of North American urban sprawl? To date, the omens are positive. Calgary and Edmonton admittedly have their share of sprawl, but their inner cities are reviving and revitalizing with their own sense of style. Edmonton's Whyte Avenue and Calgary's 17th Ave SW are utterly different yet equally exciting. Both cities now have a dozen little urban neighborhoods worth visiting for the shops and the scene. Suburban design is often exciting too—Calgary's Garrison Woods on the site of the former Canadian Forces Base, and McKenzie Towne in the far south, are Canadian models for neighborhood development. Both cities thrive artistically, although there's nothing in Western Canada to match the annual excitement of the Fringe theatre festival on Edmonton's south side.

The past suggests that a century from now, at the celebration of Alberta's Bicentennial, the cities will be changed beyond recognition. Who in 1905 could have imagined modern Edmonton and Calgary, two of the continent's most vigorous, energetic cities, with populations approaching a million? The very idea would have seemed absurd, even to the lively civic promoters and boosters who started these towns rolling. Let's hope that in 2105 Albertans will look at their urban landscapes and thank us for putting into place a sustainable urban heartland for the province.

9 Alberta Culture

FIL FRASER

There's a picture in the Alberta provincial archives captioned "Homesteaders Band, Thorhild, 1910." Four men stand in front of a rough homestead building, each holding an instrument; an autoharp, two violins and an accordion. They are about to make music. The image symbolizes a vital characteristic of many of the families who came to farm the prairie west. They were prepared for hard work and harsh winters. And part of that preparation was the understanding that life without music would, for them, hardly be life at all.

It was surely good luck rather than good management that brought me, in the winter of 1965, to a job in Edmonton. For 40 years the city has been the most comfortable part of Canada I could live in. When you want to do something daring, even foolhardy, no one here says "You can't do that," or, "Who do you think you are?" The more likely response is "Go for it," and, "Can we help?" The city welcomes and celebrates the diversity that has always been part of its reality. Respect for diversity and appreciation of the arts, I would argue, go together like backs and fronts. You rarely find one without the other.

I was born in Montreal, and have lived and worked in four provinces. But, for me, Alberta is the most remarkable part of our astonishing work-in-progress country. Many in the rest of Canada wonder why, with all our wealth, we complain so much. But deep beneath the bluster and bravado, all too often the face we present to the rest of Canada, a warm heart beats vigorously, often in swing time.

In the twentieth century Alberta (let us, for this occasion, leave Quebec out of this) provided some of the most compelling drama within Confederation. And all present indications are that, as we plant our (cowboy, rubber or roughneck) boots firmly in the twenty-

Author Fil Fraser found inspiration in this image of Thorhild's Homesteader's Band from 1910. Alberta's immigrants came to Alberta to start a new life, but along with them came a wealth of their own cultural influence in music and the arts (Provincial Archives of Alberta/A7642).

first, that is not about to change. We are a province of great, often theatrical, contradictions, of light and dark, of noble leaps forward and dig-in-your-heels recalcitrance. We are at once unsung leaders in the development of Canadian arts and culture, and home to the last, desperate stand against gay rights; we created the largest, most politically daring, Fringe theatre festival outside of Edinburgh, Scotland, yet we were the last Canadian jurisdiction to ratify the United Nations Convention on the Rights of the Child; we created the world renowned Banff Centre, a national and international mecca for artists in all disciplines, but we also spawned the notorious 1990 Aryan Nations cross burning in a town called Provost. We elect senators who are unlikely to ever hold office. We can be both generous and mean-spirited. We are the "havingest" of the haves. And some describe us as the crybabies of Confederation.

More than Ten Days of Fun: The Calgary Exhibition and Stampede
Max Foran

The Calgary Exhibition and Stampede bills itself as "The Greatest Show on Earth." Though understandable from a marketing point of view, the superlative is misleading, for the Stampede is far more than an entertainment extravaganza or mega event that enhances the city's visitor appeal. It should not be judged by the spending habits of the hundreds of thousands of visitors from around the world who annually visit the Stampede grounds, by the record amount of prize money to be won at the "best rodeo on the planet," by the decibels generated by rock

The Calgary Stampede's founder, Guy Weadick, in January 1906 (Glenbow Archives/NA-1483-10).

bands, or by the number of celebrities and visitors who attend the breakfasts, parties and gala events that accompany the ten days of "July madness." True, no one can deny the value of the Stampede as a genuine Canadian celebration, as a magnificent spectacle, or even as a tribute to a ritualized western mythology. Its essence, however, lies elsewhere. Over the years it has extolled agriculture and heritage. It has showcased technology and foreshadowed contemporary issues and events. And, for better or worse, the Stampede has helped articulate an ideology that continues to permeate both the corporate boardrooms and smokey bars of its host city.

Though it might be more difficult to identify from today's media coverage, the ongoing promotion of agriculture, agricultural technology and indeed the agrarian way of life has always been a primary mandate of the Exhibition and Stampede. A wide range of agricultural proponents and experts from the Big Four to Ernie Richardson, Jim Cross, Don Matthews and Bob Church, to name a few, have lent their energies and expertise to further agriculture in the province and region. Over the years a plethora of ongoing exhibitions, sales, educational programs and showcase events have made the Exhibition and Stampede a national agribusiness forum. For instance, prestigious livestock events like the World Charolais Congress in 1967 and the World Simmental Congress in 1978 were scheduled to coincide with the Exhibition and Stampede.

Guy Weadick had it right when he placed heritage first and foremost in the inaugural Stampede of 1912. His foresight has not been ignored. Though sometimes overstated and exaggerated, this emphasis on recreating a bygone era is seen as a necessary ingredient to any Stampede. Heritage reminders are present today in the annual Stampede Parade. They are observable in the public art and artifacts that adorn the grounds and indoor facilities at Stampede Park. They are honoured in the many art and craft activities sponsored by the Stampede, and according to current projections, they will soon come together in a grand display of western heritage in an on-site museum.

The Stampede has not focused solely on the past; it has also been a vehicle for the display of technological advances. The 1935 parade, for example, announced the birth of the industrial era. In the same decade, the Stampede featured a robot that answered questions, a giant television two decades before it was commercialized, car radios, wringerless washers and the latest in automobile technology. The Stampede has also functioned as a catalyst for bringing public attention to contemporary events and issues. Whether it was helping the unemployed in the depression, drawing attention to the children of the world, or promoting the war effort in the 1940s, the Canadian Centennial in 1967, and the Commonwealth Games in 1978, the Stampede has continued to reflect a wider social dimension than mere entertainment.

The Stampede has been instrumental in fusing urban and rural interests, and, some would argue, in advancing Calgary's Cowtown image. Its Board of Directors reflects a powerful blend of livestock and urban business leaders who have worked together to improve the Stampede and enhance both regional and urban economic health. It could also be argued that in no other area of civic activity is the ideological compatibility of the livestock and the oil and gas industries manifest more than in the boardroom and on the volunteer committees of the Calgary Exhibition and Stampede. In this context, the city's emblematic White Stetson represents the oilman and the rancher even more than the cowboy.

The Calgary Exhibition and Stampede faces many challenges in the new century. It needs to ensure that it retains integrity of purpose even as it strives to redefine itself as a major entertainment theme park. It must find ways to be more inclusive of other interest groups with respect to policymaking. Finally, it must continue to be mindful of both public opinion and the efficacy of its own policies with regard to animal welfare. But challenges are not new to the Stampede, and as long as it tries to embody the real and imagined spirit of the west, it should be able to meet them successfully.

The clear common denominator in all of this is that whatever the province does, for better *and* for worse, it has a mind of its own. Alberta does not follow—it leads. This chapter will try to illuminate at least some of the reasons that Alberta makes such a leading contribution to Canadian culture and the arts, and why that fact goes unheralded in the rest of Canada. It's worth noting at the outset that, while Calgary is clearly the province's financial capital, Edmonton has always led the way in cultural and artistic development. That's partly because, when the province was formed, both the political capital and the university were situated in Edmonton (unlike Saskatchewan, where Saskatoon got the university, but Regina got the provincial capital). That placed many of the province's intellectual resources in Canada's northernmost major city, where government civil servants and university academics sought and created entertainment, partly to help them get through the longer, darker, colder winters that come with life at latitude 53.

Who knows what might have evolved had the head of Imperial Oil decided to play golf in Edmonton. Leduc, Alberta, a virtual stone's through from the oil discovery that changed everything, is a suburb of Edmonton. According to a story told to me by Peter Lougheed, the then head of Imperial Oil had to decide whether to locate the company's head office in the capital city or in Calgary, less than a three-hour drive to the south. Turns out he preferred a Calgary golf course with a view of the mountains to one located in Edmonton's river valley. And the rest, as they say . . .

While Calgary tended to be Waspish, with a significant British-extract and American (and American-influenced) citizenry, Edmonton was host to a much more diverse population, with significant Eastern European influences. Calgary's ideological base was rooted in the rugged individualism of alone-on-the-range ranching. Edmonton was born with the fur trade, later becoming a centre for the more cooperative-minded pursuit of dry land farming.

During the province's "Camelot Years" in the 1970s and 80s, Edmonton had more live theatre per capita than any other city in North America. There were more theatre companies, more theatre spaces and seats, and more bottoms in those seats. Edmonton's Citadel (five stages, a waterfall and a tropical garden) is the largest, and arguably the finest, theatre complex in English Canada, and possibly surpassed only by Montreal's Place des Arts. Next door, the aesthetically pleasing Francis Winspear Centre for Music, according to trumpet virtuoso Jens Lindeman, is, acoustically, one of the top five or six concert halls in the world.

No other city in Canada boasts a civic centre in which the major concert hall, theatre complex, public library, art gallery and City Hall (with large, open, and much-used public spaces) frame a large civic square expressly designed to accommodate festivals and ceremonies of all kinds. Recently the CBC consolidated its Edmonton operations in a location overlooking the square. Big windows allow announcers to look out, and passersby to look in, putting public broadcasting on public display.

At the Fringe, the Play's the Thing!

Laura Neilson Bonikowsky

For many Canadians, summer means it's time for the Fringe, the delicious avant-garde theatrical genre dished up annually in extravagant portions to eager holiday-makers across the country. This well-loved Canadian tradition was inspired by the Edinburgh Fringe Festival and since then has assumed a distinctive Canadian flavour.

The original Fringe grew from rebellious protest in 1947. Eight disgruntled theatre groups, dissatisfied with theatric elitism, descended on the Edinburgh International Arts Festival uninvited. With the venues full, the interlopers produced their work wherever they could, promoting their work themselves in the streets. They were a resounding success. The next year Robert Kemp of the *Evening News* coined the name that now describes the world's largest festival: "Round the fringe of the official Festival drama there seems to be a more private enterprise than before . . . I'm afraid some of us are not going to be often at home during the evenings."

Canada's Fringe theatre tradition began in August 1982 in Edmonton with Brian Paisley, an artistic director frustrated by the dearth of venues for the abundance of theatrical talent that sat idle over the summer. Using the Edinburgh festival as a model, Paisley created a venue that promotes artistic freedom without creative interference. The Canadian approach to Fringe festivals differs from its international counterparts by assuming the administrative burden. Fringe theatres elsewhere offer performers only space, but Canadian Fringe events provide all the necessary resources, so performers need only to bring their shows to the site.

Canadian audiences differ, too, in their open-mindedness and sophistication. The reception of Canada's first Fringe festival worried promoters. Some of the titles and the plays were a little racy and occasionally theatrical expression pushed the limits. One of the productions was staged at night in an alley and people leaving a nearby bar sometimes drove their cars onto the "stage" mid-performance. Audiences and performers took it in stride.

Canadian Fringe audiences are wonderfully receptive; they arrive ready to be entertained. At the Fringe, performers have to work to lose their audience, unlike the traditional theatre atmosphere where

Brian Paisley, founder of the Fringe Theatre (Edmonton Journal).

performers have to win their audience. From Victoria to Halifax, the world's only Fringe circuit supports artists, stimulates new work and entertains an expanding audience in what has become a vacation option and trendy tourist attraction.

There is no hierarchy or agenda-grinding at the festival. Canadian Fringe theatre is often political, sometimes risqué, and you never know what you'll see, but you always know you'll have fun. Like Kemp, we are not often at home during the days and evenings of the Fringe festival!

The city's annual Fringe Theatre Festival is the largest in the world, and the Edmonton Heritage Festival, which celebrates the food, arts and crafts, music and dance of some 70 world cultures, has attracted as many as half a million people on a summer weekend. A cornucopia of summer festivals celebrates everything from jazz to folk music, from agriculture to visual arts, from buskers to cowboys. They pay homage to children, film, dance, the culinary arts, and even to a dragon boat festival. The first comprehensive, and truly Canadian encyclopedia, was published by Edmonton bookseller, publisher and author, Mel Hurtig. The three-volume work was substantially financed by the Government of Alberta and sent to every library in Canada as a gift to the country in celebration of the province's seventy-fifth anniversary.

Alberta Jazz
Jeffrey Jones

Alberta's jazz scene could be its best-kept secret. The province is far from being a jazz mecca, but it has long been home to a core of dedicated musicians and fans, keeping the music alive on stage and on the airwaves. From the big band sounds that filled Edmonton's lavish Trocadero Ballroom in the 1940s to avant-garde music played at today's major jazz festivals, Alberta has produced some top-flight players and attracted a Who's Who of the artform's legends.

Canadian music critic and author Mark Miller traces some of the earliest sounds in Alberta to a saxophonist named Ollie Wagner, whose six-decade career began in Edmonton in the 1920s, sowing the seeds for later generations.

During the Great Depression and war years, dancers flocked to ballrooms like Penley's Pavilion in downtown Calgary to kick up their heels to the tunes of the swing era. Old-timers talk about visiting big-name bands from the United States during World War Two, when construction of the Alaska Highway brought U.S. servicemen to the province.

When the days of the big band gave way to bebop, local players showed off their chops at small clubs like Calgary's Foggy Manor, a smokey after-hours venue known for its jam sessions in the late 1950s and early 1960s, frequented by such players as pianist Ray Petch and saxophonist Eddie Morris.

Today, fans check out their favourite homegrown musicians and visiting stars at a handful of nightclubs, like the Yardbird Suite in Edmonton and Calgary's Beatniq Jazz and Social Club. Big annual summer festivals in Calgary, Edmonton and Medicine Hat provide a showcase for local combos, and organizers have brought in such greats over the years as Sonny Rollins, Etta James, Tito Puente, Steve Lacy and Art Blakey.

Senator Tommy Banks is an integral part of Alberta's jazz scene.

Alberta has been home to some notable musicians who have made it big on the world stage. Best known is pianist, bandleader, broadcaster and Senator Tommy Banks, who has led large and small groups since the 1950s, while being an ambassador for the province's jazz scene. His big band played at the famed Montreux Jazz Festival in Switzerland in 1978, and he has been a fixture at Edmonton's Jazz City festival.

Trombonist and blues singer Clarence "Big" Miller played in Banks' Big Band and fronted his own groups. Miller, born in Sioux City, Iowa, played in orchestras led by greats Duke Ellington and Jay McShann before settling in Edmonton in the early 1970s. With his deep voice and easy stage presence, he became one of Alberta's most beloved performers until his death in 1992 at the age of 69.

Another alumnus of the Banks band is Edmonton-based alto saxophonist P.J. Perry, a fiery soloist in the bebop tradition who has toured the globe and performed with such legends as Dizzy Gillespie, Slide Hampton and Woody Shaw.

Up-and-coming players can take advantage of top-notch jazz music education at such institutions as the University of Calgary, Mount Royal College and Grant McEwen College. In 1972, stars Oscar Peterson and Phil Nimmons set up the summer jazz workshop at the renowned Banff Centre for the Arts, a program that has since been directed by such international figures as British bassist Dave Holland and American saxophonist Steve Coleman.

Perhaps the strongest supporters of jazz are Alberta's publicly funded radio stations. CKUA in Edmonton has been home to such broadcasters as "The Old-disk Jockey" John Worthington, known for his recordings from the 1930s through the 1950s, and Bill Coull, who lent his expertise to programs for 41 years before his retirement in 2003. University of Calgary's CJSW FM, meanwhile, serves up a steady, varied diet of jazz programming throughout its weekly schedule.

Another Albertan, born in Calgary, raised in Red Deer, and based in Edmonton for many years, is destined to enter the history books as one of Canada's most creative architects. Douglas Cardinal, designer of the national capital's Museum of Civilization and the National Museum of the American Indian in Washington, D.C., has left a legacy of unique and celebrated buildings throughout Alberta. They include the famous St. Mary's Church in Red Deer, the Edmonton Space Sciences Centre, Grande Prairie College, the St. Albert Civic Centre, and many more. Still active, his Native Studies Centre on the campus of the University of Alberta is a work in progress.

During those Camelot years, Alberta, with 30 publishers, had the second largest publishing industry in English Canada, and the second largest indigenous film and video industry. Albertans took out more library books and in fact were considered to be, on a per capita basis, the largest consumers of cultural products in English Canada. Calgary made its own contributions. The city's Glenbow Museum mounts some of the finest exhibits in the province, and its Centre for the Performing Arts, animated by a lively theatre scene, is a jewel in its own right.

The internationally celebrated Banff International Television Festival has attracted as many as 2000 delegates from countries around the world for its annual event in the Rockies. Launched in 1979, the festival continues as one of the top two or three events in the world celebrating excellence on television.

But the province's greatest arts jewel is the Banff Centre. Founded in the early 1930s as part of the University of Alberta's Department of Extension, the Banff Summer School of Fine Arts, under the leadership of Senator Donald Cameron grew to considerable prominence during the post-war years. But it was not until the

1970s that it reached for and achieved its highest pinnacle of success. With Cameron's successor, Dr. David Leighton, as president, Banff, which had by then become an extension of the University of Calgary, sought autonomy. Leighton, with no small measure of support from Jeanne Lougheed, an accomplished singer who had studied at Banff during her university years, persuaded the government to give the school stand-alone university status. The Banff Centre Act passed the legislature in 1979, and the Centre, already an internationally recognized sanctuary and training ground for artists, became a year-round educational institution, offering them the opportunity to complete their post academic training, studying under senior artists who embodied the highest world standards. In 1985 the Banff Centre celebrated its fiftieth anniversary by hosting an International Symposium on the Arts, which saw 100 leading artists from some 38 countries spend an intense week discussing their role in addressing world issues and crises.

The Banff Centre: Alberta's Creative Catalyst

Mary Hofstetter

An opera about bootlegging, murder, and the last woman hanged in Alberta; a music/theatre performance at dawn on a mountain lake; an experiential artwork that took the Venice Biennale by storm—all part of the legacy of Alberta's campus in the clouds, The Banff Centre.

Creative works as diverse as the critically acclaimed opera *Filumena*, R. Murray Schaefter's environmental music/theatre work *Princess of the Stars*, and Janet Cardiff and George Bures Miller's groundbreaking *The Paradise Institute*, recipient of the 2001 La Biennale di Venezia Special Award, are but a few examples of the Centre's enduring impact on Albertan and Canadian culture.

Since 1933, The Banff Centre has inspired the creation of new artistic works in all disciplines—dance, music, opera, theatre, Aboriginal arts, creative writing, visual arts, and new media. Founded as an extension of the University of Alberta with a single course in drama, the Centre has nurtured the development of Albertan, Canadian, and international artists for over seven decades.

Filumena is just the latest new opera to be developed at the Centre. Over the years, the Centre has premiered *Dido and Aeneas*, *Tornrak*,

David Moroni and Nadia Potts, guest artists in the Festival Ballet, 1971 (Paul D. Fleck/Banff Centre Library and Archives).

Ubu, *Boiler Room Suite*, *Jackie O.*, *Zurich 1916*, and a re-orchestration of *Wozzeck*.

Visual artists have been coming to the Centre since the 1930s—A.Y. Jackson, Walter Phillips, Marion Nicoll, and more recently Takao Tanabe, and David Rokeby. In their footsteps, artists are inventing and exploring new media, including online art, video, and virtual reality, and researchers are exploring convergences between art and technology.

Over the years, the Centre's writing programs have attracted the stars of Canadian letters, from Margaret Laurence, W.O. Mitchell, and Timothy Findley to Booker Prize-winning author Yann Martel. In music, the Centre has welcomed the world's most accomplished composers and musicians to teach and perform in Banff, including Aaron Copland, Krzysztof Penderecki, Lorand Fenyves, Zoltan Szekely, Edgar Meyer, Anton Kuerti, and Jon Kimura Parker. In the early 1970s Oscar Peterson and Phil Nimmons arrived at the Centre to create an innovative program for jazz musicians.

In addition to training young classical dancers and up-and-coming Canadian choreographers as part of its summer dance program, the Centre also hosts some of the country's top dance companies every year for development residencies. Ballet BC, Les Ballets Jazz de Montreal, the National Ballet, and Decidedly Jazz Danceworks have all developed new works in Banff.

Leadership is also fostered at The Banff Centre. Since 1953, the Centre has offered leadership development programs to generations of business leaders. Conference services at the Centre generate essential revenue to support artistic programs.

Leaders and artists in all disciplines continue to travel to Banff because it offers something rare in today's world—an environment dedicated to creative work. Every year, 4000 to 5000 participants come to Banff for professional and creative development. One of the cultural jewels of Alberta, The Banff Centre brings together artists, business and community leaders, and researchers from across the province and around the world. The talent nurtured, the new work created, the alliances forged at Banff have significantly shaped the social and cultural heritage of Alberta—and will continue to lead the way in the second century.

One of the interesting things about Alberta's artistic development is the role played by women. The first dean of the Banff Centre was a remarkable woman named Elizabeth Sterling Haynes. To quote David and Peggy Leighton's history of the Banff Centre, *Artists, Builders and Dreamers*:

Her contribution to the Banff Theatre School was immeasurable. Had it not been for her talent and her ability to inspire others, the venture might easily have collapsed in those first years. As it was, she established high standards and provided energetic leadership that captured the imagination of those who were to follow. It was Elizabeth Haynes who built the base upon which the future Banff School would grow.

Two other notable women, both teachers, Betty Mitchell in Calgary and Eva Osyth Howard in Edmonton, were pioneers in the development of Alberta theatre. Mitchell was honoured by a theatre named for her in the Calgary Jubilee Auditorium. Howard, who taught at the Victoria High School, which became renowned, with support from such luminous graduates as Arthur Hiller, has a theatre named for her in the school complex.

The Visual Arts
Russell Bingham

In the early days, most of the art made in Alberta was created by outsiders. This, of course, doesn't take into account the beautiful decorative artwork created by the indigenous peoples. But the first examples of artwork made in the European tradition were crafted by the early visitors—surveyors, adventurers, itinerant artists—who discovered Alberta's rugged and varied beauty in the nineteenth century. Probably the most famous of this group, painter Paul Kane, passed through Alberta twice, documenting on his way the trading forts in Calgary and Edmonton and sketching the daily lives of the native people. His paintings were among the first to reveal the territory that would eventually become Alberta to the rest of the world, and many of these quick sketches (later worked up into more formal compositions in his Toronto studio) have the charm and immediacy of colour snapshots.

For much of the early period, the main attraction for visiting artists was the Rocky Mountains, and when the Canadian Pacific Railway established passenger service to the west, the Rockies became a convenient destination. In 1887, the Railway even sponsored a painting tour for four members of the newly formed Royal Canadian Academy: F.M. Bell-Smith, Lucius O'Brien, T. Mower Martin and Marmaduke Matthews. Their rather academic interpretations of the scenery emphasized the majestic grandeur of the mountains and helped to publicize the tourist potential of rail travel. A few decades later, members of the Group of Seven also managed to take advantage of the CPR's generosity to put their own, more modern stamp on the Rocky Mountain subject matter. Some, like J.E.H. MacDonald, returned again and again.

Artists were slower to come to terms with the subtle power of Alberta's prairie flatlands. The prairies, with their vast skies and clear light, require a nurtured intimacy of the type that evolves from actually living in a place. Many of the first interpreters of Alberta's farmland and cattle country came from outside as well, but they settled and remained, making their living off the land or in various other pursuits, with painting as a secondary occupation. Several, including the Norwegian Lars Haukaness and the Englishmen A.C. Leighton, W.J. Phillips and H.G. Glyde, were instrumental in establishing the various art schools and colleges that sprang up here in the twenties and thirties. Without taking away from their accomplishment as artists, which was considerable, their enormous contribution as educators to the development of a home-grown Alberta art scene can hardly be over-stated.

Despite the developing professionalism of the visual arts scene in Alberta in the first half of the twentieth century, it was still mired to a large extent in the kind of conservative academicism that one would expect to prevail in a region largely cut off from the vital centres of art production. Nationally, the Group of Seven had crafted a Canadian form of modernism that exploited free paint handling and expressive colour, but by the thirties, even the innovations of the Group had ossified into something of a national style, one that for the most part was unsuited to prairie subject-matter. Alberta artists began to seek freer—and more authentic—means of expression. Two of them, Calgary painters William Leroy Stevenson and Maxwell Bates, turned their attention to the world outside, looking to the work of the masters of French modernism for challenge and inspiration. Together, they would meet to discuss the illustrations that they had seen in art magazines or critique each others' works and in 1929 they travelled together to the Art Institute of Chicago to see works by Monet, Seurat, Cézanne and Van Gogh.

Condemned by their peers for their progressive tendencies, Bates and Stevenson were kicked out of the Calgary Art Club, but went on to become by mid-century two of the Province's finest painters. They found for their own art an alternative to regionalism and provided a challenge to a generation of young Alberta painters with their expressive landscape and (in Bates's case) figurative paintings.

By the seventies, artists in the province had become more aware of their art in relation to art nationally and even internationally. Some, such as Sylvain Voyer and Harry Savage, sought to identify their art as specifically Albertan, by consciously depicting recognizably Albertan subject matter, or by including provocative text that would reflect its regional origin. Others, however, began to go in the other direction, seeking to situate their art within the broader context of late twentieth century modernism. Through the exhibition and collection activities of the Edmonton Art Gallery, many became exposed to progressive developments in American and European modernist art and this had an enormously stimulating effect on art making in Edmonton in particular. An eruption of challenging modernist abstraction occurred throughout the last decades of the century with painters such as Douglas Haynes, Phil Darrah, Graham Peacock, Terrence Keller and others making their mark. Today, the tradition has been maintained and invigorated by many younger artists, including Mitchel Smith and Sheila Luck, to name just two.

During the seventies, too, sculpture began to take on a more prominent role—again, especially in Edmonton. Prior to this time, a small group of figurative artists such as Ollie Ohlmstead had created monuments in bronze to commemorate famous people and events, but practitioners of the genre were few. The first focused sculptural movement in Alberta took the form of assembled abstract sculpture. Its first adherents, artists such as Alan Reynolds and Catherine Burgess, worked in wood, but with the arrival of British sculptor Peter Hide to teach at the University of Alberta in 1977, welded steel became the medium of choice.

An artist of international stature, Hide has had a major influence on sculptural art in the province, both through his teaching and through the quality of his work. Characterized by dense, rather than open, arrangement of parts, and verticality, Hide's abstract sculptures have attracted attention in North America and abroad, and many of the artists who matured under his influence, including Kenneth Macklin,

Inside Balzac, by Peter Hide (Mild steel, rusted, 1986 (Courtesy of the artist. Photographed by Russell Bingham).

Clay Ellis, Isla Burns, Katherine Sicotte, Royden Mills and others, have developed uniquely personal styles.

In the meantime, "conventional" landscape painting has continued to flourish. Drawing inspiration from the power of the natural environment and from its own firmly established roots, it was nurtured through the sixties, seventies and eighties by practitioners such as J.D. Turner, Illingworth Kerr, Euphemia McNaught and Ron L. Myren, and has seen revitalization and renewal through the work of Barbara Ballachey, Ken Christopher, Hendrik Bres, Hilary Prince, Gerald Faulder and many others leading up to the present day.

Installation, the hybrid zone that combines three-dimensional arrangement of objects with intellectual conception, along with other types of idea-based art of the kind that has dominated late twentieth-century art making, has also found a place in Alberta's art world, especially in southern Alberta. Calgary artists such as Walter May, John Hall, Joyce Hall, Ron Moppett, Mary Scott, Chris Cran, and Arlene Stamp have achieved national prominence. As well, in Edmonton a group of printmakers, many of whom have taught or studied at the University of Alberta, have attracted attention for their surrealist-flavoured works.

The pervading presence of Alberta's natural environment, as well as our cultural isolation, has influenced our visual expression, but art in Alberta has been shaped by many influences. Not least of these has been a supportive infrastructure of public galleries, teaching institutions and funding agencies. As we advance into our second century, there is talk of a new building for the Edmonton Art Gallery, which will allow the museum to host major travelling exhibitions of contemporary and historical art. With ambitious initiatives such as this, the future looks bright.

Much of the Camelot era's cultural development was the direct result of the funding programs generated by the Lougheed government, and led by its peripatetic and energetic Minister of Culture, Horst Schmid. Schmid, the first minister of culture in English Canada (with the backing of both Premier Lougheed, and, just as important, that of his artist wife, Jeanne) developed a series of support programs that stimulated a flowering of arts, culture and multiculturalism across the province. In the most important of these programs, the province matched, dollar for dollar, the money that arts and cultural organizations could raise from private sources. The program attracted unprecedented support from individuals and corporations who thought that, with the government effectively doubling their contributions, they were getting very good bang for the buck. Some of the more creative arts organizations found ways, during part of the era, to get the federal government to match the provincial contributions.

So, Alberta's deep involvement in and commitment to the arts didn't happen yesterday. Why doesn't the rest of Canada, for the most part, know this? Part of the reason is clearly the messages that have come out of the Alberta government over the past decade. We experienced shattering political changes in the tectonic shift between the Lougheed era's "red Tory," arts-friendly administration, and Ralph Klein's deficit- and debt-slaying regime. Arts and culture were cut along with everything else. Budgets bled. Many programs were decimated; some were decapitated. The arts were left in a situation not unlike the bloodied, dismembered knight in the film, *Monty Python and the Holy Grail*. With arms and legs hacked off, he vows to fight on, threatening to chew his opponents to pieces. What he was really doing was demonstrating his will to survive.

Now that the deficit is gone and the debt erased, there is a chance, and a challenge, for the government to rebuild programs and infrastructure in education, health and the arts. This is being written during Alberta's centennial year. What better chance to show the world who we are and what we are made of? Yet many Albertans are still waiting to hear what the main focus of the celebration will be— what "big idea" will commemorate our first century. To celebrate the province's fiftieth anniversary in 1955, the government of Ernest Manning built the Jubilee Auditoriums, identical, then state-of-the-art palaces to big stage entertainment, in Edmonton and Calgary. In 1980, on the province's seventy-fifth anniversary, the Lougheed government funded *The Canadian Encyclopedia*.

Gary Mar, who held the Ministry during the budget slashing mid-1990s, is again the Minister of Community Development, the closest thing Alberta now has to a Ministry of Culture. I asked Mar what future he saw for the arts in Alberta. The Minister is a fan of the work of Richard Florida, whose best-seller *The Rise of the Creative Class* was cited by the *Harvard Business Review* as containing one of the top breakthrough ideas of 2004. Florida's "creative class" is made up of writers, artists and entertainers, as well as scientists,

Albertan Mel Hurtig published the country's first all-Canadian reference work, *The Canadian Encyclopedia*, in 1984. It included authors and illustrators from across the country, but the bulk of the editing and compilation was done in Edmonton under the guidance of Editor-in-chief, James H. Marsh (*The Canadian Encyclopedia*).

engineers, architects and educators, all of them stirred to create new ideas, new technology and, in the broadest sense, new creative content. The new creators, Mar suggested, will be the driving force behind the development of communities and economies in this century. Government support for creators, he said, should be an investment that will bring returns in both the quality of citizenship and in economic development.

The Music Scene

Holger Petersen

I would love to see a music industry infrastructure in Alberta that would help musicians who need guidance and professional support along the way. When there is some success, we hope that they would stay in the province because there would be a business and management structure. That would include a full recording industry, labels and music publishers.

A stronger case has to be made to the politicians for the economic spin-off as a result of the music industry. Those spin-offs, like any other industry, could show huge payoffs economically and culturally. This would show how we value culture and how it touches your soul and your sense of identity in this province. For example, a little seed money to the Edmonton Folk Festival turned it into an internationally acclaimed event. The Calgary Folk Festival is establishing its own identity as well.

It's wonderful to know that Ian Tyson in his 70s is creating what many consider the best music of his career. My philosophy at Stony Plain Records is that artists get better with age. Ian's music shows we have a very deep-rooted music community in Alberta. Probably the next star of Ian's calibre is Corb Lund. As Ian says, he's been waiting 30 years for Corb Lund to come along. Corb brings another element to song-writing from a western base. His family is a long-time Alberta family; in 1902 they moved to ranch near Taber.

Alberta has really made its mark in country and the singer-songwriter areas—kd lang; Wilf Carter and Terry Clark; Carolyn Dawn Johnson. Of course, there's Nickleback's huge success in the area of pop music, and prior to that, Loverboy. Also, Joni Mitchell was born in Fort Macleod.

There are a lot of people who have come to Alberta because, like Ian Tyson, they admire our geography and wonderful mountains and, like Amos Garrett, our fishing streams.

A lot of credit should go to the music schools at Grant MacEwan College and Mount Royal College and Alberta's wonderful arts culture. There are other contributors, like Senator Tommy Banks, the internationally acclaimed artist who chose to stay in Alberta.

In the Blues world, there was the incredible Big Miller, who was also an educator. While all these artists are dedicated, they don't make much money. PJ Perry is another institution, as is Bill Bourne.

The Calgary Philharmonic Orchestra at the Jack Singer Concert Hall, 2005 (Photo by Garry Kan/Calgary Philharmonic).

The media support in this province has been very strong in all forms. In the case of CKUA, it is the voice of Alberta's culture and a unifying factor for all the cultural organizations. The best thing that could happen to Canadian culture would be for each province to have a CKUA, a truly community radio.

I'm in Alberta because I just didn't feel a compelling reason to move. I love Edmonton, and I love Alberta. I didn't see a good reason to leave. I was very lucky early on to get a part-time job at CKUA that kept me here and helped me make ends meet.

It gave me an opportunity to learn about different kinds of music.

"Economies are changing," he told me, "Successful cities like Philadelphia, Austin and Dublin attract people and jobs because of their culture." Will this view drive a new approach to the arts by the Alberta government? Mar's reply was cautious. He knows that, within the Conservative caucus, he has a selling job to do. But he said he's optimistically thinking through the means of creating a new cultural policy framework.

First on his agenda, he told me, will be to do his best to sell the idea of doubling the budget for the Alberta Foundation for the Arts (AFA). The Foundation, fuelled by the lottery money that has become an important (some say dangerous, some say immoral) part of the province's revenues, is the major funder of the arts in the province. With a budget that has barely increased since it was established in the early 90s, the Foundation struggles to meet the demands of the province's hungry and growing arts organizations. A petition circulated by arts groups gathered 100,000 signatures calling for the fund to be, at least, doubled. Minister Mar has committed himself, if not the government, to responding.

It may take as long as a generation to rebuild Alberta's ambivalent relationship with the arts. Meanwhile, at least one centennial year initiative was designed to showcase the province's creative talent before the rest of the country. With the National Arts Centre as host, Alberta Scene sent a cultural armada of some 600 musicians, dancers, writers and other artists to descend on the National Capital Region at the end of April 2005 for a series of performances and exhibitions that captured the national spotlight. Over 13 days in April and May, Alberta artists performed at more than 95 events in 19 venues across the National Capital region. The event presented everything from ballet to opera, classical music to folk, jazz, blues, roots, country, rock and hip-hop, theatre to comedy, and included visual and culinary arts, literature and film.

The Honens International Piano Competition
Julie Wright

Calgary's Honens International Piano Competition, founded in 1992, has grown to be one of the world's great music competitions. Every three years 21 pianists from all parts of the globe compete for more than $100,000 in prizes, including a unique three-season Artistic and Career Development Program. Honens is an extraordinary experience for pianists and audiences alike—not a series of tests, but a compelling festival of music.

The event's roots are deeply Albertan. In 1991, philanthropist and music enthusiast Esther Honens made a gift of $5 million towards her dream of building one of the world's great piano competitions in Calgary. Today, after only four competitions, the Honens International Piano Competition has become one of the most prestigious events of its kind.

Born in Pittsburgh in 1903, Esther Honens was raised in Calgary and studied piano as a child. Later she took a post at Henry Birks and Sons jewellers, where she worked for 25 years. She expanded her own investments and was considered a successful businesswoman when, in her 50s, she married John Hillier. After Hillier's death in the 1970s, she met and married Harold Honens. Harold was then 81, Esther 72. Together they developed their real estate holdings along Calgary's 17th Avenue SW. Esther Honens died five days after the first competition in 1992.

Today, Honens enriches the lives of Calgarians and Canadians through innovative community outreach programs and concerts by the finest young concert artists. Honens Community offers in-school programs, piano master classes, and community outreach activities like the innovative Community Concerts program that brings the excitement of young, world-class concert artists to audiences normally unable to attend live performances for mobility, financial or health reasons.

Through the Laureates in the Classroom program, Honens laureates collaborate with elementary, middle and high school teachers to develop and present in-school laureate performances and lectures based on a core curriculum. No two projects are alike.

Similarly, the Honens Young Composers Project, in collaboration with Allan Gordon Bell and the Calgary Public and Catholic School Boards, gives students in grades four, five and six opportunities to explore composition and music through a core curriculum. The program reaches more than 400 students in Calgary each year.

In addition to these programs, Honens offers piano students and piano–voice student teams from across Alberta the chance to learn from international concert artists who come to Calgary to serve as competition jurors.

Honens continues to build classical music audiences through Honens Concerts, a concert series dedicated to showcasing the competition's philosophy of "Discovering the Complete Artist"—musicians who challenge, communicate and inspire through performance.

Esther Honens would have been proud to see the Honens International Piano Competition take its place among the world's most important classical music events, and to observe her legacy to Alberta's cultural heritage.

Honens' First Laureate, Xiang Zou, brought the audience to its feet after his performance of Rachmaninov's Third Piano Concerto at the 2003 Honens Competition (Honens).

Those who took in the events came away knowing that Alberta is not just about oil rigs, wheat fields, and cowboys.

For Albertans in their own province, one of the greatest celebrations of the arts took place at the Banff Centre on April 16. Most Albertans agree that the most loved individual to grace the province's public life in its hundred-year history was the late Lieutenant Governor Lois Hole, affectionately known as the Queen of Hugs. Part of her impressive legacy, in which her remarkable human touch inspired support for education, literacy and women's health as well as the arts, is the Lieutenant Governor of Alberta Arts Awards. The Gala celebration on April 16 was tinged with sadness as participants paid tribute to the Honourable Lois E. Hole, the first patron and greatest supporter of the awards. Mrs. Hole died on January 6, in the first days of the Alberta Centennial year she had looked forward to with such anticipation. Her term had been extended to allow her to preside over the celebrations, and to host the Queen during her visit to the province.

The Arts Awards will remain one of Lois Hole's most important legacies. During her last public event, where she officially launched the awards program, she said;

The arts bring meaning to our lives; they prick our consciences, excite the senses, inspire our own creativity…they make us think and feel and strive to do better. The arts bring comfort when we need it, and they make us uncomfortable when we need it, too. They are a reflection of all we are, an image of what we were, and a call to what we could be.

Some $1.2 million raised in the private sector was matched by a $1 million government of Alberta centennial grant to create an endowment that will fund the Awards in perpetuity, offering one of Canada's richest prizes for excellence in the arts. Initially, up to three $30,000 prizes will be awarded every other year. With the addition of the centennial grant, the value or number of the prizes may grow in subsequent years. Following this launch at Banff, the program will be held in different parts of the province, possibly as part of a continuing biennial Alberta Arts Festival. Planners are working on an initiative that would see municipalities bid for the festival, in much the same way that they bid for the right to hold the winter and summer games, in which the provincial treasury provides a foundation grant, and the municipalities raise the additional funds required to stage the event.

Within its borders, Alberta's commitment to the arts is solid, sophisticated and sometimes surprising, even to those of us who live here. Quick now—name the greatest original Canadian opera!

100 Years of Sports 10

DAVID MILLS

On 1 September 1905, the creation of the Province of Alberta was heralded in Edmonton with much pomp and military pageantry by a ceremony, attended by the Governor General, Earl Grey; the Prime Minister, Sir Wilfrid Laurier; and the new Lieutenant Governor, G.H.V. Bulyea. Thousands of people watched a festive parade, featuring native groups of Cree and Stoney; Franco-Albertans; veterans of the Boer War; early pioneers, or "Old-Timers"; and floats representing the business community. The holiday spirit in Edmonton was not dampened by a storm that dumped 3 inches of snow on the capital city, but a number of sporting events that had been scheduled to celebrate Alberta's birthday had to be cancelled.

Sports were well established in Alberta by the time the province was proclaimed. New Albertans enthusiastically embraced and promoted sports. Sports provided recreation and physical activity; they turned "boys into men" who would share the progressive values of the new century. Sports provided a diversion for farmers carving out a homestead on the frontier, railway workers building the transportation links across the Prairies, or miners in the company towns. The early settlers also held sporting competitions to coincide with important holidays. In Vulcan, a small farming community in southern Alberta, baseball games against neighbouring communities were played on Victoria Day in May, Dominion Day on July 1st, and Labour Day in September. Sports encouraged competition among the new communities seeking an identity in the new province. Long before "the battle of Alberta" between Calgary and Edmonton, the municipal rivalry between neighbouring Edmonton and Strathcona was played out on the rink during an annual hockey game on New Year's Day.

In 1905, most Alberta villages and towns had at least one playing field; schools, police associations, sporting clubs and private businessmen were building the baseball and lacrosse fields, the running tracks, and hockey arenas to meet the demands of the local population. Those were the good old days when athletes played for the love of the game and communities engaged in friendly competitions where locals pitted their skills against each other. Winners were toasted and losers ribbed in fun as athletes and fans retired to a local hotel after the contests.

Amateur Hockey in Alberta

Larry Wood and Ken King

Chasing pucks on ponds was a practice much in vogue even prior to the turn of the twentieth century in Alberta. In 1902, the largest indoor ice rink of any account in what was then the Northwest Territories was constructed in Edmonton. It bore a large sign that read, Thistle Roller and Ice Rink. It included curling ice as well as a skating rink adaptable for hockey.

A completely organized version of hockey was established on November 29, 1907 when the Alberta Amateur Hockey Association was formed in Red Deer. The AAHA originally oversaw senior and quasi-professional hockey, then instituted an intermediate level in 1913 and a junior level in 1914.

In 1913, Edmonton hockey fans welcomed the opening of an arena that dwarfed the Thistle. The first puck was dropped in the Edmonton Arena on Christmas Day. Calgary's Sherman Rink was constructed in 1904. A cement addition was tacked on to the building in 1907, but fire demolished the entire edifice on February 24, 1915. Within three years, a building on the exhibition grounds that had been used by the military was renovated and became Victoria Arena, a genuine ice palace for those days.

Edmonton's Waterloo-Mercurys won gold at the Oslo Olympic Games in 1952, Canada's last until 2002. They are shown here returning from Olso to waiting fans (Edmonton Archives/ EA-600-2228a).

The brand of amateur hockey that eventually proved to be most successful over the years was played at the junior level. And the most successful franchise was that of the Edmonton Oil Kings. The Edmonton Beavers won the very first provincial junior title in 1915. No champion was declared in 1916 and the Calgary Crystals won the crown in 1917.

The first junior team to play an interprovincial series was the Calgary Monarchs in 1920, who defeated the Vancouver Blue Birds in two games and nine goals. The Monarchs subsequently bowed to the Selkirk Fishermen.

Calgary proved to be the junior hockey hotbed in the early years and sent the first Alberta team to contest the Memorial Cup, a trophy originally donated by the Ontario Hockey Association in 1919. The Calgary Canadians failed in a challenge for the trophy in 1924, losing to the Owen Sound Greys. But two years later, the Canadians won a best-of-three affair against the Queen's University Golden Gaels. Queen's won the first game 4–2, then lost successive 3–2 decisions to Calgary.

The Memorial Cup went to the national junior champs until 1934 when the junior division was divided into tiers and the trophy remained the property of the A tier. In 1971, with the addition of a major junior division, that winner became Memorial Cup champion. The Edmonton Athletics lost a pair of Cup finals, to Toronto's St. Michael's in 1934 and to the Oshawa Generals in 1939. Then, in the early fifties, the Oil Kings franchise was formed and absorbed the best players from a four-team Edmonton junior league. The Kings produced many National Hockey League performers and, over a span of 18 years, qualified for no fewer than nine Memorial Cup finals and two national championships.

A colourful, flamboyant, sometimes controversial character named Leo LeClerc managed the Kings at the beginning—1951 to 1965—and was tagged with many nicknames by his players: Leo The Lip, The Skulker, The Pipe-Cleaner, The Hockey Stick. His Oil Kings won the junior title in 1963 against the Niagara Falls Flyers and lost in the national finals of 1954 (St. Catharines Teepees), 1960 (St. Catharines Teepees), 1961 (St. Michael's), 1962 (Hamilton Red Wings), 1964 (Toronto Marlboros) and 1965 (Niagara Falls).

But if the team's colour could be said to have come from its manager up to that point, his replacement in 1966 could be termed kaleidoscopic. That was the season (Wild) Bill Hunter took over as the Oil Kings' boss and he led them to an immediate championship in a final series against the Oshawa Generals.

Hunter's Kings proceeded to lose a subsequent Cup final to the Quebec Remparts in 1971.

Hunter was a bellowing boulevardier extraordinaire and a legend among hockey builders. He was a born pitchman who once called a press conference to announce that he was calling a press conference.

The Memorial Cup format was altered to a three-team round-robin tournament in 1972. A fourth team (the host) was added in 1983. And 20 years after the Oil Kings' second success, the Medicine Hat Tigers embarked on two straight Memorial Cup-winning seasons in 1986 and 1987. The Red Deer Rebels, one year after the turn of the twenty-first century, became the fourth Alberta team to win the junior prize. Two other Alberta teams reached the tournament stage but lost in final matches, the Lethbridge Hurricanes (to Hull Olympique) in 1997 and the Calgary Hitmen (to the Ottawa 67s) in 1999.

Play for the Allan Cup, the trophy donated by Sir H. Montague Allan in recognition of national senior amateur hockey supremacy, began in 1908. Like the Stanley Cup, it was a challenge affair for many years before the Canadian Amateur Hockey Association assumed responsibility for eliminations some two decades later.

Teams from outside the boundaries of Edmonton and Calgary dominated provincial eliminations in the early days, specifically teams from High River and mining towns like Bellevue, Blairmore, Coleman and Canmore. The trend toward more successful city teams started with the Edmonton Superiors in 1930–31, followed by the Calgary Bronks in 1931–32. And the next season, the Superiors represented Canada in the unofficial world championship at St. Moritz. During their 38-game tour of Great Britain and Europe, the Superiors won 34, tied three and lost one match.

No Alberta team was close to winning the Allan Cup, however, until the Calgary Stampeders triumphed in 1946, exactly ten years after artificial ice was installed in that city. Lack of the latter to that point was the primary reason for the lack of success of Alberta teams at the national level.

The Stampeders were the first Alberta team to reach the Allan Cup final but lost the 1940 best-of-five series at Maple Leaf Gardens in Toronto to the Kirkland Lake Blue Devils. Following restricted action due to World War II, the Jack Arbour-coached Stampeders won it all.

The Calgary entry defeated the Edmonton Flyers in five games of a best-of-seven series, then eliminated the Winnipeg Orioles, Trail Smokeaters and Hamilton Tigers to win the championship. The final series was played at Edmonton. The next year, the Stampeders lost the Cup final in seven games to the Montreal Royals in the eastern city.

Not to be outdone, the Edmonton Flyers defeated the Stampeders,

Regina Caps, Trail Smokeaters, Winnipeg Reo Flyers and, finally, the Ottawa Senators to win the Cup in 1948. The final series was wrapped up at Calgary's Victoria Arena, which was replaced by the Stampede Corral in 1950, soon after the Stampeders lost the Allan Cup to the Toronto Marlboros.

Minor-league professional hockey returned to the province in 1951 and the Stampeders won the Western Hockey League title and Edinburgh Cup in 1954. The Flyers rebounded the next year to defeat Calgary in the WHL final but lost the Edinburgh Cup to the Shawinigan Falls Cataracts.

Eight years later the Flyers again won the WHL title. The Stampeders won the league in 1959 and 1961 but lost in playoff rounds.

Alberta senior-level hockey was weakened for many seasons following the ceding of the top teams to the pros in the early fifties. For the most part, intermediate-class teams aspired to Allan Cup play but failed, sometimes miserably. Still, the Lacombe Rockets were nominated to represent Canada for a 25-day, 14-game exhibition tour of Europe in 1965 and surprised many by amassing an 11–3 record.

Then came the 1965–66 Drumheller Miners, a rough, tough team coached by Roy Kelly that erased memories of many Allan Cup failures and moved into the Calgary Corral as a home playoff base once it eliminated the Calgary Spurs in playdowns. The Miners advanced to defeat the Sherbrooke Beavers in the final. In 1967, the Spurs battled all the way to the Allan Cup final but lost four straight to the Drummondville Eagles in Drummondville. A new-look Calgary Stampeders team travelled east to the final in 1971 and, again, lost four straight, this time to the Galt Hornets. Times changed for the Allan Cup in its later years. Only two Alberta teams were successful, the Stony Plain Eagles in 1999 and the Lloydminster Border Kings in 2001.

Edmonton's Waterloo-Mercurys likely would win any nomination as the province's top intermediate-level team of the twentieth century. The squad represented Canada at the 1950 world championship, won eight straight games and outscored the opposition 88–5. Two years later it represented Canada at the Winter Olympics and won the last gold medal Canada would harvest in 50 years of Olympic puck-chasing.

In 1951, the Lethbridge Maple Leafs won the world title, winning six straight games and outscoring the opposition 62–6. Alberta tier-two junior A clubs won seven gold medals in the Royal Bank Cup (formerly the Centennial Cup) play, which began in 1971.

The Red Deer Rustlers won the title in its first year, then finished as runner-up in 1972. The Spruce Grove Mets repeated that success in 1975 and 1976. The Rustlers won the title again in 1980 and the Olds Grizzlys followed in 1994, the Calgary Canucks in 1995, the Fort MacMurray Oil Barons in 2000 and the Camrose Kodiacs in 2001.

During the final two decades of the century, triple-A midget hockey grew by leaps and bounds and produced a pair of Alberta-built Canadian champions, the Calgary Buffaloes in 1989 and the Calgary Northstars in 1991. The Northstars repeated their victory in the late spring of 2003.

It wasn't until 1982, with legendary Canadian sportswoman Abby Hoffman providing the impetus, that women's hockey came into its own. The Edmonton Chimos won the third renewal of the Canadian championship in 1984 and repeated the feat in 1985, 1992 and 1997. Calgary's Oval X-Treme has since picked up the torch, winning national titles in 1998, 2001 and 2003.

There has been a tendency to romanticize our sporting past; somehow sports were more authentic, untainted by the greed of the present-day players and the bottom-line obsession of modern team owners. Today when we open the sports pages we read stories about lockouts and salary caps; players making multi-million dollar contracts; selling the product, revenue sources and profit margins; the problems of small franchises and the prospect of teams moving to larger and richer markets unless they are offered tax breaks, subsidies and new buildings to stay.

Over the last 100 years, Albertans' love of sports has grown. They participate in a variety of sports, like old-timers' hockey and ladies' ringette; skiing and curling, tennis and golf; marathons and jogging. They cheer enthusiastically for their children figure skating or playing hockey, shooting baskets or kicking soccer balls. Although there has always been female participation in sports, now girls and women are involved in every sport, and one of Alberta's best teams ever was the Edmonton Grads, who dominated the world of basketball over 60 years ago.

Sports figures became important in the province. Two of Alberta's premiers, Peter Lougheed and Don Getty, played football for the Edmonton Eskimos, as did the current Lieutenant Governor, Norman Kwong. Percy Page, coach of the Edmonton Grads basketball team, also served as Lieutenant Governor, from 1959 to 1965. Peter Pocklington, former owner of the Edmonton Oilers, ran for the leadership of the national Progressive Conservative Party in 1983 simply because team ownership had raised his public profile. Sports also link Albertans to the community and give us an identity, which can be defined by the clothing that we wear or the memories of a player or a game in our hometown. Alberta's centennial has a fostered a renewed sense of commemoration about the past and the accomplishments of the province and its teams have been celebrated. An examination of Alberta's sporting culture over the last 100 years must look at all these developments and in the process it might tell us a bit more about who we were as Albertans. First let us look at sports in Alberta a century ago.

In the first decade of the twentieth century, Alberta's population was growing rapidly as settlers poured into the province from other parts of Canada, the United States and Europe. In 1901, the census recorded just over 73,000 people; only ten years later, the population had increased to 274,000 and about two-thirds lived in rural areas. When Alberta became a province, there were two major cities, with Calgary having a larger population than the provincial capital. The 1906 census listed almost 12,000 people compared to over 11,000 for Edmonton and another 2900 for Strathcona. Lethbridge and Medicine Hat had about 3000 inhabitants each, while Red Deer was listed at about 1400 people.

Sports gave the local elites in both the small towns and the cities a means of recreation and an opportunity for social interaction with their new neighbours. High River, a small village south of Calgary, had the first polo field in Western Canada, as a number of the early ranchers were from minor British aristocratic families. In the new city of Edmonton, which had been incorporated in 1904, the sporting activities of the business and professional class and their offspring were reported in the recently-established *Edmonton Journal*. It had a small column most days called "The Sporting Life," which included items about sporting events elsewhere but concentrated upon local contests. Less than ten years earlier, the Edmonton Golf and Country had been founded, its five holes laid out on the site of the current legislature grounds. (It would move further west to what would become the Victoria Golf Club in 1906 and then to its current site in south Edmonton, opening the new

A women's hockey team from Medicine Hat poses for a team photo at the turn of the 20th century (Provincial Archives of Alberta/B6536).

layout, far removed from the riff-raff, in 1913.) The *Journal* would report that the male golfers would play and the women members would serve the lunch at the Club.

Hockey was also a popular sport during the pioneer period. As early as 1893, Calgary had several teams, each representing a different occupational group, including policemen, firemen, bankers, railway workers and ranchers. By 1895, the Calgary Fire Brigade was playing an out-of-province team from Golden, B.C. In 1897, there was a game between two women's teams but there were no male spectators because of concerns that it was "unladylike." In Edmonton, traders from the Hudson's Bay Company challenged local merchants to a game on the frozen North Saskatchewan River in 1894, and by 1905 towns like Carvale, Camrose, Wetaskiwin, Red Deer and Spruce Grove all had teams.

In 1902, the barn-like, but covered, Thistle Rink was built in downtown Edmonton. Hockey could now be played indoors, though on natural ice, rather than on the frozen North Saskatchewan River or outdoor rinks, as it had been before. With the completion of the Low Level Bridge across the river, Edmontonians now had an easier trip by rail to Strathcona, their southern neighbour and chief sporting rival.

Each New Year's Day saw a hockey game between the two communities. Although men would pay 25 cents and women 15 to see the game, the games could attract crowds of almost 2000 people. In one game, Edmonton, represented by the Thistle Hockey Club, tied Strathcona's Shamrocks 4–4, a result that was disputed by the Strathcona team, which argued that the referee missed an offside call on the tying goal. A second series was scheduled, best three of five. Edmonton won all three games in overtime, overcoming not just the Shamrocks but temperatures in the Thistle Rink that dipped to –28 degrees C. Later in the season, the same teams played for the Stephens Cup and again Edmonton was victorious, with no serious injuries to the players, just a black eye and a sore chin. It was reported that a couple of hundred Edmonton fans made the trip across the river by rail to watch a game at the new covered rink in Strathcona that had opened in December 1904. (The first covered arena in Calgary, the Auditorium Rink, also opened in the same year.) On the south side, spectators would beat the opposing players with canes, fists and purses whenever they came near the boards. Back in Edmonton after the game, three carriages, taking some well-refreshed and exuberant fans home, overturned, causing more embarrassment than injury, it seems.

The hockey competition between Edmonton and Strathcona was not matched by a similar rivalry with Calgary—there was no "Battle of Alberta" in 1905. The Thistle Club's junior team had to go to Calgary to play in the Jackson Cup Challenge, named after the hotel owner who had donated it. As no opponent wanted to play them, the Edmonton team was allowed to take the Cup, "if they could find it."

If there was no "Battle of Alberta" in hockey, there certainly was in curling. Curling thrived throughout Alberta in spite of problems, usually caused by the rapidly changing weather that affected outdoor ice. The Edmonton Curling Club was established in 1888 and city rinks played Calgary foursomes well before the turn of the century. Local curling matches and bonspiels were covered in the newspapers and when a number of Edmonton rinks went to Calgary for a week-long bonspiel in 1904, the stories knocked news of the war between Russia and Japan off the front page for four straight days. When the Edmonton rinks returned triumphant, capturing all the trophies Calgary had up for grabs, the CPR train that carried them home did not have to stop for any other train between the two cities, an honour never before accorded to sportsmen. In southern Alberta, curlers in the 1920s formed a league along the railway line and the small town of Vulcan built an indoor rink in 1922, although falling wheat prices made it difficult for the local farmers to pay for it. Curling provided isolated homesteaders the opportunity to socialize and therefore it was widely played in Alberta. As Paul Voisey notes in his book *Vulcan*, "it also stimulated the highest level of skill of any sport played in the region. For decades, the Canadian prairies produced the world's best curlers, and Ron Northcott, three-time world champion in the 1960s, learned his craft at the Vulcan Curling Club."

Sweeping Up: Alberta Curling

Larry Wood and Ken King

The first curling clubs in what was to become Alberta were formally organized in Edmonton and Calgary in 1888. Both were affiliated with the Manitoba branch of the Royal Caledonian Curling Club. Prior to that, the game was played in Calgary's ramshackle Claxton's Star Rink as early as 1886. The Thistle rink, constructed in Edmonton in 1902, made room for curling. By the year 2000, Alberta boasted 197 registered curling clubs.

The Brier, the national men's championship, began in 1927. In its first 75 years, teams from Alberta won the Canadian championship 21 times, second only to Manitoba's victory total of 26. Edmonton's Randy Ferbey is a five-time Brier winner whose endeavours have eclipsed those of every other Brier curler. Ferbey played third for Pat Ryan during Brier successes in 1988 and 1989, then skipped and threw third rocks for champion teams in 2001, 2002 and 2003.

Cliff Manahan, also of Edmonton, was Alberta's first big-time Brier competitor, competing in five Briers and winning two. He was Alberta's first Brier winner, winning six of seven games in 1933. In 1937, he was back with a 9–1 record. In the mid-fifties, the flamboyant Matt Baldwin of Edmonton and in the sixties the bespectacled and studious Ron Northcott of Calgary skipped in five Briers and won three apiece.

But Kevin Martin of Edmonton skipped more Alberta standard-bearers at the Brier than any other player. He led his team six times, won the title twice and recorded the most Brier game victories of any Alberta skip—55. He exceeded the wins of several champions, including the 42 that were won by Ed Lukowich of Medicine Hat and Calgary, another five-time provincial champion, Northcott's 40, Baldwin's 38 and Ryan's 38. Manahan won 35 games all told, one more than Hector Gervais of Edmonton, who appeared in four Briers and won two of them.

Calgary's Howard Palmer won the 1941 Brier with an 8–1 record and Billy Rose of rural Sedgewick won one of the most exciting championships in history following a three-way playoff at the 1946 Brier at Saskatoon, the first of the post-war era. Baldwin began his domination of the fifties by winning the 1954 renewal at the Edmonton Gardens. Three years later, in 1957 at Kingston, Baldwin became Alberta's first undefeated Brier winner. The next year he completed the triple at Victoria, defeating Manitoba's Terry Braunstein in a playoff.

Ladies Curling Team from Vulcan, Alberta, participates at a Calgary bonspiel in 1925. Curling was a popular early sport for women and Alberta's cooler winters provided ample opportunity to play (Glenbow Archives/NA-2685-80).

Hec Gervais won his first Brier at Calgary in 1961 and was the first Alberta skip to win the world championship. Then Northcott performed his legendary triple in four years, 1966 through 1969. He won his first Brier at Halifax by defeating Ontario in a playoff, then two years later at Kelowna won 9–1 and the next year at Oshawa sailed through unbeaten at 10–0. Following each Brier win, Northcott added world championship laurels.

Gervais completed his Brier double in 1974 at London, Ontario, but failed to win the subsequent world event. The same fate befell Lukowich, then of Medicine Hat, following his first Brier victory in 1978 at Vancouver. He didn't return to the Brier throne until 1986, when he added the world title to his list of accomplishments. Like Lukowich, Ryan flunked out in worlds following his initial Brier victory in 1988 at Chicoutimi. It took Ryan far less time to make amends, though. He was back winning the Saskatoon Brier in 1989 and the world title in Milwaukee, Wisconsin.

Martin was the Alberta strongman of the nineties. He won the Brier in his first try, at Hamilton in 1991, but was beaten in the world final. He then scored near-misses at three subsequent Briers before winning his second at Calgary in 1997—his fifth try in seven years. That brings the Alberta story around to Ferbey, whose team of Dave Nedohin (throwing last rocks), Scott Pfeifer and Marcel Rocque won an unprecedented three straight Briers starting in 2001 and narrowly missed making it four straight, losing the 2004 championship final match at Saskatoon. The team lost in the 2001 world semi-finals but rebounded to claim world titles in 2002 and 2003. In 2005, Edmonton was again the site of the Brier. Alberta cities have provided the stage for 10 Briers (Calgary 5, Edmonton 4, Red Deer 1) and established attendance records at five of them. The 10 events attracted more than 1.15 million fans, ranging from 30,000 at the first event at Calgary's Victoria Arena in 1948 to 245,296 at the Saddledome in 2002.

National competition for women began in 1961 and Alberta produced five champions during the balance of the 20th century. The first two winners were "family" teams comprising Hazel Jamieson and her daughters Gale Lee and June Coyle from Edmonton. Lee skipped in 1966 with sister Coyle at lead and Jamieson called the shots in 1968 with three daughters — Lee, Cole and Jackie Spencer.

Medicine Hat native Myrna (Adams) McQuarrie, with a Lethbridge team, won the 1977 Canadian women's title. Susan (Shields) Seitz, also from Medicine Hat, skipped a Calgary team to the title in 1981. And, in 1998, after some years of battling, Cathy (King) Borst directed her Edmonton team to the top of the national heap. It was the third Canadian title for King who, in 1977 and 1978, became the only Albertan ever to skip two national junior champion teams. A member of King's 1988 team, vice-skip Heather Godberson directed a Grande Prairie team to the Canadian and subsequent world junior titles in 1984. Dorothy Thompson of Edmonton skipped her teams to five provincial titles, more than any other Alberta curler, but failed to win the national title.

Skip Paul Gowsell of Calgary and his lead Kelly Stearne are the only two Alberta curlers to win two Canadian and world junior championships (1975, 1977). Scott Pfeifer of Edmonton played for two national junior champions but won only one world title. Other Alberta teams to win Canadian junior championships included those of Stan Trout of Edmonton in 1959 and 1967, Tom Kroeger of Stettler in 1960, Wayne Saboe of Edmonton in 1963, Brian Howes of Calgary in 1966, Shelby MacKenzie of Calgary in 1971, Lawrence Niven of Edmonton in 1972, Robb King of Edmonton in 1974, Darren Fish of Edmonton in 1978, Kevin Martin of Edmonton in 1985, LaDawn Funk of Spruce Grove in 1989, Colin Davison of Edmonton in 1994 and Ryan Keane of Edmonton in 1997. Only the teams of Funk and Davison advanced to win the world championship.

Alberta senior teams that won national titles included those skipped by Hadie Manley of Edmonton (1976, 1978), Cliff Forry of Lethbridge (1979), Beatrice Mayer of Calgary (1981), Bill Clark of Calgary (1988),

Mountain and Dead Trees. Oil on panel, 2004, by RFM McInnis (RFM McInnis).

Prairie Fence Line by Illingworth Kerr. Oil on canvas, 1987 (Glenbow Museum).

Chuckwagon racing continues to be the premier event of the Stampede. The Stampede's founder, Guy Weadick, was inspired to create the event while witnessing the round up crews who raced to the nearest saloon at the end of the day (Photograph by Gerry Thomas).

Raising of the Olympic flag at the Opening Ceremonies of Calgary's 1988 Olympic Winter Games (City of Calgary).

Calgary's Mark Tewksbury was the pride of Canada at the 1992 Olympics, taking a gold and setting an Olympic record in swimming (Photograph by Gerry Thomas).

Originally from Rocky Mountain House, champion figure skater Kurt Browning stunned the figure skating world at the 1988 World Championships by executing the first successful quadruple toe loop in competition (Photograph by Gerry Thomas).

Jamie Salé of Red Deer and her partner David Pelletier charmed skating fans in Canada and worldwide with the grace with which they endured a judging error that resulted in a silver medal in the 2002 Olympics. Later awarded the gold, Salé and Pelletier have since turned professional (Photograph by Gerry Thomas)

The Calgary Flames with team captain, Jarome Iginla, celebrate a win. In 2004, the Flames had their most successful season in nearly a decade, playing the Tampa Bay Lightning in the Stanley Cup finals (Photograph by Gerry Thomas).

Reminiscent of hockey's origins on the frozen ponds and outdoor rinks of Canada, the Oilers and Canadiens played in the first-ever NHL hockey game played outdoors, the Molson Canadian Heritage Classic on November 22, 2003 (Photograph by Gerry Thomas).

Telus Centre, University of Alberta. The U of A is one of Canada's largest major research-intensive universities, serving more than 29,000 students (Photograph by James H. Marsh).

Ian Tyson is one of the most original and enduring artistic voices of Alberta (Photograph by George Goodwin).

Patrons visit an Elephant at the Calgary Zoo. Incorporated in 1929, the Calgary Zoological Society continues to stress the importance of conservation and biodiversity both in Alberta and worldwide (Travel Alberta).

Golfing, Paradise Canyon, Lethbridge (Travel Alberta).

In 1884, surveyor and explorer Joseph Burr Tyrrell discovered dinosaur remains near the present Dinosaur Provincial Park, near Brooks. Paleontologists from around the world travel to the park to continue his legacy (Travel Alberta).

The Edmonton Folk Music Festival in Gallagher Park began in 1980 and has since grown into one of the leading Folk Festivals in the world, attracting a range of diverse music interests from African drums to the blues (Travel Alberta).

The tornado that devastated Edmonton on July 31, 1987 forever changed the way Albertans look up at the sky during a summer storm. It was one of Alberta's worst natural disasters (*Edmonton Journal*).

Queen Elizabeth II visited Alberta for the centennial celebrations in late May, 2005. In this photograph by *Edmonton Journal* photographer Rick MacWilliam, Her Majesty descends the steps of the legislature grounds with Premier Klein and his wife Colleen (*Edmonton Journal*).

Len Erickson of Edmonton (1993), Cordella Schwengler of Calgary (1994) and Tom Reed of Edmonton (2003). National champion mixed teams from Alberta were skipped by Lee Green of Calgary (1965), Don Anderson of Edmonton (1969), Bill Mitchell of Edmonton (1970), Les Rowland of Calgary (1975), Marvin Wirth of Edmonton (1990), Kurt Balderston of Grande Prairie (1992), Kevin Koe of Calgary (2000) and Shannon Kleibrink of Calgary, the first woman ever to skip a national mixed champion team (2004).

There was one more worthy sporting event during the winter of 1905. In March, there was a ladies' hockey game between Alberta College and the Edmonton High School, with the high school taking the contest, 2–0. "The young maidens are sports," it was reported in the Edmonton *Journal*, "and fight the battle with a determination that many boys would never rise to were they handicapped with skirts." Equally important apparently was the fact that the Alberta College girls wore white sweaters with a red A C on the front, while the high school players wore dark red. Both "looked chic." The Edmonton *Bulletin* reported another game in the city "bristling with fast skating on both sides and exceptionally good goalkeeping." In the period before World War I, there were women's hockey games at the Banff Winter Carnival and Calgary had a women's league that included teams from a community club, six technical and normal schools, and a host of local businesses, including P. Burns Company, Robin Hood Mills, Great West Saddlery, Imperial Oil, and Shelly's Bakery. After the war, women's teams from Alberta played in the Dominion Women's Hockey Championship. One of the best teams ever formed, the Edmonton–Jasper Place Rustlers, coached by C.R. Tufford, won the title in 1933.

During the spring, summer and fall there were stories about the organizations, and contests featured baseball, lacrosse and football (soccer) clubs. The Edmonton lacrosse club did face an initial obstacle: its first couple of practices had to be cancelled because there were no sticks to be found in the town. The Edmonton Cricket Club had matches between married members and bachelors on Good Friday and Arbour Day; and there were competitions with clubs from the small towns surrounding the city. There were also reports about polo and horse-racing, the rifle club, boxing and athletics.

The Elks' baseball team from Foremost, Alberta, sit for a team shot in 1937 (Glenbow Archives/ NA-2604-22).

There were running races that were sometimes challenge affairs that attracted not just spectators but bettors as well. But most were part of track and field days, some sponsored by the local police, some by local businessmen, or men's fraternal societies, or organizations like the YMCA, and others by the schools.

Sports and sportsmen remained local in Alberta during the early twentieth century. Small towns could still challenge the "big boys," if only for a short period of time. Many Americans who took up homesteads continued to play baseball, their national pastime, in their leisure hours. Early black settlers in the Amber Valley created ball teams that dominated northern Alberta. Baseball was such a popular sport in southern Alberta that shopkeepers in Carmangay closed their businesses at noon so that everyone in the town could watch a game against Cleverville in 1910. Sometimes fans would travel 40 to 50 miles to see a game and spectators from Vulcan might outnumber those of the home team in Lethbridge.

In 1907 the Western Canada League was established in Alberta, with teams in Calgary, Medicine Hat, Lethbridge and Edmonton. It was the lowest professional level, Class D, and its popularity ebbed and flowed in this period. By 1909, the WCL had expanded to include teams from Moose Jaw, Regina, Brandon and Winnipeg. But only three years later, the teams from Saskatchewan and Manitoba were playing elsewhere, and the League had only four teams; two were old, Edmonton and Calgary, and two new, Red Deer and Bassano. Lethbridge had folded and the Calgary owners financed a team in Red Deer. The mayor of Bassano (a community of 1400 on the main CPR line) put up his own money to field a team that would raise the visibility and stimulate the growth of the town. The Bassano Boosters were born, prompting Medicine Hat to quit the league, as it was unwilling to complete against such a small-town rival. Bassano built a new stadium for $3000 but attracted only 500 fans to its home opener, and it was suggested that the one dollar tickets throughout the League were simply too expensive. They had been only 25 cents a year earlier. Although ticket prices dropped, Bassano's attendance fell throughout the season as bad weather, the demands of agriculture and poor team play made the games unattractive. At the end of the season, Bassano dismantled its stadium and the wood was used to construct a railway trestle.

That the provincial sporting life was still small time in this period is also revealed through the career of the "Father of Baseball in Alberta," Alf "Old Hoss" Fidler. Alfred Davis Fidler was born in Ontario and came west with his family in the 1880s. The Fidlers were a railway family and Alf worked as a conductor for the Canadian Pacific Railway before joining the Alberta Government as an inspector of local improvements. But he was best known for organizing baseball teams in Canmore and Calgary, and acting as an umpire when his playing days were over. "Old Hoss," who earned his nickname at the end of his career when he hit a game-winning home run and slowly lumbered around the bases, was well-regarded in the Calgary sporting community before his death in 1927. His obituary called him the "Father of Baseball in Alberta" because he had played professionally before he returned home to work on the railway. The label is an exaggeration, although it does indicate how small the baseball world in Alberta was.

Fidler's reputation was won after he played one season at first base for the Fort Worth Panthers, in the D-level Texas League in 1892. He was also a catcher, first baseman and outfielder for teams in Medicine Hat, Canmore and Calgary, although the Canmore team, which he also organized, only played six games in 1895. He played for the Canadian Pacific Railway team in Calgary's amateur league and was asked to hit the ceremonial first pitch when Calgary played its first home game in the Western Canadian League in 1907. Although he was a gifted and respected athlete who was remembered as one of the "squarest shooters in the game," his reputation was enhanced by the fact that there were so few good Canadian ballplayers in Alberta at this time. (Edmonton's "Mr. Baseball" was John Ducey, who was a player, coach, umpire, and promoter. An early baseball stadium in the capital was named Ducey Park after the "Rajah of Renfrew"; Ducey was among the first inductees to the Canadian Baseball Hall of Fame.)

Gone were the days, even by this early date, when games meant gathering spontaneously on newly-cleared river ice for curling matches with whatever equipment was handy; or when organizing a hockey game meant getting together enough Edmonton men to play a New Year's game against a team of Mounties from Fort Saskatchewan as they had in the early 1890s. Teams were now playing in large centres and small towns, and the sports themselves were organized. The Alberta Amateur Hockey Association was established, for example, in 1907. Sports had larger social purposes—sports, especially amateur sports, were seen a social good. In 1905, sporting clubs were organized by the local elites but the games and the clubs were, in theory, accessible to a broader social spectrum; players wishing to share in "the pleasure and recreation" of hockey could join Edmonton's Thistle Club for a dollar membership fee. The only criterion was whether one could play hockey well. By the 1920s, twenty community leagues had been organized in Edmonton, first to represent local districts as they applied for municipal services and schools, and then to organize social, cultural and sporting activities for their members. The city leased grounds to the community leagues and appointed an unpaid "sports supervisor" to organize scheduling. The purpose of sport, as argued from the pulpit, in newspaper stories, and by the athletes themselves, was to demonstrate the proper virtues and challenge the body, mind and morality. Alf Fidler, in Calgary, for example, was a muscular Christian, admired as much for the character he exhibited as the skills he demonstrated.

In truth, though, sports, then as now, were about winning. Competitions are about winners and losers—whether those competitions are between teams or between communities. Therefore, the second purpose of sports was to build the community and boost the local community, as the Bassano baseball team illustrated. Boosterism expressed the need for growth, the idea that for a city to become better it had to become bigger. Boosterism was also optimistic; there was faith in the city and its destiny because boosters envisioned their community becoming the pre-eminent metropolis in the region. Consequently communities in Alberta were in constant competition with their rivals for economic advantage and prestige. The result was close cooperation between the boosters and the local government to ensure success. There was a high degree of co-ordination among the boosters. Not to be a booster—not to be part of the team—showed a lack of community spirit and a lack of business sense. Boosters also sought status. They gained their identity from the city in which they lived and therefore boosters fostered local pride and civic spirit through such activities as support for cultural and sporting endeavours. The progress of Alberta's towns and cities was measured not just in terms of its economic growth but also its success in the sports arena.

The Edmonton *Bulletin* reported that the Edmonton Football Club lost its first game to the Calgary team in October 1891, but bounced back in the return match to win 5–0. It was reported that most of Edmonton's inhabitants "rejoiced" at the news. An Edmonton hockey team challenged for the Stanley Cup for the first time in December 1908. The city's business community, led by J. H. Morris, who owned the department store, financed the team in order to advertise Edmonton across the country. And he was willing to pay good players to join the team. There was only one Edmontonian on the club; the rest were imported "ringers," including Lester Patrick, who had been playing in British Columbia. It was generally recognized, though, that the players were brought in only for the Stanley Cup challenge; as one Montreal newspaper wrote: "If those players ever go back to Edmonton their chances for filthy lucre will disappear." Edmonton lost to the Montreal Wanderers in a two-game total goal series. Edmonton challenged for the Stanley Cup again in 1910, losing two games to the Ottawa Senators. They might have done better had Lester Patrick, the best player their money could buy, not jumped to the Renfrew Millionaires just before the series began.

Swimmer Graham Smith won a record six gold medals at the Commonwealth Games in 1978 (Edmonton Archives/ET-14-173).

Edmonton businessmen and politicians sat on the board of the Edmonton Exhibition Association, whose goal was to promote events and attractions that would boost the city's image. In 1913, the Edmonton Stock Pavilion was built to provide a large venue for indoor events. Its arena floor was described as being "larger than Madison Square Garden in New York" and could seat 6000 spectators "as comfortably as in a modern theatre." The facility and the atmosphere it created became part of the event. The purpose was to make a statement about the city's drive and boldness of vision and like similar edifices today, such as the Olympic Stadium in Montreal or Skydome in Toronto, it was costly to build and maintain.

To the south, Tommy Burns, former heavyweight champion, came to live in Calgary in 1910. The Calgary business community, though, was more interested in the commercial potential of his fame than his boxing ability. Calgary promoters also began the Exhibition and Stampede in 1912, hoping the construction of a "Wild West" identity would boost the city, making it attractive to investment, business and tourism. The Stampede grounds would come to include a racetrack, a convention centre and an arena. (The Park would also become the home of the Calgary Saddledome in the 1980s.) According to Howard Palmer, the Stampede " became such a successful event and tourist attraction that it became a key part of the image of Alberta in the rest of the world." Over time the Stampede attracted rodeo cowboys and cowgirls from all over North America and would stimulate the growth of rodeo in the province. In the aboriginal community of Hobbema, for example, the Panee Agriplex was built for rodeo events. Native cowboys took part in local and international competitions and a Native Rodeo Association was created. Todd Buffalo, an aboriginal from Hobbema, said: "Rodeo has become part of our heritage. Part of our ability as athletes is to be able to compete one on one with the animal that was set here on earth by the Creator . . . . We have a bond . . . . Once you're a cowboy you have to be proud to be a cowboy, but most important, you have to be proud to be an Indian cowboy."

During the 1920s, amateur athletics continued to flourish in Alberta. In the capital, the Civil Service Athletic Association organized recreational activities for government officials, both men and women. On a field adjacent to the Legislature, there were "four tennis courts, a putting green, a practice cricket pitch, a baseball diamond and two basketball courts." Employees for the railways organized bowling, baseball, hockey and soccer in the rapidly growing cities and towns. Organizations like the YMCA sponsored teams in basketball, rugby, volleyball and cricket leagues. Minor hockey became organized to the point that after the First World War, Edmonton had juvenile, junior, intermediate and senior city leagues; junior and senior church leagues, including a Catholic league; a league for the community league teams; and a girls' league. All this was in a city of fewer than 60,000 people in 1921.

Edmonton and Calgary also had professional hockey teams in the newly formed Western Canada Hockey League, whose champion had the right to contest the Stanley Cup. Lloyd Turner, who was known as "Mr. Hockey" in Calgary, helped organize the WCHL. Turner, who built arenas, teams and leagues in the 1920s, would also play an important role in the resurgence of competition for the Allan Cup, which went to Canada's senior hockey champions, in the 1930s. These efforts led to his induction into the Hockey Hall of Fame in 1958. Alberta clubs would again challenge for the trophy. In 1923, the Edmonton Eskimos, led by Gordon Blanchard "Duke"

Keats and "Bullet" Joe Simpson, the League's leading scorer, lost to the Ottawa Senators in the final. The following year the Calgary Tigers, with star player Cully Wilson, were defeated by the Montreal Canadiens, prompting the Calgary *Herald* to seek a "plainsman" who would put the "effete East in its place."

1924 marked the last time that an Alberta team would play for the Stanley Cup until the 1980s. In that year, Boston became the first American team to join the NHL and within a few short years there were teams in Detroit, Chicago, New York, Pittsburgh and Philadelphia. The end was near. In 1926, the NHL purchased the reorganized Western Hockey League and dispersed its players, including Keats and Eddie Shore "the Edmonton Express"; five future Hall of Famers who played in Calgary—Mervyn "Red" Dutton, Barney Stanley, Rusty Crawford, Herb Gardiner and Harry Oliver went to new teams in the NHL. Edmontonians who would make the NHL were the Colville brothers, Mac and Neil; Neil would be elected to the Hockey Hall of Fame. The Edmonton *Journal* noted that: "New York pro hockey outdrew the combined attendance of any four cities in the Western league."

An Alberta team first won the Memorial Cup in this period, as well. The Calgary Canadians, with future NHLer Paul Thompson, were victorious in 1926; it would not be until the 1960s that the Edmonton Oil Kings would again bring back the Memorial Cup, on two occasions: in 1963 and 1966. The only other Alberta teams to win the Memorial Cup were the Medicine Hat Tigers in 1987 and 1988, and the Red Deer Rebels in 2001. An Edmonton team achieved some international success as well when the Superiors won the World Hockey Championship in 1932 in Switzerland.

The rise and fall of professional hockey in Alberta saw a parallel in football. In 1911, the Western Canada Rugby Football Union was formed with teams in the three Prairies provinces. When the WCRFU sought to challenge for the Grey Cup, donated by the Governor General, Earl Grey, and to be awarded to the championship team in the Dominion, it was denied on the grounds that it was too far for Eastern teams to travel to the West. It was not until 1921 that Alberta teams finally played a club from the east, the Hamilton Tigers. For Edmonton, the game was about more than football; it was another opportunity to boost the city. The Edmonton *Bulletin* proudly reported that: "The fact that they are coming shows

The world champion Edmonton Grads, with the support of their coach, J. Percy Page, dominated women's basketball from 1915 to 1940, winning 93% of their games (Provincial Archives of Alberta/BL2636).

that Edmonton is getting to be a centre of importance. Big enough to attract the best in anything." In December 1921, the first Grey Cup game between east and west was played. William F. "Deacon" White, who organized the Edmonton Eskimo football team, borrowed money from the Rotary Club, a fraternal order of local businessmen looking to promote the city, for travel. The Eskimos lost to the Toronto Argonauts by a score of 23–0. The next year, the Edmonton club, now called the Elks (after another fraternal order that sponsored them) challenged Queen's University for the Grey Cup and again lost.

In order to compete with their Eastern rivals, the Western teams adopted the forward pass to open up the game and began to import American players; the Calgary Tigers, for example, brought in a passing quarterback from the United States in 1929. Winnipeg, though, became the first team from the west to win the Grey Cup, in 1935. The next year, the Western Interprovincial Football Union was organized with teams in Winnipeg, Regina and Calgary. Joe Clarke, mayor of Edmonton back in 1920–21 and then again from 1935 to 1937 had been an athlete in his youth and supported sports, especially football. Under his leadership, the stadium that bears his name was constructed and the Eskimos football team was revived by a group of businessmen in 1938. The franchise, and the league as a whole, disbanded at the outbreak of World War II in 1939. Professional football would not return to Alberta until 1946.

The 1920s and 1930s also saw the dominance of perhaps the most successful team the city has ever produced—the Edmonton Grads Basketball team, coached by Percy Page. They were provincial champions 23 out of 24 years, and Canadian champs from their first title attempt in 1922 until they disbanded in 1940. They never lost the Underwood Trophy for competition between teams from Canada and the United States and swept all 27 international exhibition games over four sets of Olympics. All told, the Grads won 502 of the 522 games they played. The team originated with the desire of the 1915 graduates of the McDougall Commercial High School team to continue playing after winning the provincial championship. Page, born in the United States to Canadian parents, came to Edmonton in 1912 to teach commercial classes at the McDougall school. He insisted that his players be of the "highest moral character"—they were "ladies first, and athletes second." The Grads dominated local women's basketball, although, to be honest, there wasn't much competition. In 1922 they won their first Canadian championship and after they repeated the next year, "Deacon" White, one of the prominent sportsmen in the city, decided to promote the team, with the support of the local business community through its service clubs. A Cleveland team, self-proclaimed world champions, were brought to Edmonton and the games were played before a few thousand spectators in the Edmonton Gardens. The Grads won a second world championship in 1923, and played exhibition games against European teams during the Olympics the next year, winning them all. They were expected to boost their hometown and the name "Edmonton" was featured prominently on their luggage and uniforms. By 1926 they were world famous, and back home they were congratulated for representing the honour of the city and "the finest type of Canadian womanhood." Local businessmen sponsored their trip to the 1928 Olympics and civic officials recognized that the Grads "had given the city more advertising and good publicity than all the money that had been spent by the city for this purpose."

James Naismith, the Canadian who invented basketball, wrote the team in 1936: "My admiration and respect go to you because you have remained unspoiled by your successes, and have retained the womanly graces notwithstanding your participation in a strenuous game." Percy Page said that the Grads were "champions because they are the most whole-hearted, sport-loving gals that it would be possible to find; they have won because the spirit of the Prairie is born and bred in them." Noel MacDonald Robertson, a centre for the Grads, who was elected to the Canadian Sports Hall of Fame, perhaps offered a more perceptive insight: ". . . on the floor we were not individuals, we were a team."

Basketball, of course, was not just played by the Grads in Edmonton. In southern Alberta communities like Cardston, Magrath and Raymond, which had been settled largely by Mormons migrating north from the United States, basketball was more popular than hockey. It was argued that "the spirit and the moral tone of the members (of the Church of Latter-Day Saints) can be elevated and maintained on a higher plane if an adequate program for recreational activity can be provided." Therefore, most churches were built with a gymnasium attached and in some towns the local arena did not even put in ice over the winter, as Saturday night was "Basketball Night in Alberta." During the 1920s and 1930s the Raymond Union Jacks won a national men's title and 15 provincial championships.

After World War II, the sports scene in Alberta revived. In hockey, provincial teams made an impact on both the national and international levels. In 1946, the Calgary Stampeders won the Allan Cup, followed by the Edmonton Flyers, led by local boy "Big Bud" MacPherson, two years later. Other Alberta winners would include the Drumheller Miners in 1966; the Stony Plain Eagles in 1999 and the Lloydminster Border Kings in 2001. The Flyers would move on to the Western Hockey League and claim three titles between 1953 and 1962. The Edmonton Mercurys brought home Olympic gold medals from Oslo, Norway in 1952. (The Mercurys were celebrated on the 50th anniversary of their victory, which coincided with the victory of the Canadian men's and women's hockey teams at the Salt Lake City Olympics, to the point that their sweater was commemorated on a beer can.)

Football resumed competition in 1946 with the original three in the West from Winnipeg, Regina and Calgary. The Edmonton franchise was revived in 1949 by local businessmen Henry Singer and Moe Lieberman; although the club would lose in the Grey Cup game in 1952, the Eskimos won three in a row from 1954 to 1956 with stars like Jackie Parker, John Bright and "Normie" Kwong. Perhaps the most important contribution an Alberta team made to the Grey Cup was not on the field but off. In 1948 the Calgary Stampeders travelled to Toronto by train to play the Ottawa Rough Riders. Three hundred fans, dressed in cowboy garb, accompanied the team on the "Grey Cup Special," equipped with a bar and a square-dancing car. They continued the party in downtown Toronto, prompting one resident to say, "I thought that the business of cowboy hats and Indians was a lot of newspaper talk. But these guys really meant it." There was even a parade to Varsity Stadium where the game was played. The Stampeders upset the Rough Riders 12–7, prompting further celebrations by the Calgarians that included one fan riding a horse in the lobby of the Royal York Hotel. It was the beginning of a Grey Cup tradition that former Prime Minister John Diefenbaker said was "the greatest unifying force in Canada."

The Edmonton Eskimos Football Dynasty

Larry Wood and Ken King

Since the era of leather helmets and skinny padding, the Edmonton
Eskimos organization has grown to become the Canadian Football
League's icon, piling up the most Grey Cup appearances and victories.
The Eskimos won 11 of the 19 championship games they played
between 1952 and 1996. Through 2004, their record is 12 wins in 21
kicks at the lord's battered old mug. The Green and Gold sent teams,
and legendary names like Jackie Parker, Johnny Bright, Rollie Miles,
Frankie Morris and Normie Kwong, to four Grey Cup games in the
1950s and won three of them, consecutively, in fact, over a celebrated
Montreal team.

Yet it was the Eskimo teams of the period from 1973 through 1982
that will be remembered as the Canadian Football League's best. The
club qualified for nine Grey Cup games in 10 years and won six of them,
including the last five in succession. The five-in-a-row performance
(1978 through 1982) was Canadian football's crowning achievement. It
truly was a dynasty, fashioned by coach Hugh Campbell, who was hired
in 1977, general manager Norm Kimball, and defensive assistant Don
Matthews.

In Campbell's Grey Cup coaching debut the Eskimos faced the
Alouettes at Olympic Stadium in the infamous "Ice Bowl." A
record crowd (68,205) watched the sorry spectacle which
ended 41–6 in favour of Montreal. When the same teams met
in the 1978 showdown, Joe Scannella had replaced Marv
Levy as the Alouettes' head coach. Edmonton won 20–13. In
1979, the Eskimos beat the Alouettes 17–9. Before the
string of victories was complete, the team from Edmonton
had conquered every franchise in the CFL's eastern conference: 48–10 over Hamilton in 1980; 26–23 over Ottawa in
1981; and 32–16 over Toronto in 1982. The Eskimos moved
into new accommodations at Commonwealth Stadium
(seating capacity 60,217) in 1978. They also signed a quarterback with a Rose Bowl victory on his resume. His name
was Warren Moon, and his talents more than complemented
those of veterans Tom Wilkinson and Bruce Lemmerman in
constructing Edmonton's gridiron dynasty.

Edmonton Eskimo quarterback Jackie
Parker and running back Normie
Kwong holding the 1954 Grey Cup
(Canadian Football Hall of Fame and
Museum).

Over the 1979–81 period, the Eskimos lost only six games. Over the span of their five immaculate seasons, including a perfect 10–0 in play-offs, their record was 70 wins, 15 losses. In the wake of that golden half-decade, the Eskimos appeared in just five more Grey Cup games of the late 1990s, winning twice.

And Calgary? Well, the Stampeders had their moments but they were few and far between by comparison. In short, it took the Stampeders 54 years to win as many Grey Cups as the Eskimos did in five. During the last half of the century, the Stampeders played in eight Grey Cups, winning three (1971, 1992, 1998) titles. The franchise added its fifth title in 2001.

For the past generation, sports, especially professional football and hockey, have been dominated by the so-called "Battle of Alberta." The long-standing rivalry between Edmonton and Calgary revealed in politics and economics is also expressed through sports. The Eskimos and the Stampeders have one of the strongest rivalries in the Canadian Football League, highlighted by the Labour Day Classic in Calgary. The Oilers and the Flames have been bitter rivals since Calgary gained its NHL franchise in 1980.

The Edmonton Oilers, called the Alberta Oilers, were first owned by "Wild Bill" Hunter, a junior hockey promoter who had acquired the franchise when the World Hockey Association was incorporated in 1971. The Oilers were not very successful on the ice and the financial losses were high, in spite of the fact that the team had moved into the new city-owned Northlands Coliseum. Peter Pocklington, a car dealer, real estate promoter and entrepreneur, bought the team in March 1977 and his ownership marked the beginning of a turnaround for the franchise. Pocklington appointed Glen Sather, then a player with the club, as coach and later put him in charge of all hockey operations. The Oilers made the playoffs in the 1977–78 season and finished first in the WHA in 1978–79, after having acquired teenage phenomenon Wayne Gretzky, only to lose the Avco Cup to the Winnipeg Jets.

Alberta's Stanley Cup Decade: 1981–1990

Larry Wood

Alberta's most memorable hockey dynasty was fashioned during an eight-year span from 1983 through 1990. It was an unforgettable period in the province's sports history as the Edmonton Oilers played in six Stanley Cup finals in eight years and won five of them. The Calgary Flames skated in both the Stanley Cup finals that the Oilers missed during that period, winning one of them.

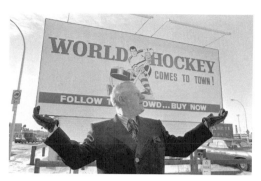

When avid promoter "Wild Bill" Hunter brought a World Hockey Association franchise, the Alberta Oilers, to Edmonton in February 1972, he started a hockey dynasty that would result in five Stanley Cup victories by the renamed Edmonton Oilers (Provincial Archives of Alberta/J784).

During the Edmonton Oilers' last season in the WHA, owner Peter Pocklington acquired the rights to a 17-year-old phenomenon named Wayne Gretzky. Glen Sather was elevated to the position of coach in 1977 and to president and general manager in 1980. During the Oilers' first NHL draft session (1979), the team selected Kevin Lowe, Mark Messier and Glenn Anderson. The next year, the team drafted Paul Coffey, Jari Kurri and Andy Moog. And the next year, goalie Grant Fuhr was added to the lineup.

In 1981 the Oilers won their first playoff series by upsetting the legendary Montreal Canadiens 3–0 in three games, but they lost to the defending champion New York Islanders in six games, 4–2. In 1984 the Oilers defeated their provincial rival Calgary Flames in seven games before going on to hammer Minnesota in four games and then to dethrone the champion Islanders in five. The Oilers lost only three games in four series the next year and wiped out Philadelphia 4–1 in the final. In 1987 they needed seven games to subdue Philly again. But in 1988, perhaps their greatest season ever, they lost only twice in four series and swept the Flames (in Round Two) and Boston (in Round Four) four straight.

The Flames, meanwhile, finally won a wild series against Edmonton in the second round of the 1986 playoffs. The series was tied at three games each and 2–2 at 5:14 of the third period when Oiler defenceman Steve Smith banked the puck off goalie Grant Fuhr and into the Oilers' net, giving Calgary the series. The Flames eased past St. Louis in another seven-game round before losing the final to the Canadiens in five games.

During the summer following Oilers' fourth Cup victory, owner Pocklington stunned Edmonton by trading Gretzky to Los Angeles. The

The Edmonton Oilers dominated Stanley Cup competion in the 1980s. Here, Kevin Lowe hoists the cup during a parade in Edmonton, with Jari Kurri (left) and Mark Messier (middle) looking on (Photograph by Gerry Thomas).

immediate ramifications of the trade showed up during the 1989 playoffs. During the first round, the Oilers took a 3–1 lead over Gretzky and his L.A. Kings. But the Kings fought back with three straight victories to sideline Edmonton.

In Calgary, the Flames had won the President's Trophy as the NHL's top team in 1987–88 and 1988–89. In the latter season, they defeated Montreal in a six-game Cup final, becoming the first team ever to win a Cup-deciding game in the Canadiens' home rink.

The Oilers 1990 Stanley Cup run, although anti-climactic compared to the Gretzky years, was reminiscent of their initial success in that their toughness was put to the test at the outset, overcoming a 3–1 deficit against Winnipeg. Again, the series was a springboard, as the Oilers went on to defeat the Kings, Chicago and Boston. Years later, Gretzky told *Edmonton Sun* columnist Terry Jones: "I'll tell you one thing I'll go to my grave believing. There may have been better teams that have won the Stanley Cup, but those Edmonton teams were the most exciting teams ever to win it."

Finally, in 1979, the NHL expanded into Edmonton. Fans were eager to see NHL hockey and 1981 the Oilers had become one of the most exciting teams in the NHL; Edmonton even knocked the Montreal Canadiens out of the playoffs before losing to the eventual Stanley Cup winners, the New York Islanders. The Oilers won their first Stanley Cup in 1984, the first of five that would mark their heyday as the best team in the NHL. But it was during this run that Pocklington became personally involved in trading "the Great One," Wayne Gretzky, to the Los Angeles Kings in August 1988 for two players, three draft choices and a reported US $15 million in cash. There was a huge uproar in Edmonton, which prompted several local businesses to boycott products from Pocklington-owned companies and even made Pocklington a target on the cartoon page.

The Oilers had a disappointing season on the ice, being knocked out of the playoffs in the first round by the Gretzky-led Kings. By the early 1990s the glory days were over. After winning the Stanley Cup in 1990, the last of the stars from the 1980s were traded away or sold and success in the playoffs came less often. Threats to move the franchise to a more lucrative market, like Hamilton or Minneapolis or Houston, pressured the city to give Pocklington full control of the arena. Moreover Edmonton contributed $15 million for renovations and built a new baseball park to house Pocklington's Triple-A club, the Trappers.

Edmonton's chief rivals are located 300 kilometres to the south, in Calgary. Calgary's first brush with professional hockey came with the transfer of the WHA's Vancouver Blazers to the city in 1975. After losses totalling $6.5 million over two seasons, the Calgary Cowboys folded in August 1977. Calgary gained its NHL franchise in 1980 when Nelson Skalbania, a Vancouver real estate promoter and friend of Peter Pocklington, bought the Atlanta Flames and shifted them to Alberta. He sold his interest in the franchise to a close-knit group of Calgary businessmen, which included Daryl K. and Byron Seaman, the brothers who control Bow Valley Industries, an energy and environmental management group; Harley Hotchkiss, an oil and gas developer with interests in real estate and agriculture; and Norman Kwong, former halfback with the Edmonton Eskimos and later president of the Calgary Stampeders.

When the idea of bringing an NHL team to Calgary was first raised, it was linked to plans to celebrate Alberta's 75th anniversary and to the proposal to acquire the 1988 Winter Olympics. The success of the Flames was also due, in some measure, to the co-operation of various levels of government. The Pengrowth Saddledome, where the team plays, was built for the Winter

Olympics at a cost of $97 million, with the city, provincial and federal governments footing the bill. The Government of Alberta, headed at that time by Peter Lougheed, felt that an NHL franchise would help the Olympic bid.

The Flames' organization has proven successful on and off the ice. Calgary reached the Stanley Cup final in 1986, although the team lost to Montreal, and it has had the best record over the regular season for 1987–88 and 1988–89, culminating in its first Stanley Cup. Although the Flames were profitable from the beginning, as one of the management team said: "the name of the game is to beat Edmonton." It was not until 1986 that the Flames were able to defeat their provincial rivals; they won the seventh game of the Smythe division final when Steve Smith, an Oiler defenceman, banked a pass into his own net to give the Flames a 3–2 victory. The reactions of the Calgary players and owners were the same; Mike Vernon, the Flames' goalie, said: "I'm glad to be part of beating Edmonton. I'm a Calgarian. There's nothing that I wanted more than to beat Edmonton, except to win the Stanley Cup."

There was more to the motivation of the Calgary ownership group than simply beating the Oilers. The owners wanted to give back to their community as well. Some of the profits were used to support amateur sports because Daryl Seaman, a former director of Hockey Canada, was convinced that Canadians "needed to spend more time and money on the development of the game at all levels." Thus, money was directed towards Hockey Canada and its Centre of Excellence in Calgary. The owners of the Flames were also boosters of Calgary. In the words of Norman Kwong: "I'm glad to be able to share in a significant contribution to the betterment of the game and to the city of Calgary."

Recently, however, the Calgary ownership has adopted a more business-like orientation in its approach to the franchise. With net income shrinking because of increasing players' salaries over the past decade, the prospect of relocation to the United States was raised by a former president of the team, Bill Hay: "We don't want to move. But we need to increase our revenue so we can remain competitive. It's a business deal." Even Calgary's run for the 2004 Stanley Cup did little to offset concerns about the future of the small-market franchise. In order to increase profits, the team must win and a successful franchise generates higher operating costs.

It may be the fans, and not the owners, who have the final say about the future of the sport. Professional sports enjoy a powerful grip on our culture, our imaginations and our wallets. But fans have become increasingly disillusioned because of spiralling ticket prices, threats of franchise moves, multi-million dollar contracts, lack of team loyalty on the part of players and management, and finally, the recent lockout. During the 1990s, for example, many Oilers' fans stopped going to the games, prompting Glen Sather, then-president of the club, to say: "Edmonton is a great hockey town. . . . People just don't seem to want to see us play anymore."

Peter Pocklington was forced to sell the franchise to a group of local boosters. Cal Nichols, head of the Edmonton Investors' Group, said they bought the Oilers, not because of the profits which could be generated from an NHL team, but because "I saw in the community at that time the will to go to the wall. The common goal was to keep the team because *this is Edmonton*." The importance of the team could not be measured in dollar values. The Oilers attracted other businesses to Edmonton because corporations "want to live in major-league status towns." In the Edmonton *Journal*, a column stated: "The Oilers have a whole different balance sheet, one that has way more to do with the intensity of interest and support for NHL hockey and the value the Oilers provide to the image of the City of Edmonton. Both the city and the team look to other measures to determine the value of the club." Like their counterparts almost a century earlier, modern boosters argue that results today, whether financial or on the ice, are not as important as the potential for the future.

Loyal fans that love the game have become loyal consumers, paying for the product that professional sports teams deliver. The businessmen who own the franchises and city boosters have long tapped into the fans' sense of identification with their local teams. They have established a strong link between the popular desires to have high-profile sports teams represent the city and a narrower set of business and civic interests. Popular expressions of pride in its teams have coincided with the commercial interests of local businesses; the General Manager of the Edmonton Chamber of Commerce believed the Oilers' Cup win in 1984 was "worth millions." A report by Economic Development Edmonton a decade later would argue that the Oilers generated almost

$63 million in revenue for the city and raised almost $20 million in taxes. Other studies show that professional sports teams actually cost cities money.

The continued booster mentality helps explain the desire to establish Edmonton as a "world-class city" by hosting large international events, including the British Commonwealth Games in 1978; the 1983 World University Games; the World Figure Skating Championships, featuring four-time champion from Caroline, Kurt Browning, who trained in Edmonton; the 2001 IAAF World Championships in Athletics; the Women's Under-19 Soccer Championship and the World Ringette Championship in 2002; and the 2005 World Masters Games. Former Mayor of Edmonton Ivor Dent was instrumental, for example, in bringing the Commonwealth Games to Edmonton; he saw it as "a once in a lifetime opportunity to 'show off' to visitors." The event, therefore, was about the spectacle and monuments necessary to raise the city's international profile. The centrepiece of the Games was Commonwealth Stadium, which was built for $20 million in public funding, and afterwards became the home of the CFL's Edmonton Eskimos.

The World University Games were also intended to put Edmonton on the map. The Universiade had never before been hosted in North America; consequently there had never been much attention paid to the Games outside of Europe. The concept behind the competition was to promote "sporting values and encourage sporting practice in harmony with, and complementary to, the university spirit." Edmonton not only had the facilities for such an event, but it could build on the tradition of excellence in sports, especially in hockey, at the University of Alberta.

When the University of Alberta competed in Western Canadian championships, it did so not just on behalf of the students but on behalf of the larger community as well. The University of Alberta Golden Bears (the nickname appeared in 1929) hockey team began to play in Edmonton in 1908–09; it was not until 1911 that it played another university squad, crushing Saskatchewan in Saskatoon, 16–0. The Western Intercollegiate Athletic Union of the two universities plus Manitoba was formed in 1919; the Golden Bears would go on to win 17 straight titles and be given permanent possession of the league trophy in 1950. A new prize, the W.G. Hardy trophy, was named after a Classics

professor at the University of Alberta and coach of the Golden Bears; Hardy also served as President of the Alberta Amateur Hockey Association, the Canadian Amateur Hockey Association and the International Ice Hockey Federation between 1931 and 1951. The Golden Bears won six CIAU titles before the University Games and have been national champions six times since. The team plays in Clare Drake arena, named after the winningest coach in Canadian university history.

Hockey was not just a male preserve at the University of Alberta. From the 1920s to the 1940s, there was a women's intervarsity hockey team. The club would travel by train to Winnipeg to play the University of Manitoba and on the way home pick up games along the way, including exhibitions with boys' teams. The student newspaper, *The Gateway*, reported that the girls made "the boys step some." The hockey team, or "puckettes" as it was known, disappeared during World War II when the number of women on campus declined dramatically. There was not a resurgence of women's hockey in Edmonton until the 1970s when the Chimos appeared. With no competitive women's teams to challenge them, the club played boys' Bantam and Midget teams. In 1984, the Edmonton Chimos won a national championship. It was not until 1997 that a women's hockey team, known as the Pandas, re-appeared on campus. The team has since won eight Canada West titles and four national championships.

The World University Games led to the construction of new residences around the University of Alberta, the Butterdome, which is the athletic complex on campus, and 11,000 new seats at Commonwealth Stadium. The profile of Edmonton was also raised because Prince Charles and Princess Diana were invited to officially open the Games on July 1, 1983. Even the Calgary *Herald* was impressed by the pomp and ceremony, calling it a "triple-barrelled bash." Almost a decade later, though, sensitive Edmontonians were outraged when a British journalist sent to cover the IAAF Championships said Edmonton was "a sorry stop before dropping off the edge of the world" and lacked atmosphere; he re-named the city "Deadmonton." Citizens were much relieved when the official verdict was that Edmonton was "a capable host."

In 2002, Edmonton hosted yet another international event, the World Ringette Championship. Sam Jacks invented Ringette in Ontario in 1963; it was the first ice sport created exclusively for girls and women and it emphasizes skating, skilled play making and teamwork; for example, players must pass a blue ring, using a straight stick, over the blue lines to a teammate; they cannot carry the ring the length of the ice by themselves. By the mid-1970s ringette was being played in Alberta and today there are almost 5000 players in this province. Over the past decade, Alberta teams have proven to be the best at regional and national championships and the province has produced some of the best players in world, including Calgary's Lisa Brown and Edmonton's Laura Warner, who is the captain of Team Canada. When Canada defeated Finland 3–1 to regain the World Championship in 2002, there were nine Alberta players on the roster and head coach Lorrie Horne and assistant Phyllis Sadoway were also from this province.

The Legacy of the Calgary Olympics
Larry Wood and Ken King

The success of the Calgary Olympics was measured not only in the competition and participation of the community but also in the many and varied legacies of the games. Infrastructure directly resulting from the event included Canada Olympic Park, which remains one of the nation's top athletic training centres and the province's no. 2 tourist attraction;

the 20,000-seat Olympic Saddledome; the Nakiska ski resort; the Olympic Oval (speed skating track) on the University of Calgary campus; and the Olympic Nordic Centre at Canmore.

Since 1998, each of these facilities has been upgraded and continues to benefit hundreds of high-performance athletes training at Calgary '88 venues and receiving funding from the Calgary Olympic Development Association (CODA), which was re-structured to manage the legacy of the Games. The Canada Olympic Park (COP) venue, at the city's western edge, was the original site of ski jumping, freestyle skiing, bobsled and luge (skeleton was added later). It was the vision of the Olympic organizing committee's vice-president of sport, Brian Murphy, who had discovered the site while driving on the Trans Canada highway. The Government of Canada agreed to design and build COP for $15.2 million as part of its $200-million commitment to the Olympic Games.

The boldest recent initiative of the development association is a plan to create Canada's first Centre of Sport Excellence, where athletes can access world-leading advanced human and technical resources and training facilities.

The greatest spectacle seen in Alberta, of course, was the Calgary Winter Olympics, held in 1988. The Chair of the Organizing Committee, Frank King, announced that the Games were the most

The Olympic Games may have ended in 1988 with the extinguishing of the torch, but the event's lasting contribution to Calgary was the Olympic Park. Athletes from all over Canada continue to train at this world-class facility (Travel Alberta).

successful in history because the cost was only $525 million compared to revenues of $557 million. The profit of $32 million was not balanced against the almost half a billion dollars turned over by the provincial and federal governments for facilities which have provided a sports legacy for the city and the country. Calgary now has a speed-skating oval at the University of Calgary; ski jumps, bobsled and luge runs at Olympic Park; and, of course, the Saddledome, which houses Hockey Canada's Centre of Excellence. In addition, there were improvements to the city's infrastructure. Most Albertans, on the other hand, deem the Olympics a success because of the torch relay, the opening ceremonies and the parties that matched those of the Stampede. Even better, skaters Brian Orser and Elizabeth Manley, as well Banff's own Karen Percy, a skier, won medals for Canada. There was also the unforgettable Jamaican bobsled team that made its first-ever appearance and the inept British ski jumper, Eddie "the Eagle" Edwards—two spectacles in themselves who gained international notoriety.

There is little doubt that sports contribute to a group or community identity. Cheering for the home team, nicknamed the Tomahawks and later the Hawks, gave the aboriginal population of Hobbema, for example, a sense of cultural as well as local pride. This feeling of pride is not simply a small town response, either. Shortly after the Eskimos reeled off five straight Grey Cup victories from 1978 to 1982 and the Oilers won five Stanley Cups in seven years, Edmonton began to call itself the "City of Champions." The irony is that these clubs employ few local players and are owned by businessmen seeking to make a profit, but they are presented as important city resources and an integral part of life in the community.

These attachments to professional sports teams make it easy to mobilize support for concessions and subsidies that benefit private interests—Northlands Coliseum, now Rexall Place, was built by the City of Edmonton in the 1970s for the Oilers; the Eskimos' home is Commonwealth Stadium, a facility built with over $20 million of public funds in 1978 and millions more when the facility was renovated in 1983 and again in 2001; the construction of the Saddledome in Calgary, and its upgrading in the 1990s, benefitted the owners of the Calgary Flames.

This pattern of using sports to promote the economic development and raise the profile of local communities and the province has existed throughout Alberta's history. From the very beginning, love of the game was not the only motivation for athletes playing here. The organization of teams and their contests against rivals, whether it was Edmonton–Strathcona, Bassano–Medicine Hat or "the battle of Alberta," the persistent challenges for the Stanley Cup or the Grey Cup by Calgary and Edmonton had as much to do with the desire to boost these communities and ensure their success over other centres as it did with the desire for victory on the field of play. The emphasis on community is also linked to the connection between place and identity. Sports are not just about *where* we are, but about *who* we are as well.

Don Wetherell and Irene Kmet argue, "...sport was a means of implanting the view of the dominant culture in Alberta...[S]ome hoped that sports would integrate rural and urban society, promote social stability, and assist in creating a British society...." While the most popular sports, hockey, curling, golf and baseball, were part of the cultural baggage brought to Alberta by its early settlers, newcomers readily adopted them as a means to fit in. As Ken Dryden and Roy McGregor suggest in *The Game*, sports are also the "stuff of life." Sports provide a connection to past accomplishments and future glories. While sports pits team against team, town against town, and west against east, sports were enjoyed by all groups and so cut across class, ethnic and rural-urban lines. Sports helped create a sense of identity in the province and fostered the evolution of that identity over the last century to produce Albertans.

11 Engaging the World

Satya Das and Ken Chapman

"I can still count in Arabic," Anya declares in Polish-accented English, as a plate of truffle-scented tagliatelle is placed before her in a stylish Italian restaurant in downtown Edmonton. She proceeds to demonstrate, impressively. "Of course I only learned the colloquial language," she says of a life in Sudan nearly a half century ago, where her husband Karol conducted that nation's first census. David nods along as Anya counts. He is just back from Sudan, where he has been imparting his honed-in-Alberta medical skills to students and staff at the University of Khartoum. The conversation flows to Sudan then and now, the appalling hate-war in Darfur, as black-clad servers carry aromatic plates and frosty bottles across echoing tiles.

Everyone at the table was born somewhere else, and made a conscious choice to become Albertans and Canadians, making a new home and a new life. Anya's time in North Africa was a way station in an eventful journey that began in Poland and saw her come of age in the Warsaw Uprising of 1944. She still uses a cane, a legacy of an injury suffered in those tragic 63 days in which thousands of ordinary Poles, men and women, fought and died together in the Armia Krajowa, the Home Army, in a valiant but doomed attempt to oust the Nazis from Poland. On this sunny winter Friday, as David and Karol compare notes on everyday life in Khartoum, both Poland and Sudan seem an eternity away from the small pleasures of life in Edmonton. For all of these high-achieving immigrants who carry the modern face of Alberta to the world, it is possible to savour the civility and peace of their Canadian destination as a fragrant pour of golden Soave swirls into the wineglass.

Anyone walking by this particular table would see no obvious connection between these women and men. They range in age from their 40s to their 80s, come from varying backgrounds, both professional and ethnic, and make a point of lunching together at least once a month. Yet the connection is both cosmopolitan and typically Albertan. At some point in their lives, all of these people have been associated with one of two English universities, and that seemingly tenuous link binds them still. For anyone eavesdropping, the conversations at the table reveal the richness and breadth of the world that has come to live in Alberta, and which in turn shapes Alberta's open and curious engagement with the world. During an animated discussion on the American invasion of Iraq, Karol interjects to observe that he occupied Basra 60 years ago as a soldier at the end of World War II, "and we were taught to be very respectful of the local customs." (Karol also liberated Libya, and has the commemorative medal Colonel Gadhafi gave him six decades after.) That same cavesdropper might hear Marilyn speaking about the human genome, Mavanur describing the glories of Angkor Wat, John expressing the pleasure of inspiring children to love math and science, Robert discussing the finer points of the Hubble space telescope (his book on the subject was a New York Times Notable Book of the Year), or Philip finding a connection between Plato's ideas and the way we order our society today.

Alberta at War

Laura Neilson Bonikowsky

In a period spanning less than 50 years, Canadians were called to war three times, in South Africa in 1899 (until 1902), World War I in 1914 (until 1919) and World War II in 1939 (until 1945). Each time, the country responded with a larger force than the time before. And each time, conditions were more horrifying than the time before, as the technology of war gave armed forces more efficient ways of killing people. Those who answered the call to battle faced one ordeal after another.

Difficulties were no stranger to many of the Albertans who signed up to fight. They were from hardy stock, pioneers who had at the turn of the century, before Alberta became a province, met the challenges of homesteading, facing more hardships than their counterparts in other areas of the country. A harsh, unrelenting environment, coupled with the isolation of living in rural Alberta was the undoing of many who tried to tame the vast, raw prairie. There were few roads and fewer rail lines, leaving the early settlers far removed from towns where they could get even basic supplies, including the seed that would provide their livelihood, but also from schools, churches, doctors and the company of neighbours. Those who succeeded did so through sheer grit, hard work and self-sufficiency.

When Britain went to war in 1914, there was no question that Canada was also at war. Canadians pledged their support for the Empire. Sir Wilfrid Laurier spoke for most Canadians when he proclaimed: "It is our duty to let Great Britain know and to let the friends and foes of Great Britain know that there is in Canada but one mind and one heart and that all Canadians are behind the Mother Country." Prime Minister Robert Borden's offer of Canadian assistance was accepted, and orders were given immediately for the mobilization of an expeditionary force.

In Canadian history, World War I is a turning point. At Vimy Ridge, Canadian troops did what no other Allied force had been able to do: they broke the German lines. It was the first time in the Great War that all four Canadian divisions fought together on the same battlefield, and, despite the horror and the terrible losses, they were glorious. It has been said many times since that the battle of Vimy Ridge gave birth to Canada as a nation. It's quite sad to think of a nation like Canada being forged in the fire of battle, but certainly its warriors stood shoulder to shoulder at the vanguard of a formidable force. Canada went to war a child of the Empire, but came home matured and battle-hardened, with a sense of achievement and self-confidence.

After World War I, Canada continued to assert its independence by participating as a sovereign nation in the formation of the League of Nations. Later, the 1931 Statute of Westminster ratified Canada's de facto autonomous status within the British Empire. But Canada remained freely associated with the United Kingdom as a member of the British Commonwealth of Nations. Laurier's famous prediction that the 20th century would belong to Canada was on everyone's mind. In Canada, and indeed around the world, the 1920s were a time of postwar rebuilding and financial success. Increased industrialization fuelled economic growth and technological advances led economists to predict that growth would continue.

The economic boom was stimulated by an influx of immigrants pouring into the country to populate the West, though thousands of them were deported later when they lost their jobs. The West was built on borrowed money. Access to western products was facilitated by three railways, built in what can only be described as an orgy of track laying. Often the lines ran parallel to each other. When the railways went bust, the taxpayers were left holding the bag.

As Europe recovered from the war, there was less need for Canadian resources, such as the wheat that was integral to the economy of the West. Canada produced far more wheat than Canadians could consume and grain pools unwisely held back, hoping for bigger profits. Grain elevators were filled to bursting with unsold grain as former customers turned elsewhere, leaving Canada with a glut of grain, despite the poor crop of 1929, a byproduct of the drought that had begun to plague farmers. Grain prices fell dramatically. On October 29, 1929, the bottom fell out.

Although the Crash of 1929 did not cause the Great Depression, it did contribute to it, as did the drought. In 1929 there was grain in the elevators but not in the fields. It was only a matter of time before there was nothing to sell, even at reduced prices. The ripple effect on the economy was profound. Failing crops meant less grain in elevators to be transported by rail, fewer mill deliveries, less flour delivered to bakeries—reduced employment throughout all the industries associated with agriculture.

The Depression of the Dirty Thirties hit hard in Alberta, as it did across the prairies. Alberta farmers watched helplessly as their livelihoods blew away in clouds of fertile topsoil. Thistles were all the parched earth could produce. When the wind abated, the sun burning through the haze was all but obliterated by swarms of grasshoppers that ate their way through every bit of vegetation in their path. The drought lasted from 1929 to 1937 and devastated 7.3 million hectares, one-quarter of Canada's arable land, causing 13,900 farms to be abandoned. To cope, farmers tried fallowing, crop rotation and shallow cultivation to preserve soil moisture, unfortunately leaving the soil vulnerable to wind erosion.

All through the long years of the Depression, Albertans toughed it out. Some lost everything. Others barely scraped by. They were just beginning to pull out of it when war was declared in Europe. This time, it was not automatically assumed that Canada would take part. The memories of World War I were still fresh. The waste of a generation, the debt and the strain on the country's unity imposed by conscription deterred Canadians of all political affiliations from entertaining the thought of going to war again. When British Prime Minister Neville Chamberlain adopted a policy of appeasing Adolf Hitler, and postponed war by sacrificing Czechoslovakia in the Munich Crisis of 1938, Canadian Prime Minister Mackenzie King supported him and even thanked him publicly. However, that crisis was probably the turning point for public opinion toward seeing war as the only way to stop the Nazis. Eventually, the country's mood changed to the point where Canada saw itself taking part in another global conflict. King himself did not doubt that in a world war involving Britain, Canada could not stand aside.

In its own small way, this lunch table illustrates the three components that are central to successful and beneficial interaction with the twenty-first century world: creativity, connectivity and capability. Creativity, in a young society still discovering its intellectual muscle, with two dynamic metro cities where people are free to define themselves and pursue their dreams. Connectivity, with links and networks to circles of leadership, influence, change in nearly every part of the world, and within the world represented in Alberta—and the connectivity of information technology to enable ideas to be put into action. Capability, as a wealthy province in a wealthy country where governments are committed—albeit in fits and starts—to ensuring that every citizen has equitable opportunities to fulfill her or his potential. Add other conditions that most places in the world cannot take for granted—the rule of law, reasonably good governance and a fair degree of transparency and accountability by those who hold power—and the template is laid for success in an increasingly interconnected and interdependent world.

When it comes to its place in the world, Alberta is not so much a state of the mind as a potential model for how the world may live and thrive together. Since the first arrival of the first people perhaps as long ago as 30,000 years—the pioneers who established themselves and evolved into Alberta's First Nations—nearly every stream of human experience has found a home in this province. And at last, at the dawn of our second century, we are learning to make the most of this astonishing diversity, including the strength and vigour of our First Nations population. In the process, we are passing well beyond the "tolerance" that many societies preach, to a genuine affection for and engagement with one another. This is true not just in the social and cultural milieus, but in the economic and entrepreneurial vigour that emerges when people of different backgrounds and experiences pool their collective strengths.

Letters Home: Wartime Memories
Jim Stanton

Among Albertans first into battle were members of the Calgary Tank Regiment, part of the 2nd Canadian Division, which first met German troops during the abortive landings at Dieppe on the coast of France on August 19, 1942, the "dress rehearsal" for the invasion nearly two years later. In July 1944, the 2nd Canadian Division fought in France to liberate Caen, and then helped round up the remnants of the German army in Normandy at the Falaise Gap. During the pursuit of the defeated enemy toward the Reich, the Canadians liberated Dieppe and helped clear the Scheldt River estuary to open the port of Antwerp for the Allies.

That dark August day in 1942 saw 907 Canadians killed and another 1,500 wounded or taken prisoner. For the captured, combat was over, but the long war of internment by Hitler's Nazis had just begun. They spent 999 days in a stark, dank prison before being liberated by American forces on May 15, 1945.

A crowd gathers at the corner of Jasper Avenue and 101 Street to read the huge bulletin board set up by the *Edmonton Journal* with the latest news from Europe and Ottawa during the First World War (Glenbow Archives/ NC-6-65918).

Austin Stanton returned to his family after several years as a prisoner of war. Here, he is seated with his wife, Margaret, and eldest son, Jim (Stanton Family).

My own family's part in this was almost unbearably suspenseful and dramatic, but ended happily. My father, Austin Stanton, returned to his wife Margaret after several years as a prisoner. The little family eventually grew to include me, the eldest child, as well as my sisters Judy and Jeannie, and brother John, the founder of The Running Room stores.

Luckily, many family papers, letters and photos were preserved. They tell an incredible story that I'm delighted to be able to offer here, in honour of all the Alberta families that were divided and tormented by war.

On August 17, 1942, Austin wrote a long letter to Margaret. It would be the last one for some time. He had been overseas for 18 months. He knew he was going into battle in two days but could not tell his wife—the censors would have edited it out of the letter. What he did say was:

The regiment is training hard, we continue to practice amphibious landing techniques, I've seen enough sea water to make a prairie boy never want to see any again. It really gums up the tanks.

On a personal note I need to tell you our love has always been beautiful and very sacred to me and I still love you very much. I know this has been a funny letter but while there are many things I can't tell you, there is one thing I want you to know. I LOVE YOU.

Two days later, August 19, 1942, Austin went ashore at Dieppe in the Canadian-led invasion of occupied France. His Churchill tank was the first Allied tank to land in occupied Europe. The invasion was a disaster from the beginning. The tanks were ill-chosen for the mission. The rounded pebbles on the beach stopped many of them in their tracks as soon as they reached shore. In a few hours of terrible carnage, the war was over for these Canadians; hundreds were killed and approximately 1,500 were wounded and taken prisoner.

Margaret received a telegram from the Canadian army on August 23, stating:

Sincerely regret to inform you that Captain Austin Stanton missing in action. Stop. Further information will follow.

This was the first time the Canadian army had been in battle in Europe in World War II and confusion reigned. In a decision that could only be understood by military bureaucrats, all pay and allowances were cut off to military dependents, including Margaret Stanton.

Word was slow to come from the army, but Margaret began to receive letters from survivors who knew Austin, and the news was not good.

A fellow tanker wrote to her:

As we neared the beach, the firing was intense, I looked over at the landing craft beside me and saw Austin pull down his hatch. As he did so, he said over the radio "Tally ho the Huns" and led his tank off the landing craft onto the beaches.

On August 23, a fellow officer wrote:

Austin did a magnificent piece of work at Dieppe. His tank landed and went into action over the beaches. When his first tank was knocked out by a German shell, he got into another and kept on fighting. Austie's was one of the tanks that met the fierce German counter attack. The Canadian infantry who had landed and got into the town said that without the tanks they would not have had a chance.

On August 25, another tank officer wrote to Margaret:

I know it will mean much to you and Jimmy that Austin accomplished important things in those last few hours there. He roomed across from me and the place has not been the same since. His driver, who was wounded but survived and swam back to a navy ship, is inconsolable with the loss.

Then on August 30, the Canadian Army Chaplain wrote to say:

I am writing to offer my since condolences for the loss of your good husband. I knew Austin well and had the greatest admiration for him. He carried on his good work to the end and the part he played in the raid was one of the heroic roles of the regiment. They're singing his praises for his good work and he will always be remembered for it. I'm sure you will be consoled in being resigned to the will of God and in the knowledge that he was ready for any eventuality.

On September 19 the army confirmed that Austin was *"missing, presumed killed and we can assure you of our very deep sympathy at this time of stress and worry."*

Then came astounding and joyous news. On September 29 Margaret received a post card with a Hitler postage stamp on it, marked "Kriegsgefangenpost" (prisoner of war mail) from Germany, from Austin saying he was alive and well. He had no idea that he had been reported missing or killed. Like the rest of those captured, he had been herded off to a German Prisoner of War camp and by late September, he was allowed to write and said:

Dearest Marg, Things are going quite well. Please remember to send me some civilian clothes, chocolates, shoes, a light scarf, a bottle of olive oil, and some hair tonic. Don't worry, I am quite well. Send smokes as well. Love Austie

You can imagine her shock! For the next three years they carried on their lives by writing to each other. Margaret sent Austin food parcels and waited for war's end.

In 1945 Austin, along with the rest of his camp, was liberated by George Patton's U.S. Army and he began his journey home. The Edmonton *Bulletin* described his homecoming:

Captain Austin G. Stanton, Edmonton resident and Dieppe war hero, returns home after four years overseas for a joyous reunion with his wife Margaret and his 6 year old son Jimmy, who will get to know his dad for the first time.

For Margaret and Austin Stanton, the long wartime ordeal was over.

Many of Alberta's innovative enterprises, whether in the energy sector, manufacturing or information technology, understand that the hierarchical world is too constrained. Increasingly, the world is driven by networks—by connections between people, each building on the other's strengths. In this world, those who are nimble and adaptive and able to form connections will flourish far better than monolithic, monocultural societies or business entities that find it difficult to operate beyond their own limited view and experience of "the right way" to do things. In Alberta, we find the connection, create the network, and pursue the opportunity. In this first-name culture, cutting-edge enterprises look at merit rather than pedigree, and people at the top got there by being comfortable, observant, and open to new ideas and experiences. The centenarian province offers such a lively cultural mix that you listen to accents to separate the Albertans from the newcomers. Those who don't speak with the local accent are judged to be from somewhere else, although they are not necessarily foreigners—they might even be from another part of Canada. In Alberta's metropolitan culture, ethnicity and pigmentation are no longer the definition of whether someone "belongs" or is a newcomer who has yet to be integrated.

Emerging from a history as racist and ignorant as any in North America, modern Albertans realise the value of being in and of the world, of recognising that the whole world lives here and in turn provides networks, bridges and opportunities that open myriad possibilities. Much of that is reflected in how the population sees itself. In Edmonton and Calgary, the "two founding nations" theory of English Canada and French Canada is barely visible. In the 2001 national census, fewer than nine per cent of the people in the two metropolitan cities identified themselves as single-origin British or French. By far the greatest self-description was "Canadian." In today's Alberta, racism exists as it does everywhere, yet far fewer people are susceptible to the ignorance and xenophobia at its core. It is easy to find clear instances of racial discrimination. Yet these are the exception rather than the norm, because familiarity in Alberta tends to breed respect rather than contempt. "Racist" feeling arises more often from ignorance than malice. The co-author's late father Fred Chapman was railing away about "Pakis" one day to a close friend. "Your mean Pakis like me, Fred?" asked his brown-skinned interlocutor, clearly endowed with features readily found in Pakistan. "No, not you, Virinder—I mean Pakis!"

Fred's sentiments represent a far gentler version than the racist past that saw the deliberate deracination of First Nations, the internment of Ukrainian-origin Canadians in World War I, the displacement and internment of Japanese-origin Canadians in World War II, the persistent efforts to keep Alberta "white" and "British" even though the province's population was by definition multicultural from the start of the second wave of immigration in the mid-eighteenth century.

To understand how far we have come from that past, come to a Court of Canadian Citizenship in Edmonton. Picture the hall, with 50 or 60 people from the rainbow of humanity waiting to be sworn in. The usher calls the court to order, and in comes the judge: stately in his flowing black robes decorated with the insignia of a member of the Order of Canada, his deep red turban a vivid contrast to his judicial habit. This is Judge Gurcharan Singh Bhatia, the first turbaned Sikh ever to hold the post. Whenever he welcomes new citizens, he speaks with passion about our country, its history, its destiny, and its potential. Above all, he talks about what he calls the Canadian values that define us—the written ones in the Canadian Charter of Rights and Freedoms, and the unwritten ones that evolved in the magnificent cultural mingling that defines our country. To reflect on Gurcharan Bhatia's message is to understand the profound transformation from exclusion to inclusion, from suspicion to understanding.

Moreover, it is ever more apparent that the hierarchy implicit in ghettos and discrimination is also being overcome by the networks of relationships that drive modern Albertans. Indeed, one telling instance is seen in the 2004 Alberta provincial election. The province's then-Economic Development minister, Progressive Conservative Mark Norris, lost his Edmonton seat to Mohammad Elsalhy. The young Liberal pharmacist became the first candidate of Muslim and Arab heritage, since the September 11, 2001 terror attacks in the United States, to defeat an incumbent and win elected office in North America. When Elsalhy looks around the Alberta legislature, he will find he is not alone in reflecting the emerging face of Alberta, including other first-generation immigrants. The fact that relative newcomers to this country, that Canadians who were born elsewhere, take a rightful place in the national and provincial parliaments is a striking example of Albertans' and Canadians' ability not just to coexist, but to affirm that diversity is strength. These are selling points in the global economy. No matter what country Alberta deals with, it can present a familiar face. There will always be an Albertan who was either born in that country, or has roots there. This is a remarkable human resource, as Albertans increasingly take their globally-conscious province into the next century of its destiny.

Yet to succeed in fulfilling its potential, Alberta needs to be recognized as something more than a cliché of empty spaces and the rugged Wild West frontier. When we look beyond the mythic imagery some Albertans project to the world—cowboys, torch-and-twang, and a chilly extension of the American West—we find a richness and variety that is much more appealing to a cosmopolitan world. For modern, cosmopolitan, outward-looking Albertans who are ready to trade and engage with the world, going beyond the self-limiting imagery of the past is an essential beginning. Albertans have proven that they can excel at every endeavour, make themselves at ease with just about any culture. They have connections and networks that span the world. Yet even their own government perpetuates the myth. In the travel and tourism section of its website, the Government of Alberta's Ministry of Economic Development proclaims: "Alberta really is the True West. We aren't just putting on a show for the city slickers: this is the real thing. Our working ranches, farm families, and country towns are the spirit of western lifestyle. If you want a more extended experience, stay at a guest ranch, or saddle up with a trail riding guide and see how great Alberta looks from horseback."

It is deeply ironic that this urban, diverse, forward-looking and progressive province should insist on transmitting a Stetson and jeans image that at best captures the smallest fraction of what and who we are—or even once were. As Alberta enters its second century, it could just as easily project a different image of Alberta to engage the world—one that rings truer than the Calgary Stampede. Imagine Alberta as a Venice of the twenty-first century? Before you decree "madness" consider this. The long-term impact of what Venetian explorer Marco Polo did in Cathay was to bring ideas and technology back to Venice—everything from gunpowder to pasta to ways of organising the social order. Venice's strength was to turn the links Marco Polo opened and the knowledge he acquired to its advantage as a trading city. Marco Polo's voyages gave Venice a creative edge, because they provided the city-state—the modern equivalent is a province like Alberta—with ideas from another culture, and we all know from our own experience that diversity breeds new approaches to knowledge. If we reflect a little more deeply, and look at who we truly are, we will find Alberta is lucky enough to enjoy that particular advantage in its international engagement.

After all, Alberta is a province whose writers are acclaimed the world over, translated into all the world's major tongues. The breathtaking style of its film-makers, its audacious presence in television, video and new media build on an artistic legacy already renowned for dance, classical and popular music, painting and the plastic arts. It is one of the world's most sought-after tourist destinations, entertaining more visitors than its entire population every year.

Alberta is a clever province. The information superhighway runs strong and swift, travelled by an astonishingly learned workforce—most high-school graduates continue with some form of post-secondary training, and its proportion of university or technical college graduates is the highest in the world. This cleverness is not squandered. It ranks with Singapore, Taiwan and Hong Kong as one of the most competitive jurisdictions in the world, measured by the World Competitiveness Index.

Alberta is able to offer its citizens an estimable standard of civilization. It is one of the safest societies in the world, with a stable democracy. Its population is surprisingly cosmopolitan, particularly in its major cities, where it is possible to function in any major world language. It has a strong manufacturing base, and sells much of what it makes abroad. It is committed to open markets and open trade, and to the maintenance of a compassionate state. It has superb transportation and communications links by world standards, superb universities, and a civility to everyday life that is one of its most engaging features. Its citizens have the confidence and skill to flourish in any country in the world, and are equally confident in welcoming the world to their country.

There is ample opportunity to escape a robust metropolitan life for the less hurried pleasures of the countryside. Indeed, it is said of Alberta that the land indelibly shaped its citizens' lives, though more and more urban dwellers seem unaware of this once-intimate bond. There are places to find solitude, and places to find frenetic engagement. It is in many ways a model for the world, the epitome of a civil society built on a culture of peace. It is also a place abundant in resources, one of the world's largest exporters of wheat and sulphur and the second largest exporter of natural gas, and will become one of the world's top petroleum producers once its abundant oil sands reserves are fully exploited. A diverse population and the invaluable resources of the University of Alberta, University of Calgary,

Northern and Southern Alberta Institutes of Technology, Mount Royal and Grant MacEwan Community Colleges give Edmonton and Calgary an important edge in the global economy. So does the world-renowned distance-learning capacity offered by Athabasca University. The excellence, size and capacity of Alberta's universities set us apart. We have a tremendous opportunity to build long-term growth and prosperity by exporting brainpower and all the fruits thereof. As Alberta evolves from a producer of raw materials to processing them for export, our people's knowledge of and contacts within nearly every country make for a future of limitless possibilities. But these emerging competitive advantages wouldn't have been possible without the international character and diverse economy of Alberta and its natural hinterland.

The Other Face of Alberta

Bill Warden

Think Alberta, and one forms a mental image of the oilfield "roughneck," a cowboy wrestling a steer to the ground at the Calgary Stampede, and an urban executive in an office in a glass tower plotting the next corporate takeover. And with good reason. The image is accurate.

But Alberta is much more than oil, beef and high finance. Over four decades of travelling the world, I have encountered so many remarkable Albertans that it would take volumes to tell their stories. From k.d. lang to hockey's Sutter brothers and politicians Joe Clark and Preston Manning, Alberta natives have made their way to the top of the charts. There is something about the lofty Rockies, the endless rolling prairies, the sparkling sun and the healthy crisp fresh air that gives birth to a particular brand of hardy, risk-taking pioneer.

We all have our heroes, those whom perhaps we met or who made a special impression on us. Take Art Jenkyns. Art was your typical outgoing Calgary businessman, a first-class salesman, in the best sense of the word, for his company, his community and his faith. Back in the 60s, Art was seized by a vision on the night he heard a doctor who worked in India tell of his experience with the blind. With true Alberta pioneering spirit, he took the initiative and set out to build an

In 1963, Calgary businessman Art Jenkyns joined with fellow Calgarians to work on behalf of the blind of India. He became the founder of Operation Eyesight, an international development organization specialising in blindness prevention and treatment in South Asia, Africa and Latin America (Operation Eyesight Universal, www.operationeyesight.ca).

In 1979, Calgary's Ken Taylor helped six Americans hostages to escape from Iran by issuing them fake Canadian passports, fooling the Iranians into thinking the hostages were Canadians. (CP Archives).

organization to bring the gift of sight to the poorest of the world's poor. Today, some 40 years later, Operation Eyesight Universal has enhanced the lives of millions, thanks to Art Jenkyns's monumental efforts and those of the hardy band of loyal followers whom he gathered around him in the early years. His was not the slick public relations organization that so many of today's charities have become, but rather a down-to-earth group of Alberta's finest who first and foremost relied on their own resources and sturdy efforts to change the world for the better.

Then there was Ken Taylor, a public servant in Canada's finest tradition. Born in Calgary, Ken, like so many other Albertans, had a yen to use his talents on the national scene. He pushed Canadian products as a Trade Commissioner in places like Guatemala, London and Detroit. His career might simply have blended into the broad mosaic of Canadian diplomacy had it not been for the fortuitous set of circumstances that placed him in Iran as Canada's ambassador when the country was swept up in revolutionary turbulence. Lesser individuals might have stayed safely in the office observing the momentous events, including the taking hostage of almost the entire American embassy staff. But Ambassador Taylor was made of sterner stuff than most and he readily threw himself into the risk-laden task of hiding six American diplomats who had eluded the Iranian net, and organizing their eventual escape. The sensational event, which became known as the Canadian Caper, brought Taylor recognition across the United States, and pride to all Albertans. He was one of theirs. His action was exactly that expected of one imbued with the risk-taking spirit of Alberta.

Alberta has a way of bringing out the best in people. So many "new" Albertans have made monumental contributions in medicine, business and many other fields. Such was Camille Dow-Baker, born in Trinidad, immigrant to Canada. Not satisfied with two decades as an engineer in the energy industry, Camille's vision reached far beyond the oilfields to the deserts of Pakistan, the dusty plains of India and the rampant poverty of Haiti's slums. Her vision? Water: bringing clean, drinkable water to the millions upon millions who do not have it. Obsessed with returning to the poor some of the bounty she herself had come to enjoy, Camille gathered around her a group of the passionate and like-minded, mainly former colleagues and friends in the industry. She and her band of disciples are Alberta pioneers, bringing the discipline of a business model to the business of helping the poor to help themselves.

These are just some of my heroes, a few of Alberta's hardy

contemporary pioneers I have come across in my own wanderings around the globe. Scratch the surface of Alberta. You will find the salt of the earth, the movers and shakers, the pioneers who still have the vision and the spirit that generate optimism and bright hope for our planet's future.

The late Prime Minister Pierre Trudeau was criticized for his immigration policy, but he has enriched the fabric of Alberta immensely and enabled Calgary and Edmonton to become true international cities. He was the first prime minister after the "White Canada" immigration policy finally ended with the Immigration Act changes of 1967, and it was during his time that non-white immigration boomed. At the same time, Peter Lougheed's Multiculturalism Act in Alberta in 1973 was a landmark piece of pioneering legislation because it enshrined cultural diversity in the province's laws, enabling Alberta to reap the benefits of its growing diversity.

In a sense, turning Alberta into a centre of proactive and positive global engagement is a matter of fulfilling the province's destiny. The first immigrants waited a long time, more than 10,000 years, before others came to stake their claim to this geography, bringing notions of "ownership" that were at odds with the First Nations sense of "belonging," but which in recent years are finding a semblance of accommodation after a long and shameful history of colonialism.

The new wave of immigration began with the traders in 1795. The rivers used by the voyageurs were the highways of that time. Now, Albertans use land and sea and air to assist commerce. In the global marketplace, the advantage goes to countries that are innovative. The persistence of huge surpluses in energy-rich Alberta, and the national commitment to a dynamic, knowledge-based Canadian economy, means Alberta is supremely well positioned to adapt to the latest technology, invest in skills development and seek out new economic opportunities all over the world.

To put it into perspective, think of what all the accomplishments of Alberta's first century enable, as this province of 3.3 million people seeks to navigate a fruitful course in a world of six billion humans. Let's start with a big-picture consideration. What do health care, seniors care, research, technology, higher education, taxes, good governance, immigration, economic opportunity, investment, wages, employment, skills, mobility, airports, universities, railways, a clean environment, factories, policing, and the flowers in city parks all have in common? Now think about this answer. In its own way, each is part of the civil and prosperous society many nations aspire to but few achieve: a perspective that is able to combine all of these factors into a productive mix will flourish. That means looking at international relations in a context of the advantages we are able to tap, by virtue of the fact that we are both in and of the world. All of the factors just listed are part of innovation. In effect, they shape a country or an economy's ability to stay one step ahead of the competition, by creating new things or finding new uses for old inventions. How? By making the very best use it can of its people's skills and talents and by encouraging other talented people to come and take advantage of a well-endowed culture of opportunity and innovation.

By combining our many strengths and perspectives in the manner of Venice in the middle centuries of the second millennium, we can make our province a destination of choice for the creative and innovative people of the world.

Our population mix, our resource wealth and our economic foundation enable us to lead in innovation, with an ever-broader economic base that continues to diversify, and by encouraging an immigration surge that attracts talented high-income earners to work in the new and growing areas of the economy. Yet this future as a meeting place of the world demands an ongoing investment in innovation—creating the economic, social, political and educational policies necessary to build a smarter, safer, better-run and more inventive province. We have no choice, because people aren't going to come here merely to enjoy the winters. Smarter, because the wider the range of education, the better the prospects of innovation. Safer, because individual security (in everything from good health care to good neighbourhoods) breeds the confidence and sense of well-being necessary for innovation. Well-run, because a good, democratic, responsible government provides peace and the rule of law necessary to nurture the fruits of innovation. And inventive, because productivity demands we lead rather than follow—and inventiveness comes from a rich, culturally diverse society that unites many streams of human experience, and many different ways of looking at the same opportunities. The key is to get a handle on the many complex facets of a successful interaction with the world. In a "smart province" like Alberta, with our educational institutions, natural resources, attractive lifestyle and low costs, we are well placed to create the ideal mix that will lead to higher productivity, and thereby a better standard of living for everyone. The challenge, though, is to recognise the links, and to build on them. Social planning and economic planning can no longer run as parallel streams. They must be diverted to join one with the other, so that their interconnectedness can become more evident. Building our creative, connected and capable future demands the ability to find the important connection between things that don't seem related at first—the specific skill a rich immigrant mix gives us. It's not easy to break down divisions and find common links, but in doing so, we have already learned substantial rewards await.

If the Albertan identity is composed of so many diversities and so many complexities, urban and regional, aboriginal and recent immigrant, and all the constituent groups of that immigration, then perhaps the best way to contribute to the shaping of a Canadian identity is to identify what all those elements are. In a sense the Canadian metropolitan cities are part of a global urban culture in which the standard brands of globalisation, from McDonald's to Nike to Starbucks, offer a superficial homogeneity that defines the international urban landscape without necessarily touching the day-to-day interaction of people and their society.

Where does this complex mix of metropolitan and regional cultures of astonishing cultural diversity and plurality take us? To the recognition that in our part of Canada, the New West, a new world is taking shape: one in which the best and worst of the borderless world mingle, in cities that from their very foundation were shaped by a meeting of cultures. This is where the new sense of being Albertan and Canadian is taking shape. That collective identity, too long the province of people who insisted on dividing Canada into "two solitudes" of Anglophone and Francophone, is taking shape anew in what might be called the Third Solitude—the immigrant-built Canada that is most keenly present in Alberta. The Third Solitude is a counterpoint to the notion of Canada as a nation of two solitudes, but it is also a robust expression of a cosmopolitan and egalitarian society free of hierarchy and caste-and-class barriers.

Unbound by long tradition, created perforce from a culture of settlement and mingling, the New West represented by Alberta is the clearest expression of the evolution of a societal structure that is able to make the most of human potential, and a political structure that is pluralistic in accommodating citizen ambitions, even as it appears monolithic in its partisan political representation.

And one can only anticipate that as this model of recognizing and valuing the mingling of the world within our borders spreads out from Alberta to more fully establish itself in the rest of Canada, our national character will be shaped by an even broader understanding of who we are and what we can achieve together. Indeed, it can be argued that Alberta constitutes Canada's vanguard in globalization, and all of Canada has aspirations to be the world's vanguard nation. Our abundant resource base and our capacity to add talent and value to human resources through education, skills training and population growth truly enables Alberta to be leaders in the borderless world. We know the mission and challenge of our second century: to aspire to global leadership as a model of how human diversity can beneficially mingle, by combining the opportunities and dreams flowing from the people who call themselves Albertans.

And in the century to come, we will toast this intriguing evolution at our Edmonton lunch table, and many others like it, as the Anyas and the Karols of future generations gather to share the companionship and camaraderie that flow from the grand inclusion that is our Alberta.

Which Future for Alberta?

RUBEN NELSON

12

The great overarching question facing Albertans in 2005 is: "Will Alberta still be a great place to live in 2105?" Again and again in our work regarding societal change, this question has emerged at the root of the concerns Albertans have for their future. I am heartened by the fact that more and more Albertans, especially young people and their grandparents, are asking this question with degrees of openness, anxiety and doubt that would have been unthinkable only a generation ago. The pity is that our official leaders are not yet able to inquire with the same openness and uncertainty. At least in public, most of our business and political leaders only ask the question rhetorically. They don't yet believe that it is worth their serious attention. You won't have to listen long to those who seek to replace Ralph Klein to figure this out.

So publicly, the great overarching question haunts us not. Officially, we lose no sleep over it. Rather, we carry on as if we had not a care, as if a grand future is ours by right. As a cabinet minister said to me, "Ruben, how can we not be positive about Alberta's future? We can't miss." We are confident, even cocky, about our future.

The New Information Age
John Kendall

As we celebrate Alberta's hundredth birthday we also reach the fortieth anniversary of Moore's law, in which Gordon Moore of Intel stated that the number of transistors on an integrated circuit, a chip, would double each year. He later revised it to double every two years. There was also a corollary that stated that the price of an individual chip tends to 95

John Kendall (Photograph by David Brown).

cents! The combined increase in power and decrease in price of integrated circuits has had a profound impact on society, resulting in an age of Information Technology and a knowledge-based economy that no one could have predicted.

To understand the speed and importance of the semiconductor electronic revolution, let us look back to World War II. Vacuum tubes were state-of-the-art with their red-hot filaments emitting electrons. They were hot, power-hungry and subject to a relatively short life span. Yet, the computers of the day that enabled scientists to understand new developments in solid state physics were powered by vacuum tubes. During the war, radar detectors often used point contact detectors. After the war, Shockley *et al* used point contacts to study the electrical properties of various crystal surfaces. In their pursuit of understanding these early simple devices, they developed the point contact transistor, and in trying to understand these, developed the bipolar transistor and later the full range of transistors we now use. At some point it was observed that instead of fabricating individual transistors on germanium or silicon, cutting them out, packaging them and then soldering them back together to form electronic circuits, they could connect the transistors together on the silicon wafer. The integrated circuit was born.

To underline the impact of these developments, let me give you two examples that I witnessed personally. The first has to do with work I did in the 60s on silicon nitride and the resulting EEPROM, a memory device that retains information even when the power is turned off. This means that computers and calculators could now store their operating instructions for when the device is turned back on. The fundamental results from work we did on the materials and devices involved was fed into an old Harwell computer, usually on a Friday, and the results were ready on the Monday; that is, it took 48 hours for the computer to analyze the results. Just after arriving in Calgary, I used a new HP calculator, which employed these EEPROMs and did the same calculation at my desk in two minutes! In the 80s when LSI Logic had an Alberta presence and was helping us set up the Alberta Microelectronic Centre, they designed an ASIC (application specific integrated circuit), or a custom designed IC, for Sony. This was used in the first Sony Play Station and had more computer power for kids to play games with than NASA had in its entirety when they landed a man on the moon. This was progress indeed.

It is clear from this that Alberta has bought into the Information Age and the new knowledge based economy. Where are we headed and is our province prepared and able to be even more involved in future developments?

It is amazing how the semiconductor industry has been able to keep Moore's law valid by almost doubling the number of devices on a square centimeter of silicon every two years. It has required some exceedingly clever technological developments. The term microelectronics is used because the feature size of devices on a chip are measured in microns and even fractions of a micron. A micron is one millionth of a metre. In the end Moore's law will break down because we will run up against the laws of nature, namely quantum mechanics, at extremely small dimensions. However, there are two developments now leading the way for the continued reduction of size of the active elements on a chip.

The first is the whole area of nanotechnology and nanoelectronics in particular. Now we are talking of dimensions in terms of a billionth of a metre and we are moving into the realm of atomic dimensions. Here we start to manipulate atoms, to look at extremely tiny circuits some of which can assemble themselves. Even using simple carbon nanotubes as switches that are left on (a "1") or turned off (burnt out like a fuse for a "0") can result in ICs that hold terabytes of memory in a square centimeter of chip area. Imagine, such a small device could hold all your CD collection and film collection from which you could select your choice for replay and there are no moving parts! This technology now begins to cross over into the molecular and biotechnology areas and molecular electronics and DNA computing appear feasible. This will slowly open up the possibilities of extremely small computers that are compatible with the human body and can be used in the body for diagnosis, treatment and the correction of various conditions. The National Institute of Nanotechnology in Edmonton is already pioneering the way for Alberta and Canada to be at the forefront of future developments, developments that will make "scientific fiction" look tame.

For almost 200 years, our ideas about computing exceeded our ability to implement them. Finally the hardware available to implement computers became available and now exceeds our ability to use them effectively. A dramatic revolution is required to ensure reliable, efficient and effective software. Slowly Software Engineering is maturing, but we have a long way to go. The robust, reliable effective and efficient design of user friendly software is long over due. Again Alberta is fortunate to have the infrastructure and people to be part of these exciting and dramatic changes.

The final barrier to the ongoing application of Moore's law is quantum mechanics. However, what if instead of seeing it as a barrier, we *use* quantum mechanics to develop new computer hardware and software? In Calgary there is a group now pursuing Quantum Information Processing, which approaches quantum mechanics in this way. Incredibly efficient, effective and secure computer technology, information processing and information dissemination is now on the horizon. Consider that if two nuclear particles became entangled, whatever happens to one affects the other no matter how far apart in the Universe they are. Are we going to be able to use this property to ensure secure computing? Can we use other aspects of quantum mechanics for encryption and for information processing. The answer is, "almost certainly!" Now the development of software will become quite different.

Because of wise decisions made for the long term benefit of all Albertans, the establishment of the various heritage funds and research and development organizations, the Province is in an excellent position to become an integral part of the *new* Information Age and not only take part in its development but to immediately apply this new technology in many other areas such as medicine, natural resource discovery and recovery and the protection of our environment, to mention but a few.

In politics, long term decisions do not come easy, but if we ever needed proof of the advantage of such decisions, just look at the strength of Alberta' high tech industry because of decisions made over twenty years ago.

Should we be? Is our casual attitude towards the future warranted? Should we be awakening ourselves from our dogmatic slumbers and turning an eye to our future that tempers hope with caution, even pessimism?

I shall argue that we must take the great overarching question seriously and explore it as if our future hangs on how we come to understand and treat it—for it does.

It is salutary to remind ourselves that in 1945, just after World War II, Saskatchewan was Canada's third largest province—as measured by population, Gross Domestic Product and influence in Canada. At that time, virtually all commentators agreed that it, not Alberta, was the best place to invest in Western Canada. It was then as cocky and as confident as we are today. They, too, knew that their future would be golden. Sixty years later, all this has changed. Now there are more people from Saskatchewan in Alberta who are "net tax payers"—those who pay more to the government in taxes than they receive back from it—than there are net taxpayers left in Saskatchewan. If the Saskatchewan Chamber of Commerce is to be believed, by age 10, children in Saskatchewan know that they must leave in order to have a good life. For the people of Saskatchewan the default answer to the great overarching question has changed from "of course," to "of course not."

Could this happen to us?

Of course it could. History is littered with the dead shells of societies that did not prepare themselves for a changing future. I realize that it is quite normal for those within industrial cultures to think that they are immune to profound changes in their historical context. In this sense, it is not our fault. However, it is also quite wrongheaded. The report from the International Futures Forum—*The Enlightened Corporation*—reflects the growing suspicion that something profound is afoot:

Today's business executives have lived, matured, and succeeded in a world in which the business corporation has been essentially unchallenged—except by other business corporations. Competitiveness has been the theme. What might happen if, in the coming decade, it's less about competitiveness and more about adaptiveness—the ability to adapt to quite fundamental shifts in the social environment in which the corporations are working? What challenges does that present?

However, our record is not comforting, because it shows no such sensitivity. As Albertans we missed all of the signals that the now-mythic National Energy Program was never about energy and always about protecting the founding myth that, in Canada, the French/English compact must always trump all else, including upstart later-comer provinces. Twelve years ago, we decided, without undertaking any kind of inquiry, that BSE in Britain and Japan was no threat to us. We still "know" that we have enough water in southern Alberta to not deflect us from our present course. Worse, we are flying blind. No significant institution in any sector of our province has a developed capacity to practice strategic foresight in an integrated manner at a high professional level. In short, in 2005, we demonstrate the same arrogance and self-inflicted blindness that led to Saskatchewan's decline.

Alberta's Science and Technology: Past, Present and Future
John Kendall

Alberta was born in a relatively unsophisticated technological era, dominated by the railway and relatively straightforward agriculture. As the twentieth century progressed, the province moved into the discovery and recovery of natural resources, which brought improvements in the ways that the discovery and recovery of natural resources were made.

In the 1970s an exponential increase in the pursuit of science and technology began, initially aimed at the improvement of the two major economic platforms on which Alberta's wealth was founded. Premier Peter Lougheed led the development of a long-term vision for the province and the Heritage Fund was established. Also, it was wisely decided to push for a diversification of the province's economy in order to be less vulnerable to the fluctuations in the resource industry.

In the area of science and technology the Alberta Heritage Fund for Medical Research (AHFMR) was established, and then later under the leadership of the present premier, Ralph Klein, the Alberta Heritage Fund for Science and Engineering Research (now named Alberta Ingenuity) was created. All of this was done as the number of people in the province with higher education increased rapidly, particularly in the two major cities of Calgary and Edmonton.

This was followed by many other important initiatives relating to the diversification of the economy and the improvement of our traditional industries. The Alberta Microelectronics Centre was established, as was TR Labs, both in conjunction with industry. The cities of Edmonton and Calgary improved their Economic Development Authorities. Initiatives such as the Calgary Research Development Authority, now Calgary Inc., were undertaken not only to attract high tech industries to the province but to foster our own emerging high tech companies. Other initiatives, such as The Information Circle of Research Excellence, iCORE, followed, with its emphasis on information technology. These are just a few examples.

All of these endeavours attracted increased numbers of highly qualified people to Alberta through Research Chairs and research and development funding. Links were established across Canada and around the world, as Alberta became a driving force in a number of high tech areas. Diversification was and is working so that now substantial revenues result from high tech industries and Alberta's institutions and research labs have sufficient "currency" to be invited to join in many major international initiatives.

The National Institute of Nanotechnology at the University of Alberta (National Research Council of Canada).

As we reach the end of the province's first 100 years, there is a vibrant, exciting and very positive attitude and expectancy with respect to science and technology. It is not unusual to read of major breakthroughs in medicine or in geophysics and engineering taking place in Alberta. Examples include 3-D seismic techniques and accurate drilling techniques that improve the discovery and recovery of oil and gas; the National Institute of Nanotechnology in Edmonton and a substantial quantum information processing endeavour in Calgary that promise major breakthroughs in communications, computing and sophisticated electronics to be used in medicine, the oil and gas sectors and even in the entertainment industry.

What type of society do we hope that future science and technology will help us to achieve? First of all, nothing will be achieved if we do not put the primary emphasis on education. The "raw material" of the knowledge-based economy is a cadre of well-educated, confident, imaginative, entrepreneurial, young people. Our universities have to supply and nurture these individuals.

What could Alberta be like in 20 to 50 years if we take the correct steps with respect to education and infrastructure? Which scientific and technological advances that we anticipate will actually materialize? Here are a few of the important technical developments likely to be achieved.

A readily available, reliable, plentiful, clean and relatively cheap source of energy. This will probably in the end be in the form of nuclear fusion, which has no radioactive waste to dispose of. However, that is still a long way off. Clean efficient transportation in many ways depends on the source of energy discovered above; for example, electric cars for local journeys, which could easily hook up to monorails for longer trips.

Efficient waste disposal. For example: waterless or low water use toilets, which are odourless and sanitary; and the incineration of all waste products, without producing pollution.

Oil and gas once being burned for energy could be used to manufacture plastics that are, in principle, easy and relatively clean to recycle.

Highly secure dissemination and electronic storage of information, as well as inexpensive, easy to read flat displays, which will make electronic books and "newspapers" possible. This will enable a great reduction in the use of paper, in particular for newspapers.

Major breakthroughs in medicine, which will certainly have a major impact on our longevity and the quality of life, with major advances in cures for such diseases as cancer, heart disease and Alzheimer's disease.

We already have the science and technology to make some of these things happen, while others are further off. Future developments will be harnessed for the benefit of humankind and the protection of our environment. Even with new technologies, progress will take time because in many ways our infrastructure will require major changes. That, in itself, is expensive and time-consuming and needs careful planning. We certainly need to learn from the mistakes of the past.

No matter how we look at Alberta's situation, the future is bright and very exciting. Our possibilities are many and varied. The hardest part, of course, is the efficient, effective and creative use of our traditional and new-found resources for the benefit of all Albertans and Canadians in general.

Think about some of the questions we need to ask, but are not asking:

Will the twenty-first century be like the twentieth or profoundly different—at least as different as the twentieth century was from the nineteenth?

We need to come to terms with the fact that our present aspirations, plans, efforts and forms of governance and organization all assume that we face an essentially familiar future. Without realizing it, we are betting our grandchildren's future on whether the classic industrial view of reality, the earth and human persons will be good for another hundred years. In spite of all the talk of change, innovation and transformation that is now required from public platforms, if you scratch the surface you will find that virtually every leader of every institution is committed to a future essentially like the world they now know and take for granted.

On what underlying assumptions about the earth, history and the human race do our late modern industrial society and economy rest? Will they still be valid throughout the twenty-first century? If not, what forces are driving us to new perceptions of reality, our relationship to it and the implications for governance, wealth creation, learning and the creation of healthy persons, families and communities? What new understandings are challenging today's orthodoxy?

To the extent that we are ignorant of the well-springs of our own society and economy and out of touch with the forces that are eroding their legitimacy, we are as lambs before wolves. Yet few today can speak knowledgeably to these questions. Our CEOs, mayors, college and university presidents, bishops and deputy ministers should be thankful that they do not have to write an insightful and grounded ten-page essay on these questions in order to keep their jobs.

What unseen opportunities are hidden in today's societal noise and signals of change?

The franchise that could be ours is this—to become the world's first jurisdiction that openly embraces the challenge of consciously evolving into a post-industrial society and economy, one that truly fits the novel emerging conditions of the twenty-first century. It is ironic that this commitment would also be our best long-range economic development strategy, creating a positive global reputation and knowledge work for Albertans for several generations.

What vision could be ours in our second century?

Alberta—we are acknowledged as the world's leading pioneers of twenty-first century economies, societies and ways of living.

We are admired around the world for our courageous and explicit commitment to exploring and understanding the profoundly changing conditions of the twenty-first century; making it easy for us to access the knowledge, persons, resources and tools that we require to adapt to change; and developing the new ways of living that truly fit with and capitalize on the changing conditions—ways that allow us to sustain success regardless of the conditions we face, ways that ultimately lead to the creation of a civilization that works for all.

We are the partners of choice for companies and organizations that share our commitment to creating a world that is truly wise, courageous, secure, prosperous, innovative, inclusive, integrated, sustainable and humane.

We are, in short, the most future-savvy and influential small jurisdiction in the world. The best of the world's best willingly invest and come to live here in order to participate in the work of pioneering a great twenty-first century culture—a culture so exciting that our children and grandchildren have reasons to stay!

A Vision for the Next 100 years
Peter Lougheed

The Honourable Peter Lougheed and his wife, Jeanne (Photograph by Sara Fuller. Banff Centre Archives).

My vision of Alberta in the next century is a province that emerges as the dominant economic and political force in Canada. Why? Because the good fortune of having natural resources has led Alberta to become very skilled in technical matters. The world is changing and centres of technological enterprise will be at the forefront of every corner of the world.

Politically, Alberta will develop a more international perspective than other parts of Canada because we are such a trading area. That perspective will shift not just to the United States but to other parts of the world. For example, in agriculture, Alberta will upgrade more products at home and sell the processed products around the world.

These changes will create a different tension in Confederation because Albertans will be more in tune with world events than some other parts of the country. At home, the province will become more disparate and less cohesive in political and social terms. This will be influenced in varying degree by an influx of new Canadians from Asia and other parts of the world. The political tensions with Ottawa will continue simply because the constitution of Canada gives such an abundance of jurisdiction to the provinces as compared to individual states in America.

This naturally will create a constant tension that will vary by degrees in the decades ahead.

One factor often ignored is climate. Alberta has an unusually variable climate, including frequent severe winters. This causes the citizens to become more supportive of one another and our history has led us to become leaders in helping others as volunteers. Also, the cities will become more dominant politically, although there will no longer merely be two major centres, but as many as eight.

As well as Edmonton and Calgary, the large centres could be Fort McMurray, Grande Prairie, Red Deer, Lethbridge and some surprising newcomers over the century. For example, we have set up distance education in the town of Athabasca; it will become more important in the years ahead. Athabasca could be a surprise as a significant centre. There will be big changes in education because Albertans will demand from the provincial government that we lead Canada in supporting education. We should regain our position of having the largest percentage of students going to post secondary education in the country.

The largest political change in decades ahead could be an adjustment from dominance of one party; that will change as the province becomes more diversified and more newcomers get involved. Overall, I see an incredible future for our province. Albertans have worked hard to excel for 100 years. After many economic and political trials, their efforts are producing spectacular results.

Hopes for the Future
Jeanne Lougheed

I would like to see in the future of Alberta increased awareness, enthusiasm, acceptance and support of the cultural life of the province so that it becomes a key part of the everyday life of Albertans. The literature, art, crafts, music, and drama through which we tell the stories of our lives and our history define us as a society. They enrich our lives, whether we participate in their creation or are partakers of their beauty. Without this cultural life, our meaning and our existence are diminished.

My other profound wish for the future is the eradication of child poverty. There is no reason, and no excuse, in a society as blessed as ours, for any child to suffer from poverty. We owe our future to the nourishment, physically, mentally and spiritually, of our children.

The Future
Mercedes Zayas Sharpe

Mercedes Zayas Sharpe is 13 years old and in the Grade 8 French Immersion program at McKernan School in Edmonton.

What will make Alberta a great place to live in its next century? What is your vision for Alberta in its next 100 years?

I think that in the next century, Alberta would be great if it were able to develop its cities more. If the cities had more of a cosmopolitan

Mercedes Zayas Sharpe (Photograph by Natalie Sharpe).

atmosphere, then a lot of people will be drawn to them. If we could keep the beautiful old buildings, replace the rundown buildings, and fix up our parks, Alberta would be even more beautiful than it is now. I think that it would also be great if there were no discrimination or poverty. It would also like it if there were no smoking allowed in Alberta. That way, people would be healthier and there would be less pollution.

In the next hundred years, I hope that Alberta's post-secondary fees will be much less than they are at present. I am in grade 8, and I would really like to go to University, but I'm afraid that I won't be able to afford the large costs of getting an education. Right now, it's very hard for students to go to university because of the outrageous costs, so I believe that over the next hundred years, the government should make university more affordable.

Future Vision
Paul Edwards

Throughout the next 100 years, I envision that Alberta will continue to be the dominant province in Canada, in all repects. Alberta will continue to be economically strong and as time passes our economy will continue to grow. This growth will not be a result of the resources of our past but rather Alberta's progression into other industries. It will be this diversity that will keep our economy strong. The community of Alberta will continue to grow and we will live in a society where Albertans are proud to live in Alberta, and where other people will want to live in Alberta. Alberta will become a province where the people are passionate in their lives and are driven to become successful. It is this drive that will continue to keep Alberta strong.

As Alberta continues to grow, I believe that the health care and education systems in our province will be leaders for those throughout the world. This will happen, mainly, because of increases in funding, which will be possible through Alberta's strong economy. Alberta will continue to be led by a strong political party, which makes decisions in the best interest of the province, and not themselves. As well, Alberta will continue to expand its influence on national politics, as the province continues to grow. As many new people come to Alberta, from other parts of Canada or around the world, the cultural diversity of Alberta will continue to grow. This diversity will continue to help enrich the culture of Alberta, helping Alberta to become a more dynamic province.

As time goes on, Alberta will become a leader not only in Canada, but also throughout the world. Alberta will be seen as a role model for other countries and provinces in economic, political and social decisions. Alberta will be a province that will grow, in all aspects, and a province that will continue to go beyond its limits.

Alberta will be a great place to live throughout the next century, as this vision for Alberta comes true. Alberta has had a very strong past and as we learn from our past, we will become stronger in the future. There are many reasons Alberta will be a great place to live. In my view, Alberta offers a great education system, which will continue to promote innovation. As well Alberta offers numerous opportunities that help youth, like myself, become more involved in our community. These include opportunities such as volunteering, helping on political campaigns, or getting involved through events such as Model Parliaments and speech and debate. These opportunities also exist throughout the working field because of the numerous jobs Alberta currently has to offer. The last main reason why Alberta will be a great place to live, is because Alberta has "Nowhere to go but up." The provincial debt has been repaid, the economy continues to be strong, and our diverse population continues to grow. It is because of aspects such as these that Alberta currently is and will continue to be a great place to live throughout the next century.

Paul Edwards

Voices from Yellowhead Tribal College
Compiled by Natalie Sharpe

Since the mid-1980s Yellowhead Tribal College, located in the City of Edmonton, has been providing a variety of upgrading and post-secondary programs to First Nations students. Most of the students quoted here are from the First Nations, comprising the Yellowhead Tribal Council, namely, Alexander, Alexis, Enoch, O'Chiese, and Sunchild. They are a culturally diverse group of Stoney (Nakoda, Sioux) and Cree.

These are the voices of the Yellowhead Tribal College students in a Native Peoples course. They talk of an Alberta that embraces cultural diversity, equity and respect for First Nations people. They envision a healthy environment, a healthy and well-educated nation. They wish for resolution to long-standing land and residential school claims. Their desire is to see the First Nations have a vested interest in the future in the political, social, and economic development of Alberta.

What will make Alberta a great place to live in its next century?

Concentrate more on the environment.
Better health care for everyone.
Lower taxes.
Educate everyone to better understand others' cultures and customs.
Resolve land claims and residential school claims.
Teach every child and adult to not be prejudiced.

Joanne Sharphead

Should have more employment available in policing and security for native people so that it could be a more comfortable setting for aboriginals who visit places such as West Edmonton Mall.

Tina Cardinal

Aboriginal self-government.
No two-tiered health care.
A Liberal or New Democrat government instead of Conservative.
Greater restrictions for ecological endeavours.

Connie Nanimahoo

I believe that industry needs to be lessened; the environment should be the most important resource. So protect it, not exploit it. Farming needs to be lessened as well, to manageable plots of land. Students should be able to attend any school they like. I believe attending the district school leads to rich-richer, poor-poorer. I think policing needs a fresh new vantage point. The children of 2005 have too much disrespect for the law.

Tara Kootenay

Alberta currently has exceptional and rich resources. I believe that if resources are maintained with respect to water and minerals, our land can remain rich.

Emily Potts

For First Nations groups to have total power of own resources and government but at the same time, set up systems of government that are foolproof. Land Claims be settled.

That we live in this province having mutual respect for everyone.
To try and fix the hole in the ozone layer, to stop depleting the earth of all its minerals and resources. When there is no oil base, that is when our rivers and lakes start to dry up.

Desiree Gladue

General population of Alberta to be educated on Treaty Rights and the history of all First Nations.
Designate seats for First Nations to participate in government legislature.
Economic activities to be accessed by all, not only those who have capital.

Kathleen Alexis

Protect mother earth.
Reduce pollutants to help future generations.
Reduce poverty.
Equality for jobs and job creation.
Stop racism—achieve healing concepts for natives that were affected by colonization.
Better educate children, adults, society on native genocide, the truths, changed perceived notions based on stereotypical views.

Lesley Anderson

What is your vision for Alberta in its next 100 years?

Peace and Harmony!

Joanne Sharphead

There will be more aboriginal people in job areas that are presently non-existent.

Tina Cardinal

A University with aboriginal content in mainstream "canons."

Connie Nanimahoo

I would like to see true cultural diversity, not this pretended one we say Canada is now. All are one species (human being); let's forget the socially constructed identification.

Tara Kootenay

Alberta's native communities are becoming more developed with economics and politics with the mainstream society. Native communities are challenging the mainstream by keeping up with modern technology and its benefits toward production. Alberta in retrospect has a great agricultural system. Issues on our native communities can either get better or worse. My focus is mostly on my native communities because I'm First Nations myself.

Emily Potts

I hope that Alberta comes up with a collective effort to clean the environment and save the planet.

Desiree Gladue

A concerted effort to ensure the environment and resources are preserved.
To ensure health, education are available to all.
To live in a society where equality is a must and racism will not be tolerated.
For our society to not glorify violence and so that a paradigm shift.
occurs in our views regarding this topic.

Kathleen Alexis

An egalitarian society.
Good health, share of riches, communities of support.
No crime, no drugs, no alcohol.
Improvise our ancestors' teachings.
For all races.

Lesley Anderson

Laura E. Simon is a retired teacher who taught starting in the 1950s on reserves and Métis colonies as far west as the Queen Charlotte Islands and as far north as the Northwest Territories. She advocates political government change; she also calls for social and educational equity to eradicate racial inequalities, homelessness, and discrimination.

What will make Alberta a great place to live in its next century?

We need a political party that does not act as a dictatorship. We also need strong opposition parties that will and can hold the government to account.

There should be no university fees.
Social programs should eliminate homelessness!!

Laura E. Simon

What is your vision for Alberta in its next 100 years?

There will be no homelessness nor hunger.
Racial discrimination will not exist.
Status Indians and members of Métis colonies will have greater job opportunities and there should not be a need for out-of-province employees.

Laura E. Simon

What of Alberta?
Rielle Braid

I've lived in Alberta my whole life, and until now, I always thought it would be the easiest place to leave. Now that I'm faced with the reality of *actually* being someplace else at school, suddenly everything about Alberta has a new degree of meaning for me. I'll miss things; I'll miss the same people who run by me on their morning jog when I walk to school. I'll miss my mom insisting we drive by the mountain view when we're riding home from grocery shopping, and I'll miss that view (even if I pretended that mountain view was lame). I'll miss the look of the Calgary Tower when I come home at the end of August after summer vacation. I'll miss Alberta Theatre Projects and their beautiful shows.

At the same time, I know there's so much about Alberta I wish could change. The familiarity of things I love shares a place with things that make me angry. I remember working at the video store one night, and a young couple strutted into the store, cackling about a homeless man sitting outside in the cold. That was sick. It's one thing to complain about a person asking you for change, and it's another to make fun of him when you can go inside, to warmth, and spend your money on trivial little wants.

I hate how unemployment and homelessness are serious problems in Alberta. What's worse is that so many Albertans don't take an interest. We walk by and insist we have no spare change. Even if it's true, even if

Rielle Braid (Photograph by Don Braid).

you don't have a dime in your pocket, what's the harm in stopping and saying hello? There isn't any. Once we as Albertans take a rising interest in this problem, then maybe the politicians will, too.

It's so confusing loving one part of Calgary and then being so disappointed in another. I hope that we can perhaps find a way to believe in people, regardless of sexuality, gender and race. I've seen a city that can stay up late, all night, and party down on 17th Avenue to support a Hockey Team. Could we not also show that support for the Calgary Philharmonic Orchestra? Or the Women's Shelter? I know we as Albertans have it in us to show love and enthusiasm for *something*. That's a start, right? And if we can start here, then it can spread. All it takes is that small spark and suddenly, there's a chance for change.

Alberta has been a wonderful experience for me, and a hard one at the same time. I've come to be disappointed in a lack of interest in the arts from the majority, yet have seen incredible support from the people who really love the arts. I remember seeing the same people in the audience every day last summer, when I performed in Fiddler On the Roof with Summerstock, a youth-theatre company in Calgary. It's an incredible feeling, recognizing people who come to believe in you.

I understand these problems are everywhere. Is that any excuse not do something about it? What are we, weak? No. We have books and phones and even paper and pens to make SIGNS that can protest for what we believe. My mother makes a difference by trying to help people, any people, no matter who they are. My father makes a difference by writing what he believes, no matter what people may think of him after he's written it. My brother makes a difference by going out and protesting, by teaching, by understanding everyone and their differences, by putting out a newsletter.

Considering what I have seen Albertans accomplish during my entire life, I know what we can do. I know we are strong enough to create a truly happy, equal province. I know we can be an influence. I hope you believe a little more now, too, because if a little smart alec like *me* can, then you can give it a try, can't you? Get out of your chair, and get *out* there.

But finish this book first.

Albertans: Our Citizenship and Identity

13

Aritha van Herk

The concept of citizenship is one that Canadians, especially we wealthy, happy-go-lucky Albertans, often take for granted. Unless our parents or grandparents were born elsewhere (and chances are that they were, since only the First Nations people are original Albertans), we don't examine and celebrate our citizenship and its legacy of tolerance and freedom enough.

My own birthright has never been a privilege that I take for granted. A child of immigrant parents who came to this country from the Netherlands, I am reminded over and over again of the multiple advantages of being Canadian. My parents were citizens of the Netherlands in the spring of 1945 when they were liberated from five years of Nazi oppression and occupation by Canadian soldiers. Those

A group of Dutch immigrants new to Alberta pose outside the building for Canadian National Railways, Departments of Colonization and Agriculture, Canadian National Land Settlement Association, Edmonton, Alberta (Glenbow Archives/ND-3-4564).

Canadians not only liberated the Netherlands, but through sheer presence exerted a huge moral and social impact on the people of the Netherlands, who had suffered long and hard, especially during the last year of the war, the Hunger Winter of 1945. These liberating soldiers were proud of their country, and they represented Canada well—they were polite, generous, proud, and although they were homesick, proceeded with the job that they had been sent to do, to help clean up and feed a horrifically battered and starving people. It was because of those soldiers that my parents decided to immigrate to Canada and become Canadian—citizens by choice.

In light of that life-lesson, I have always cherished my citizenship, so much so that I feel every jolt and creak in the fragile Canadian craft, especially in the last ten years, in my bones. This Canada, however fraught and subject to stress, is an idea worth fighting for, worth keeping, despite the assiduous efforts of politicians or interest groups who seem intent on destroying its integrity. The identity it bestows on us, multicultural children of the world, is almost magical, a gift far beyond geography, a gift of the ideal home and citizenship.

The western world's concept of citizenship was profoundly changed by the French Revolution and its after-effects. On October 10, 1792, the French Convention decreed that the employment of *whit* and *monsieur* (marks of respect and thus class markers) was a form of address now to be replaced by *citoyen* and *citoyenne*, more egalitarian titles. Did this change the attitudes of the French caught up in the frenzy of the revolution with its many twists and turns? Perhaps they were more concerned about food and shelter than the forms of address that proclaimed a distinct equality. Certainly that small development was only a signal of the chain of events that dominoed from the 1774 American War of Independence through famine and grain riots in northern France to the 1776 American Declaration of Independence, with France supporting the Americans from 1778 until the 1783 Peace of Versailles. Most of us have learned about the highlights, if not the low points, of the French Revolution. The Fall of the Bastille on July 14, 1789, the peasant revolt against feudalism, and the Declaration of the Rights of Man and of the Citizen. Citizenship was an idea that was born out of oppression and conflict, out of bloodshed and battle, and changed as it came to represent much more than a designation for one who simply lived in a particular place, an occupant or inhabitant. It means now one who enjoys the rights and privileges of a state or country, one who can vote and who is entitled to full protection under that state's laws. More than that, it implies responsibility, a responsibility to contribute to the place called home.

The home we know as Alberta did not always have so clear-cut an identity as it does now, although the people who lived here were always restless, passionately curious, eager to discover not only the beauty of this landscape but its mysteries, what lies beneath the surface of this blessed province. At the end of the nineteenth century, the Northwest Territories, which was the designation the west wore after Rupert's Land had been purchased from the Hudson's Bay Company by Canada, was a place that felt it deserved greater independence than it had been accorded by Ottawa. In 1885, elected members to the Northwest Territorial Council drew up a list of requests for the citizens of the west whom, they felt, were getting the short end of the stick in terms of services and attention. That list is both dated and resonant, a litany of dissatisfaction. They desired:

Canadian troops celebrate the liberation of Holland with Dutch citizens, 1945. Many Dutch decided to immigrate to Canada after their experience with Canadian soldiers in WWII (Department of Nation Defence/Library and Archives Canada/PA-136176).

1. The privilege of incorporating companies with strictly territorial aims.
2. The right to survey and supervise all old and established trails.
3. Claims by settlers and squatters who settled before the survey to be given titles.
4. The government to take a strong stand against the high freight rates being charged by the C.P.R.
5. Settlers to be granted permission to cut trees for lumber and fuel on Crown land.
6. The right of *habeas corpus* for the Territories.
7. The North Saskatchewan River to be improved for navigation.
8. A territorial court of appeal.
9. The construction of a wagon road to Peace River.
10. Territorial representation in the House of Commons and the Senate.
11. Provision of pre-emption or second homestead privileges.
12. Provision of new railways running north and south.
13. Revenue from customs duties on machinery to be shared with the Territories.

Albertans: Our Citizenship and Identity

14. Money voted by parliament for western spending to be under the authority of the council [the Territorial council, based in Regina].
15. The early completion of a railway to Hudson Bay.
16. Appointment without delay of a commission to settle half-breed claims.
17. The early settlement of rebellion losses.
18. Livestock production and tree-planting to be considered in fulfillment of homestead duties.
19. Residents of the Territories to be appointed to fill local positions of trust.
20. Food supplies for police and Indians to be purchased as far as possible in the West.
21. More Canadian beef to be bought instead of United States pork in filling orders for Indian needs.

Oddly, some of these items comprise matters that are still disputatious here in Alberta. We have better than a wagon road to Peace River, but we continue to argue about representation to the House of Commons and the Senate. So much time, so little change.

But the struggle for representative government in the territories was a long and hard one, a step by step progress that reflects our home today. Frederick Haultain, the father of provincial autonomy for Alberta and Saskatchewan, was its most dedicated advocate, and he fought long and hard for the citizens' rights that had first been so carefully listed in 1885. Elected to the Territorial Council (representing southern Alberta, the area around Lethbridge, Pincher Creek and Fort Macleod) in 1887, he consistently called for responsible government for this part of the world. Political progress then was slow, and the Dominion was not inclined to pay much attention to the protests and demands that came from the west. We were the squeaky wheel within Canada and Frederick Haultain was the hub arguing for the rights of westerners. "Self-government" was the watchword, and while we might now take for granted provincial powers within the larger Confederation of Canada, at that time they garnered considerable friction and fury.

Power and privilege for the west. Such a long story. Back and forth they argued through the final years of the nineteenth century, Haultain and his supporters battling Ottawa, until finally, in 1897, the Territorial Legislative Assembly was given some power over its own governance. But that small victory was quickly followed by the boundary debate, the hunger for the established provinces to acquire more territory, and the argument over which of the cities would enjoy the role of capital. The pinnacle of the debate probably occurred on December 18, 1901, at Indian Head, Assiniboia. It took place between Rodmond Roblin, then Premier of Manitoba, and Frederick Haultain, then Premier of the Northwest Territories. On the one side Roblin defended the Manitoba legislature's desire to transfer a portion of the Northwest Territories to their provincial jurisdiction. On the other side Haultain argued against annexation to Manitoba and for Territorial autonomy. Five hundred signatures had petitioned Roblin to come to Indian Head for the debate, and more than double that were actually present, a five-hour marathon meeting in a log hall lit by smoky tapers and burning pitch, the audience sweating and yet mesmerized by the long but eloquent debate. Haultain, although the more subtle and less entertaining of the two, seems to have won the day, for Manitoba's plan to annex parts of the territory was not sustained.

A man of the centre, Frederick Haultain strongly deplored the influence of partyism in politics and always insisted that it had no place in the West (Glenbow Archives/NA-510-2).

Still, it would take another turbulent and dogged three years of work on Haultain's part before Ottawa would consent to the granting of provincial status, and even then, that would be accomplished on Ottawa's terms, not Haultain's, and only because Wilfrid Laurier used provincehood as a re-election promise. Haultain had dreamed of one big province called Buffalo, but there would be two, Alberta and Saskatchewan. Other issues relevant to provincial autonomy were contingent as well: crown lands, school jurisdiction, and the contentious railway tax exemption. But to add insult to hard work, Haultain was not offered one of the premierships; he was not even invited to the inaugural ceremonies. He had served as leader and exemplary citizen but he was bypassed at the very moment that gave other westerners the pride of provincial autonomy.

His example recites the true calling of citizenship. We enjoy the rights and privileges of being Albertan, and we cannot imagine ourselves isolated from the concept and its practice, its rights and responsibilities, throughout history and the larger world. But then we face the question of identity, and a whole other complex of questions arises. If our identity is tied to nation, how does that balance with our allegiance to our province first and our locality second?

After all, we live locally. It is in the local world where we sleep and eat, where we drive and take transit and go to school, where we visit historical sites and remark our childhood memories, where our identities (in terms of daily life) are forged. The result is that the national and the local exert differing pressures on identity. The larger citizen declares herself Canadian, but the quotidian, feet-on-the-ground and living the schedule of breakfast to bedtime citizen identifies herself as western Canadian, Albertan, Calgarian.

This distinction would not be an issue were the two not frequently in conflict. The centre's view of the west, as a peripheral region not to be taken seriously, has caused severe disaffection, some of it exaggerated and some just. Haultain's deliberate snub might stand as a metaphor for the distinctions in desire between the local and the national. We are, here in Alberta, always uneasy about the lineaments of provincehood and how those lines are drawn. The result is that our western identity is shaded by a mistrust of our national identity; subject to so much pressure, we westerners react by becoming relatively defensive about our local identity in contrast to our national identity—elevating its importance to our actions.

So do Albertans consider themselves western Canadians before they consider themselves Canadians? Absolutely and yet not. But what then, does that mean? Most Albertans are utterly committed to the "idea" of Canada, but long for a Canada that is committed to the "idea" of their region—Alberta as a political entity to be taken seriously. The centre seldom whole-heartedly embraces the west, but seeks always to distance, disallow and debunk the energy and the ideas that come out of the regions. We've all heard the jokes about Alberta culture as oxymoron, about Albertans voting like lemmings, about Alberta's greed. Those judgmental readings do not make for a coherent bridge between the local and the national. The result is, for anyone, a disparity between allegiance to a nation and to the place where one lives, not necessarily the same place, and not necessarily in search of a similar outcome.

And there are further stresses on our loyalties; the demands and pressures that accompany both citizenship and identity are not entirely internal. We Canadians will likely, within 20 years, be sharing a common currency with the United States of America, and it is only a short step from that usage toward variations on amalgamation with the United States. What turn then will our identities and our sense of citizenship take?

Canada is a global country, made up of many different peoples from many parts of the world. If we are intelligent, that global character can be to our benefit—we have contacts and connections all over the globe, and we ought to be using those linkages to our benefit. Instead, we seem only vaguely aware of global movements, facts that are bound to affect us in future. For example, China is home to 1.3 billion people. In terms of world influence, the sheer mathematics of that number has to make us question our role as global citizens. Should we not be doing everything in our power to forge a strong connection with China and other countries? We cannot simply sit back and believe that globalization is a benign or neutral force that we do not have to think about. The new global energy (this large world growing smaller) will certainly have an effect on our lives, our identities, our citizenship. Our challenge for the future is to conduct ourselves as citizens of the world even as we cherish our distinctive and our definitive home. A citizen of the world is one who is at home and claims his/her rights everywhere in that world. A citizen of the world is one who is cosmopolitan, tolerant, curious, gracious and courteous to strangers, gracious and courteous when s/he is a stranger.

Our regional identity is mostly related to home, home as the most complicated and least erasable of sites, home both elemental and nostalgic, the place where the world begins and ends. Calgary is my home, the site where I live and play, sleep and eat. The condition of the roads, the schools, the air, the plays and concerts and bookstores that I attend or visit are integral to my life, my outlook, my identity, my citizenship. My identity is tied to the west and my citizenship is tied to Canada, but both are inflected by this place, my home. This beautiful, wild, out of control city is more than home, it is HOME. And before anything else, that home, both literal and metaphorical, incites allegiance. More than cultural, religious or national identity, home in all its forms becomes the most private of citizenships, but the one that we will always wish to protect and to cherish.

14 The Alberta State of Mind

On Being Albertan, and Calgarian
Heather Bala Edwards

Heather Bala Edwards

I am Albertan and I am a Calgarian. Yes, I was one of the ten people who were actually born in Calgary. My first exposure to politics was around age seven at the dinner table where I would hear about "the evil Trudeau government robbing Alberta with the national energy program," or how Premier Peter Lougheed was "the most amazing person in the world" (which he is). It was all quite far away from my focus at the time—recess, my new bike and grade two hot-dog lunches. My first real brush with politics was at a pancake breakfast. Mom dug out our red western kerchiefs and plastic cowboy hats with the whistles attached, packed us up in the car, and dragged us to the Bay parking lot for the quintessential Stampede experience.

While trying to find my Mom in the midst of a sea of jean-clad knees and whining that my eggs were touching the syrup, I tugged on what I thought was my Mom's pant leg. It wasn't. It was Joe Clark's. I remember my Mom saying later "That was Joe Clark," and she explained who he was. Not only was this my first experience with politics, but in hindsight it symbolized much more: these breakfasts epitomize the egalitarian, down-to-earth Albertan approach to politics. In Alberta, it's normal for politicians to stand in parking lots with regular folks eating soggy pancakes on paper plates. It took many years away from Alberta to recognize and appreciate this difference.

My political life continued from there as I was perpetually and involuntarily signed up for the Young Conservatives by my father. Every year he'd proudly hand me my membership card, which I would put in the back of my drawer, never to see it again. It wasn't until university that

I stumbled on my own politics. Through friends, I was enlisted as a delegate to the 1990 Liberal Leadership convention, and was intrigued by the people and process of politics. I spent many campaigns bravely knocking on doors, surreptitiously leaving Liberal pamphlets in mailboxes, learning new swear words as they were hurled toward whichever Liberal candidate I was with. Other times, I watched as the candidates spent time sharing views with individuals, each learning from the other. The process taught me to have a thick skin, but it also demonstrated that most Albertans will listen to other views if they are presented rationally and logically. It also taught me that not many people in Calgary will actually vote Liberal.

But I had the political bug. I worked summer jobs in Ottawa on Parliament Hill and took my Masters in Political Science theory at the University of Calgary. I studied under a very right-wing group of professors, which turned out to be an education in more ways than one—I learned from each one of them that, no matter your opinion, it deserves respect. Armed with this Albertan approach to respecting other views, I moved to Ottawa full-time. After all, as a Liberal with a Political Science background, I had to leave the province to get a job.

I was honestly ready to leave Alberta and thought I would never come back. I took for granted the opportunities that Alberta had to offer. Excellent schools, the Banff Centre where I aspired to play violin and piano, the Glenbow Museum, the Calgary Philharmonic, the beautiful Lake Louise ski slopes, Spruce Meadows, a chance for every high school student to get a Rutherford Scholarship, two international airports, the Royal Tyrell Museum in Drumheller . . . the list goes on. There is something new and interesting to do and to learn literally every minute of the day. I thought it would be the same, or better, everywhere else.

I went to work in Ottawa full time in 1998. I had heard so many times that Alberta was ignored, or alienated, or other expletives that I recognized from my door-knocking days. I thought this was ridiculous—Alberta was treated very well, I told myself. All these people are whining and complaining and making up stuff about us being alienated—how could we not be respected?! I went to Ottawa wide-eyed and naïve to work for a Senator for a year and then for four years as a press secretary to a cabinet minister. Ottawa was an enlightening experience. I learned through an embarrassing social faux-pas that people in Ottawa are more formal and like to be referred to by their title and not their first name. I saw that it's not a perfect system, that people and provinces are not treated equally.

I was surprised to see that things were different in Ottawa. For instance, Joe Clark is a very tall man in person, and Brian Mulroney is not—they look different on TV. Perhaps more important, I quickly saw that Alberta didn't have the voice that I liked to think that it had. Because of the fact that Alberta has few seats compared to other provinces, it will never have the influence needed to sway decisions. Governments can afford to lose seats in Alberta if they can win over voter-rich Ontario and Quebec. It was disillusioning to have issues dismissed simply because they are "only Albertan" issues.

This is not to say that Alberta is never factored into political decision-making, but its weight is not proportional to its actual resources and contribution. Will this incongruity ever balance out? It's highly unlikely, unless there are massive changes to our political system. The only change that is possible is for Alberta to change its view of itself within the system. If you can't beat them, or join them, then change your attitude and lead through example. Alberta is a province rich with resources, people, innovation, motivation and ideas. Albertans may complain about health-care, about potholes, or about the price of gas, but with each complaint comes a novel solution to dealing with old challenges. We can no longer afford to whine about alienation and wait for someone in Ottawa to fix it. More and more, Alberta is challenging the status quo, demanding respect, and not being surprised when it gets it.

During my time working in Ottawa, I attended a July 1 Citizenship Ceremony in Lethbridge. I will never forget that moment, watching new Canadians from all over the globe proudly receiving their official papers and their Canadian flag. They chose to come to Canada, and to Alberta. The best choice I ever made was to leave Alberta. It was only by being away that I realized how special this province truly is. Even though I lived in Ottawa for awhile and could have been seen as a traitor, I was allowed back over the border and am living in Alberta again.

I look on our province now with fresh eyes and I see the gifts that are all around us. I love not paying provincial sales tax. I like wearing sandals in January when it's +25 degrees during a warm Chinook. More than that, I enjoy the energy and optimism of Albertans. Sure, for a few weeks a year during Stampede we revert to a cliché, but wearing cowboy boots, jeans and bolo ties reminds us that we are all equal and we're in this together. We call each other by our first names, no matter how rich or famous or powerful anyone is.

At a dinner table with all kinds of people from the arts, business and politics, the question was recently raised: what is your favourite city in the world? Everyone thought for a brief moment and then blurted out "Calgary!" We had to change the question to be: "what is your favourite city besides Calgary?"

Every trip we go on, anywhere in the world, when we return we always say "it's so good to be home." Like Dorothy in *The Wizard of Oz*, we know there is no place like home. There is no place like Alberta, no people like Albertans, and no future like ours.

My Life as an Albertan

Roger Gibbins

Roger Gibbins

Alberta was a distant, unknown place when I was growing up in northern British Columbia. It was part of that vast expanse of emptiness that swept in my mind from the Rockies to Toronto, the source of Ernest Manning's Sunday gospel broadcasts that I sometimes stumbled across on the local Prince George radio station. When I was twelve my family went on a short holiday to Banff, and I was both amazed and more than a little disturbed to find that Banff was in Alberta, not British Columbia. In the jargon of a much later time, mountains in Alberta simply did not compute.

As I worked my way through university in Vancouver and then California, the possibility of living in Alberta never crossed my mind. So, what happened?

Like hundreds of thousands of others over the years, my wife and I became economic migrants. At the time that I completed my graduate work at Stanford University in 1973, there were only two political science job openings in Canada, one at the University of Calgary and one in Sackville, New Brunswick. We chose Calgary for the simple reason that it was closer to our families in B.C., and we never looked back.

Alberta's "state of mind" in the early 1970s was chippy and somewhat rough around the edges. If Alberta was no longer the agrarian frontier, that frontier had just recently left the building. The oil wealth was just beginning to flow, courtesy of OPEC, and the new Alberta premier, Peter Lougheed, was just beginning to move Alberta to the centre of the national stage.

Calgary restaurants at the time specialized in steaks or, just for something a bit wild and exotic, prime rib. If today's Calgary is often described as a big city with a small city heart, it was then a small city with the heart and sometimes the emotional maturity of a teenager with jingle in his jeans. Nonetheless, it was a good place to live, to raise a family, to pursue a career, to touch nature in its many varied forms. Above all else, Alberta was a province packed with opportunity, a place of fresh starts where just about everyone seemed new.

Over the thirty-some years between then and now, Alberta matured and mellowed, or maybe I came to see the province differently through eyes that had certainly matured, and probably mellowed. What has not waned, however, is the frontier spirit. This phrase, I know, sounds like a cliché, but it does capture a sense of open horizons of the mind, a sense that everything and anything is possible, a belief in innovation and creativity.

So, is Alberta the best place in Canada to live? Certainly there are days when I believe so, days when the morning sun catches the tips of the Rockies, clear as glass although 100 kilometres away. But I realize that Canada is full of great communities, of compelling vistas, even of coasts and beaches. What perhaps sets Alberta apart is its state of mind, a mix of edginess and openness, of entrepreneurial zeal coupled with deep community engagement. If not necessarily the greatest place in Canada, it is unquestionably a good place to live, and a wonderful platform from which to participate in the broader Canadian community. Above all else, it has truly become home for me. Northern B.C., where are you now?

In the Alberta State of Mind
James H. Marsh

It was Alberta's 75th anniversary that brought me to Edmonton in 1980 to work on its most enduring legacy—*The Canadian Encyclopedia*. The encyclopedia was created through an unusual partnership between the nationalist publisher Mel Hurtig, who had once run for the Trudeau Liberals, and Conservative Premier Peter Lougheed, who was at that time locked in mortal combat over energy policy with those same Liberals. It was a noble idea, to celebrate Alberta by creating a reference work as a gift to *all* the people of Canada. Mel advertised nationally for an editor and hired me, a Toronto boy (via Ottawa). I was not a popular choice. As well as being condemned by the right-wing *Alberta Report* for being a "socialist" (I am not), I was criticized to my face for taking the place of unidentified locals who could have done the job just as well.

So from the day I arrived in Alberta in June of 1980 I had a much more complex view of Alberta than the simplistic image portrayed not only in the national media but by many Albertans themselves. It was epitomized by those two men: the nationalist Hurtig who was always a fierce promoter of his home city and province, and the forceful defender of provincial rights Lougheed, who always proclaimed himself a Canadian first.

James H. Marsh

Perhaps because I have remained something of an outsider, I have never sympathized with the cranky side of Alberta politics. I don't mean so much the ideological, "all government is bad government" conservatives or even the aggrieved sectionalists, but more the righteous who treat their opponents with derision. There is a lot of talk of getting Alberta's "voice" heard on the national stage, but sadly when many Canadians hear that voice they hear the kind of offensive attacks like those directed, without apology or stricture, against Belinda Stronach when she defected to the hated Liberals in May of 2005.

The truth is that Alberta politics is far more complex than that. It has radicals, populists, environmentalists, nationalists and, yes, federalists. When the occasion calls for it, our provincial premiers have "come in from the cold" and participated constructively, and even decisively, in the national debates. The province has lively local politics and even elects a few Liberals and socialists.

And so I have learned over the years that Alberta society is a lot more nuanced than its redneck image allows. It might suit some image-makers to paint Alberta as "Texas North," but the province does not have a long waiting list on death row and is not tying up its legislature with a debate on banning high-school cheerleaders. Alberta's oil industry has its share of mavericks—the business demands it—but it also has a conscience and a sense of responsibility that can only be called characteristically "Canadian." The description, in this book, of the initiatives that Syncrude and others have taken to include First Nations is an inspiring model for the future.

Something else that does not fit the Alberta stereotype of hard-nosed materialism is its vibrant artistic community. There is plenty to celebrate the inner cowboy in us—the genius of Ian Tyson—"think I'll go out to Alberta/weather's good there in the fall"—but there are also two beautiful new concert halls in Edmonton and Calgary, two superb orchestras, two opera companies, several ballet and dance companies, publishers, writers, painters and an impressive array of theatre. Canada's most prestigious folk festival takes place in my own neighbourhood and the renowned Fringe not far away. The Banff Centre is an integral part of not just Alberta's cultural life, but of the whole nation. The longer you live here, the less the image of the unsophisticated roughneck sticks.

It is my own politics, I suppose, but my wish for the future is that Alberta will find more ways to have its many virtues known nationally and to have its other "voices" heard. We already have a single-minded "Bloc" operating out of Quebec threatening our national survival. Even supporters of the federal Liberals understand the need for a viable second option at the national level and Alberta is perhaps best equipped to provide that option.

I have in my 25 years here in Alberta seen our society mature and grow. Even in 1980 I still saw remnants of a racist and anti-Semitic past. I found a society that still talked more about diversity than actually respected it. (It was not until 1972 that the Lougheed government finally eradicated the odious eugenics law.) Now imagine how our ancestors of 100 years ago would have reacted to our current situation, in which our primary immigration comes from Asia. Something magical has happened as we continue to transform ourselves into a truly tolerant society, celebrating diversity while more and more just checking that census box that says "Canadian."

No personal reflection on being Albertan can ignore the dominating force that geography has on the imagination. Any trip out onto the prairie or into the foothills, mountains, forests or badlands deepens a sense of connection and wonder. Returning home is always an anticipated pleasure: the space, the air, the oil "donkeys" dipping, the clouds of dust kicked up from country roads. Inexorably Alberta becomes home and pride overcomes ambivalence. I have turned down numerous offers to move back east. I have asked my tempters "How can you match this?" Yes, I now believe that I have earned the right to say that Alberta belongs as much to me as to the radicals of any stripe. Since OPEC, Peter Lougheed, Reform and the Klein revolution we cannot say that we are "not being heard." In fact, Alberta has probably done more to set the national agenda than any other province.

One last birthday wish? That we return to that idea in which *The Canadian Encyclopedia* and this book were conceived, that if we knew ourselves and each other better, we could celebrate being Albertan and see that we have so much more to offer to the confederation.

In The Alberta State of Mind

Sydney Sharpe

If I'd staked a claim on every piece of Alberta land where I've visited or lived, I'd be a wealthy woman—not in cash, but in experience and adventure. I am rich beyond measure from walking, hiking, riding, biking, flying, canoeing and even some canoodling within this bountiful province.

Alberta is a land that seems to loom far larger than its space on the map. The wondrous light slides throughout the exuberant skies and infuses the countryside with a vivid clarity. It defines every part of the province and even illuminates our provincial psyche; like the light, we are clear, direct, and sharp around the edges.

One midnight many years ago, my dad insisted on reading the *Grande Prairie Herald Tribune* by the beam of the moon as we sat outside during the soft summer solstice. We were living in the Peace Country, where the nights blur into days in high summer. The Wapiti River slept in the winter and then roared awake after the spring blizzards, once catching two canoeloads of foolish Sharpe kids and their friends in its torrents. We survived by clinging to broken tree branches.

In the Medicine Hat area, where we lived twice, nobody dared toy with the South Saskatchewan except the bull snakes. The river that carved the coulees will camp out in my mind forever, a stark and splendid landscape of water and bare hills, cottonwoods and teeming wildlife. And rattlesnakes. One day as my brother Noel and I walked to school with the Rathwell kids, a rattler slithered from the bush before us and coiled, ready to strike. I grabbed a stick and whacked the sinister viper to death. We proudly carried the corpse to school and showed it to incredulous kids. When I tell the story now, I'm asked a thoroughly modern question: Did I feel badly for the snake? I did not. To a bunch of ragged kids on the prairie, it was him or us.

I vividly remember the stacks of the glass factory on the skyway to the Hat. For us, the Trans-Canada stopped at Redcliff and the community life that often settled around the Legion, where friends and family gathered for a brew or just a smoke and a talk. As a connector of town

Sydney Sharpe: "This is a book about the Alberta way as an impetus for doing and for being who we are" (Don Braid).

life, the Legion housed the memories of fallen friends and fresh horrors, for the war was all too recent. Two crews of the South Alberta Regiment had been captured in the battle of the Hochwald near the end of the war. On another battlefield, my Uncle Howard Osgood was left for dead as German troops bayoneted the wounded around him. He was still less than 18 years old; like many another Alberta boy, he'd lied about his age to join the battle, following his older brother, Gordon, and sister, Norma. After the terror was over, these men and women began to rebuild the dreams that their bravery had rescued from the abyss of war.

My son, who loves the wild with a passion, once had a dangerous brush with the Bow River. He survived and so did his expensive hiking boot. The canoe crept on the water, bulging with camping gear and food. When it rounded a bend, the sloping vessel slunk to its side, then slid through the frosty waters on its belly. The two canoeists clung to its hulk until the bank broke the river's grip. By the time Gabriel had climbed the bank, one boot was missing, but his frozen feet couldn't tell which one. He and his pal made their way through the bush and later rendezvoused with their group downriver. And then my son saw his other boot sitting beside the campfire, drying out.

There is nothing like the North Saskatchewan River breaking free of winter. Its icy chains hang onto the river and refuse to release their grip until the April sun cracks their command. The ice is cunning in its control, beguiling the one that walks on the bank to cross over to the other side. "I'm strong," it says. "You can walk on me." And leave that bank forever.

These are some of the pieces of Alberta that travel with me across the country and around the globe. When I'm away from the province, I wonder if the spirit of the land is really just a mélange of misguided dreams, a mirage in my mind. So many other places have their own unique beauty.

Then I return and immediately relax. It was only culture shock. Alberta truly is a state of mind, sharply defined by unique qualities of light, landscape and culture.

Suggested Readings

COMPILED BY JAMES H. MARSH

General History and Pictorial

Benson, Daryl. *Alberta—Images*. Edmonton: Culler Books, 2004.

Bunner, Paul, ed. *Alberta in the 20th Century*, 12 vols. Edmonton: History Book Publications, Ltd., 1992–2004.

Cashman, Tony. *A Picture History of Alberta*. Edmonton: Hurtig Publishers, 1979.

Francis, R. Douglas, and Howard Palmer. *The Prairie West: Historical Readings*. Edmonton: Pica Pica Press, 1992.

Friesen, Gerald. *The Canadian Prairies: A History*. Toronto: University of Toronto Press, 1984.

Harris, R. Cole [*et al.*]. *Historical Atlas of Canada*, 3 vols. Toronto: University of Toronto Press, 1987–1993.

Holt, Faye Reinberg. *Alberta: A History in Photographs*. Vancouver: Altitude Publishing, 1996.

Owram, Doug. *Promise of Eden: The Canadian Expansionist Movement and the Idea of the West, 1865–1900*. Toronto: University of Toronto Press, 1980.

Thomas, Lewis G. *The Prairie West to 1905: A Canadian Sourcebook*. Toronto: Oxford University Press, 1975.

Palmer, Howard and Tamara Palmer. *Alberta: A New History*. Edmonton: Hurtig Publishers, 1990.

Thompson, John Herd. *Forging the Prairie West*. Toronto: Oxford University Press, 1998.

van Herk, Aritha. *Mavericks: An Incorrigible History of Alberta*. Toronto: Viking/Penguin, 2001.

First Nations

Allen, Robert S. "The Breaking of Big Bear." *Horizon Canada*, vol. 5 (1987): 1190–1195.

Barron, F. Laurie. "A Summary of Federal Indian Policy in the Canadian West, 1867–1984." *Native Studies Review*, vol. 1, no. 1 (1984): 28–39.

Barron, F. Laurie and James B. Waldrum, eds. *1885 and After: Native Society in Transition*. Regina: Canadian Plains Research Centre, 1986.

Brown, Jennifer S.H. *Stranger in Blood: Fur Trade Families in Indian Country*. Vancouver: University of British Columbia Press, 1980.

Brown, Jennifer S.H., and Elizabeth Vibert, eds. *Reading Beyond Words: Contexts for Native History*. Peterborough: Broadview Press, 1996.

Cardinal, Harold. *The Unjust Society: The Tragedy of Canada's Indians*. Edmonton: Hurtig Publishers, 1969.

Campbell, Maria. *Halfbreed*. Toronto: McClelland & Stewart, 1973.

Chalmers, John W. "Treaty No. Six." *Alberta History*, vol. 25 (spring 1977): 23–27.

Dempsey, L. James. *Warriors of the King: Prairie Indians in World War I*. Regina: Canadian Plains Research Center, 1999.

Dickason, Olive P. *Canada's First Nations: A History of Founding Peoples from Earliest Times*. Toronto: McClelland and Stewart, 1992.

Fumoleau, René. *As Long as This Land Shall Last: A History of Treaty 8 and Treaty 11, 1870–1939*. Toronto: McClelland and Stewart Limited, [1973].

Miller, Jim R. *Skyscrapers Hid the Heavens: A History of Indian–White Relations in Canada*. Toronto: University of Toronto Press, 1989.

Peterson, Jacqueline, and Jennifer S.H. Brown, eds. *The New Peoples: Being and Becoming Métis in North America*. Winnipeg: University of Manitoba Press, 1985.

Ray, Arthur J. *I Have Lived Here Since the World Began*. Toronto: Key Porter, 1996.

Ray, Arthur J., Jim R. Miller, and Frank J. Tough. *Bounty and Benevolence: A History of Saskatchewan Treaties*. Montreal: McGill-Queen's University Press, 2000.

Sprague, D.N. *Canada and the Métis, 1869–1885*. Waterloo: Wilfrid Laurier University Press, 1988.

Ward, Donald. *The People: A Historical Guide to the First Nations of Alberta, Saskatchewan, and Manitoba*. Toronto: Fitzhenry & Whiteside, 1995.

Fur Trade Era

Binnema, Ted and Rod Macleod, eds. *From Rupert's Land to Canada: Essays in Honour of John E. Foster*. Edmonton: University of Alberta Press, 2001.

Francis, Dan. *Battle for the West: Fur Traders and the Birth of Western Canada*. Edmonton: Hurtig, 1982.

Glover, Richard, ed. *David Thompson's Narrative 1784–1812*. Toronto: Champlain Society, 1962.

Harper, J. Russell. "William Hind and the Overlanders." *The Beaver*, outfit 302, no. 3 (1971): 4–15.

Innis, Harold A. *The Fur Trade in Canada: An Introduction to Canadian Economic History*. Toronto: University of Toronto Press, 1962.

Johnson, Alice M., ed. *Saskatchewan Journals and Correspondence: Edmonton House 1795–1800; Chesterfield House 1800–1802*. London: Hudson's Bay Record Society, 1967.

Pannekoek, Frits. *The Fur Trade and Western Canadian Society, 1670–1870*. Ottawa: Canadian Historical Association, 1987.

Payne, Michael, *The Most Respectable Place in the Territory: Everyday Life in Hudson's Bay Company Service, 1788 to 1870*. Ottawa: Canadian Parks Service, 1989.

Ray, Arthur. *Indians in the Fur Trade: Their Role as Trappers, Hunters, and Middlemen in the Lands Southwest of Hudson Bay, 1660–1870*. Toronto: University of Toronto Press, 1974.

Ray, Arthur. *"Give us Good Measure:" An Economic Analysis of Relations between the*

Indians and the Hudson's Bay Company before 1763. Toronto: University of Toronto Press, 1978.

Rich, E.E. *The Fur Trade and the North West to 1857*. Toronto: McClelland & Stewart, 1967.

Ruggles, Richard I. *A Country so Interesting: The Hudson's Bay Company and Two Centuries of Mapping, 1670–1870*. Montreal: McGill-Queen's University Press, 1991.

Van Kirk, Sylvia. *Many Tender Ties: Women in Fur Trade Society in Western Canada*. Winnipeg: Watson and Dyer, 1980.

Van Kirk, Sylvia. "Women in Between: Indian Women in Fur Trade Society in Western Canada." *Historical Papers* (Canadian Historical Association), 1977: 30–47.

Scientific Expeditions to the West

Birrell, Andrew. *Into the Silent Land: Survey Photography in the Canadian West, 1858–1900*. Ottawa: Public Archives of Canada, 1975.

Cavell, E. *Journeys to the Far West*. Toronto: James Lorimer and Company, 1979.

Gough, Barry. *The Northwest Coast: British Navigation, Trade, and Discoveries to 1812*. Vancouver: University of British Columbia Press, 1992.

Graebner, Norman A., ed. *Manifest Destiny*. Indianapolis: Bobbs-Merrill, 1968.

Huyda, Richard. *H.L. Hime. Photographer: The Assiniboine and Saskatchewan Exploring Expedition*. Toronto: The Coach House Press, 1975.

Jackson, C. *With Lens and Brush: Images of the Western Canadian Landscape 1845–1890*. Calgary: Glenbow Museum, 1989.

Spry, Irene M., ed. *The Papers of the Palliser Expedition*. Toronto: Champlain Society, 1968.

Zeller, Suzanne. *Inventing Canada: Early Victorian Science and the Idea of a Transcontinental Nation*. Toronto: University of Toronto Press, 1987.

The North-West Territory

Baker, William. *The Mounted Police and Prairie Society 1873–1919*. Regina: Canadian Plains Research Centre, 1998.

Beal, Bob, and Rod Macleod. *Prairie Fire: The 1885 North-West Rebellion*. Edmonton: Hurtig Publishers, 1984.

Beahen, William and Stan Horrall. *Red Coats on the Prairies: The North-West Mounted Police, 1886–1900*. Regina: Centax Books, 1998.

Birrell, Andrew J. "The North American Boundary Commission: Three Photographic Expeditions, 1872–74." *History of Photography*, vol. 20, no. 2 (1996): 113–121.

Brown, Jennifer S.H. *Documentary Editing: Whose Voices?* Toronto: Champlain Society, 1992.

Bumstead, J.M. *The Red River Rebellion*. Winnipeg: Watson and Dwyer, 1996.

Cook, Owen, and Peter Roberston. "James Peters, Military Photography and the Northwest Campaign." *Canadian Military History*, vol. 9 (Winter 2000): 23–29.

Hall, D.J. *Clifford Sifton*, 2 vols. Vancouver: University of British Columbia Press, 1981–1985.

Lambrecht, Kirk N. *The Administration of Dominion Lands, 1870–1930*. Regina: Canadian Plains Research Center, 1991.

Macleod, R.G. *The North-West Mounted Police and Law Enforcement 1873–1905*. Toronto: University of Toronto Press, 1976.

McLaren, John, Hamar Foster and Chet Orloff. *Law for the Elephant, Law for the Beaver: Essays in the Legal History of the North American West*. Regina: Canadian Plains Research Center, 1992.

McLean, Don. *1885: Métis Rebellion or Government Conspiracy?* Winnipeg: Pemmican Publications, 1985.

Monaghan, D. *Oliver Buell (1844–1910) Photographer*. Montreal: Concordia Art Gallery, 1984.

Morton, Desmond. *The Last War Drum: The North West Campaign of 1885*. Toronto: Hakkert, 1972.

Oppen, William A. *The Riel Rebellions: A Cartographic History*. Toronto: University of Toronto Press, 1979.

Public Archives of Canada. *Western Odyssey 1881: With the Marquis of Lorne, Pencil Sketches by Sydney Prior Hall*. Ottawa: Public Archives of Canada, 1975.

Robertson, Peter. "The New Amateur/ 1885–1990." *Private Realms of Light: Amateur Photography in Canada/1839–1940*. Lilly Koltun, ed., pp. 16–31. Markham: Fitzhenry and Whiteside, 1984.

Silversides, Brock V. *Looking West: Photographing the Canadian Prairies*. Calgary: Fifth House, 1999.

Sprague, D.N. *Canada and the Métis, 1869–1885*. Waterloo: Wilfrid Laurier University Press, 1988.

Spry, Irene M., and Bennett McCardle. *The Records of the Department of the Interior and Research Concerning Canada's Western Frontier of Settlement*. Regina: Canadian Plains Research Center, 1993.

Stanley, George F.G. *The Birth of Western Canada: A History of the Riel Rebellions*. Toronto: University of Toronto Press, 1970.

Stanley, George F.G. *Toil and Trouble: Military Expeditions to Red River*. Toronto: Dundurn Press, 1989.

Stanley, George F.G. "The Man Who Sketched the Great March." *Men in Scarlet*. Hugh A. Dempsey, ed., pp. 27–49. Calgary: McClelland and Stewart West, 1974.

Tobias, John L. "Canada's Subjugation of the Plains Cree, 1879–1885." *Canadian Historical Review*, vol. 64, no. 4 (1983): 519–548.

Immigration and Settlement

Bell, Keith. "Representing the Prairie, Private and Commercial Photography in Western Canada, 1880–1980." *Thirteen Essays on Photography*, pp. 13–32. Ottawa: Canadian Museum of Photography, 1988.

Breen, David H. *The Canadian Prairie West and the Ranching Frontier, 1874–1924*. Toronto: University of Toronto Press, 1983.

Broadfoot, Barry. *The Pioneer Years, 1895–1914: Memories of Settlers Who Opened the West*. Toronto: Doubleday Canada, 1976.

Burnet, Jean. *Next Year Country: A Study of Rural Social Organization in Alberta*. Toronto: University of Toronto Press, 1978.

Dawson, Carl A., and Eva Younge. *Pioneering in the Prairie Provinces: The Social Side of the Settlement Process*. Toronto: Macmillan, 1940.

Minifie, James M. *Homesteader: A Prairie Boyhood Recalled*. Toronto: Macmillan of Canada, 1972.

Palmer, Howard, and Tamara Palmer. *Peoples of Alberta: Portraits of Cultural Diversity*. Saskatoon: Western Producer Prairie Books, 1985.

Rasmussen, Linda, et al. *A Harvest Yet to Reap: A History of Prairie Women*. Toronto: Women's Press, 1975.

Rees, Ronald. *New and Naked Land: Making the Prairies Home*. Saskatoon: Western Producer Prairie Books, 1988.

Robertson, Heather. *Salt of the Earth*. Toronto: James Lorimer and Company, 1974.

Thomas, Greg, and Ian Clarke. "The Garrison Mentality and the Canadian West." *Prairie Forum*, vol. 4 (1979): 83–104.

Tracie, Carl J. *"Toil and Peaceful Life:" Doukhobor Village Settlement in Saskatchewan, 1899–1918*. Regina: Canadian Plains Research Center, 1996.

Transportation

Berton, Pierre. *The Last Spike: The Great Railway, 1881–1885.* Toronto: McClelland and Stewart, 1971.

Berton, Pierre. *The National Dream: The Great Railway, 1871–1881.* Toronto: McClelland and Stewart, 1970.

Dempsey, Hugh A., ed. *The CPR West: The Iron Road and the Making of a Nation.* Vancouver: Douglas and McIntyre, 1984.

Eagle, John A. *The Canadian Pacific Railway and the Development of Western Canada, 1896–1914.* Montreal: McGill-Queen's University Press, 1989.

Hart, E.J. *The Selling of Canada: The CPR and the Beginning of Canadian Tourism.* Banff: Altitude Publishing Limited, 1983.

Innis, Harold A. *A History of the Canadian Pacific Railway.* Toronto: University of Toronto Press, 1971.

Lamb, W. Kaye. *History of the Canadian Pacific Railway.* New York: Macmillan, 1977.

Regher, T.D. *Canadian Northern Railway: Pioneer Road of the Northern Prairies, 1895–1918.* Toronto: Macmillan, 1986.

Multicultural Life

Allen, Richard. "The Social Gospel as the Religion of the Agrarian Revolt." *The West and the Nation: Essays in Honour of W.L. Morton.* Carl Berger and Ramsay Cook, eds., pp. 174–186. Toronto: McClelland & Stewart, 1976.

Bennett, J.W. *Hutterian Brethren: The Agricultural Economy and Social Organization of a Communal People.* Stanford: Stanford University Press, 1967.

Brown, R.C., ed. *Minorities, Schools, and Politics.* Toronto: University of Toronto Press, 1969.

Cook, Ramsay. *The Regenerators: Social Criticism in Late Victorian English Canada.* Toronto: University of Toronto Press, 1985.

England, Robert. "Ethnic Settlers in Western Canada: Reminiscences of a Pioneer." *Canadian Ethnic Studies,* vol. 8 (1976): 18–33.

Entz, W. "The Suppression of the German Language Press in September 1918 (with Special Reference to the Secular German Language Papers in Western Canada)." *Canadian Ethnic Studies,* vol. 8 (1976): 56–70.

Epp, F.H. *Mennonites in Canada, 1786–1920: The History of a Separate People.* Toronto: Macmillan of Canada, 1974.

Epp, George K., ed. *Harvest: An Anthology of Mennonite Writing in Canada, 1874–1914.*
Winnipeg: Centennial Publications, 1974.

Flint, David. *The Hutterites: A Study in Prejudice.* Toronto: Oxford University Press, 1975.

Foster, W. Garland. "Canadian Communists: The Doukhobor Experiment." *American Journal of Sociology,* vol. 41 (1935): 327–340.

Gross, Paul S. *The Hutterite Way: The Inside Story of the Life, Customs, Religion, and Traditions of the Hutterites.* Saskatoon: Freeman Publishing, 1965.

Nancy Sheehan, *et al,* eds., pp. 155–173. Calgary: Destselig, 1986.

Kordan, Bohdan S., and Peter Melnycky, eds. *In the Shadow of the Rockies: Diary of the Castle Mountain Internment Camp, 1915–1917.* Edmonton: Canadian Institute of Ukrainian Studies Press, 1991.

Loewen, Royden K. *Family, Church, and Market: A Mennonite Community in the Old and the New Worlds, 1850–1930.* Urbana: University of Illinois Press, 1993.

Lohrenz, Gerhard. *The Mennonites of Western Canada.* Winnipeg: Centennial Publications, 1974.

Palmer, Howard. *Land of the Second Chance: A History of Ethnic Groups in Southern Alberta.* Lethbridge: Lethbridge Herald, 1972.

Palmer, Howard. "Strangers and Stereotypes: The Rise of Nativism, 1880–1920." *Patterns of Prejudice: A History of Nativism in Alberta.* Howard Palmer, ed., pp. 17–60. Toronto: McClelland & Stewart, 1982.

Petryshyn, Jaroslav. *Peasants in the Promised Land: Canada and the Ukrainians, 1891–1914.* Toronto: James Lorimer, 1985.

Rasporich, A.W. "Utopian Ideals and Community Settlements in Western Canada, 1880–1914." *The Settlement of the West.* Howard Palmer, ed., pp. 114–129. Calgary: Comprint, 1977.

Swyripa, Frances. *Wedded to the Cause: Ukrainian-Canadian Women and Ethnic Identity, 1891–1991.* Toronto: University of Toronto Press, 1993.

Tarasoff, K. *A Pictorial History of the Doukhobors.* Saskatoon: Western Producer, 1969.

Thompson, John Herd, and Allen Seager. *Canada, 1922–1939: Decades of Discord.* Toronto: McClelland & Stewart, 1985.

Tracie, C.J. "Ethnicity and the Prairie Environment: Patterns of Old Colony Mennonite and Doukhobor Settlement." *Man and Nature on the Prairies.* Richard Allen, ed., pp. 46–65. Regina: Canadian Plains Research Centre, 1976.

White, Donny. *In Search of Geraldine Moodie.* Regina: Canadian Plains Research Centre, 1998.

Woodcock, George, and Ivan Avakumovic. *The Doukhobors.* Toronto: Oxford University Press, 1968.

Woodsworth, J.S. *Strangers Within our Gates; or Coming Canadians.* Toronto: University of Toronto Press, 1972.

Urbanization

Artibise, Alan F.J. "Boosterism and the Development of Prairie Cities, 1871–1913." *Town and City: Aspects of Western Canadian Urban Development.* A.F.J. Artibise, ed., pp. 209–235. Regina: Canadian Plains Research Center, 1981.

Artibise, Alan F.J. "City-Building in the Canadian West: From Boosterism to Corporatism." *Journal of Canadian Studies,* vol. 17, no. 3 (1982): 35–44.

Foran, Max. *Calgary: an Illustrated History.* Toronto: James Lorimer, 1978.

Goyette, Linda. *Edmonton in Our Own Words.* Edmonton: University of Alberta Press, 2004.

Hesketh, Bob and Frances Swyripa, eds. *Edmonton, Life of a City.* Edmonton: Alberta Historical Resource Foundation, 1995.

Melnyk, Bryan P. *Calgary Builds: The Emergence of an Urban Landscape, 1905–1914.* Regina: Canadian Plains Research Center, 1985.

Merrett, Kathryn Chase. *A History of the Edmonton City Market 1900–2000: Urban Values and Urban Culture.* Calgary: University of Calgary Press, 2001.

Voisey, Paul. "The Urbanization of the Canadian Prairies, 1871–1916." *Histoire Sociale/Social History,* vol. 8 (1975): 77–101.

Western Protests

Avery, Donald H. *Dangerous Foreigners: European Immigrant Workers and Labour Radicalism in Canada, 1896–1932.* Toronto: McClelland and Stewart, 1979.

Bell, Edward. *Social Classes and Social Credit in Alberta.* Montreal and Kingston: McGill-Queen's University Press, 1993.

Bercuson, David J. *Confrontation at Winnipeg: Labour, Industrial Relations, and the General Strike.* Montreal: McGill-Queen's University Press, 1990.

Berger, Carl, ed. *Conscription 1917.* Toronto: University of Toronto Press, 1969.

Bumstead, J.M. *The Winnipeg General Strike of 1919: An Illustrated History.* Winnipeg: Watson and Dwyer, 1994.

Cherwinski, Joe. "Early Working-Class Life on the Prairies." *The Prairie West: Historical Readings*. R. Douglas Francis and Howard Palmer, eds., pp. 544–556. Edmonton: Pica Pica Press, 1992.

Danysk, Cecilia. *Hired Hands: Labour and the Development of Prairie Agriculture, 1880–1930*. Toronto: McClelland & Stewart, 1995.

Elliot, David Raymond. *Bible Bill: A Biography of William Aberhart*. Edmonton: Reidmore Books, 1987.

Fairbanks, Carol. *Prairie Women: Images in American and Canadian Fiction*. New Haven: Yale University Press, 1986.

Fairbanks, Carol, and Sara Brooks Sundberg. *Farm Women on the Prairie Frontier*. New Jersey: Scarecrow, 1983.

Gibbins, Roger. *Prairie Politics and Society: Regionalism in Decline*. Toronto: Butterworth, 1980.

Irving, John. *The Social Credit Movement in Alberta*. Toronto: University of Toronto Press, 1959.

Kealey, Gregory S. "1919: The Canadian Labour Revolt." *Labour/Le Travail*, vol. 13 (1984): 11–44.

Laycock, David. *Populism and Democratic Thought in the Canadian Prairies, 1910–1945*. Toronto: University of Toronto Press, 1990.

Mardon, Ernest G. and Austin A. *Alberta in Revolt: The Social Credit William "Bible Bill" Aberhart Years, 1935–1943*. Edmonton: Fisher House Publishers, 1996.

McClung, Nellie. *In Times Like These*. Toronto: University of Toronto Press, [1972].

Morton, W.L. *The Progressive Party in Canada*. Toronto: University of Toronto Press, 1950.

Rasmussen, Linda, *et al.*, eds. *A Harvest Yet to Reap: A History of Prairie Women*. Toronto: Women's Press, 1976.

Sharp, Paul F. *The Agrarian Revolt in Western Canada*. Minneapolis: University of Minnesota Press, 1948.

Silverman, Elaine. *The Last Best West: Women on the Alberta Frontier, 1880–1930*. Montreal: Eden Press, 1984.

Strong-Boag, Veronica. "'Ever a Crusader': Nellie McClung, First-Wave Feminist." *Rethinking Canada: The Promise of Women's History*. Veronica Strong-Boag and Anita Clair Fellman, eds., pp. 178–190. Toronto: Copp Clark Pitman, 1991.

Strong-Boag, Veronica. "Pulling in Double Harness or Hauling a Double Load: Women, Work and Feminism on the Canadian Prairie." *Journal of Canadian Studies*, vol. 21, no. 3 (1986): 32–52.

Thomas, Lewis H. *William Aberhart and Social Credit in Alberta*. Toronto: Copp Clark Publishers, 1977.

Thompson, John Herd. "'The Beginning of our Regeneration': The Great War and Western Canadian Reform Movements." *Canadian Historical Association Historical Papers*, 1972.

Thompson, John Herd. *The Harvests of War: The Prairie West, 1914–1918*. Toronto: McClelland and Stewart, 1978.

Voisey, Paul. "The 'Votes for Women' Movement." *Alberta History*, vol. 23 (1975): 10–23.

Young, Walter D. *Democracy and Discontent: Progressivism, Socialism and Social Credit in the Canadian West*. Toronto: McGraw-Hill Ryerson, 1978.

Politics and Economics

Bell, Edward. "The Rise of the Lougheed Conservatives and the Demise of Social Credit in Alberta: A Reconsideration," *Canadian Journal of Political Science* 26 (1993).

Carmichael, E.A. and C. Herrera, eds. *Canada's Energy Policy: 1985 and Beyond*. C.D. Howe Institute, 1984.

Doern, Bruce and Glen Toner. *The Politics of Energy: The Development and Implementation of the National Energy Program*. Toronto: Methuen, 1985.

Gibbins, Roger. "Political Discontent in the Prairie West: Patterns of Continuity and Change," in *The Prairie West: Historical Readings*, ed. R. Douglas Francis and Howard Palmer. Edmonton: University of Alberta Press, 1992, 693–694.

J.D. House. *The Last of the Free Enterprisers: The Oilmen of Calgary*. Toronto: Macmillan of Canada, 1980.

Hurtig, Mel. *At Twilight in the Country: Memoirs of a Canadian Nationalist*. Toronto: Stoddart, 1996.

Hustack, Alan. *Peter Lougheed: A Biography*. Toronto: McClelland & Stewart, 1979.

Klassen, Henry C. *A Business History of Alberta*. Calgary: University of Calgary Press, 1999.

Milne, David. *Tug of War: Ottawa and the Provinces Under Trudeau and Mulroney*. Toronto: Lorimer, 1986, 86–87.

Norrie, Ken and Doug Owram. *A History of the Canadian Economy*, 2nd Edition. Toronto: Harcourt & Brace, 1996.

Norrie, Ken. "Energy, Federalism, and the West," *Publius: The Journal of Federalism* 14 (Winter 1984): 83.

Owram, Doug. "Reluctant Hinterland," in *Western Separatism*, ed. Larry Pratt and Garth Stevenson. Edmonton: Hurtig Publishers, 1981, 45.

Romney Paul. *Getting It Wrong: How Canadians Forgot their Past and Imperilled Confederation*. Toronto: University of Toronto Press, 1999.

Sharpe, Sydney. *A Patch Of Green: Canada's Oil Patch Makes Peace with the Environment*. Dublin, NH: Yankee Publishing, 2002.

Sharpe, Sydney and Don Braid. *Storming Babylon: Preston Manning and the Rise of the Reform Party*. Toronto: Key Porter, 1991.

Sharpe, Sydney. *The Gilded Ghetto: Women and Political Power in Canada*. Toronto: Harper Collins, 1995.

Sharpe, Sydney. *Breakup: Why The West Feels Left Out of Canada*. Toronto: Key Porter, 1990.

Wood, David G. *The Lougheed Legacy*. Toronto: Key Porter Books Ltd., 1985.

Arts and Culture

Goto, Hiromi. *Chorus of Mushrooms*. Edmonton: NeWest Press, 1994.

Fraser, Fil. *Alberta's Camelot: Culture and the Arts in the Lougheed Years*. Edmonton: Lone Pine, 2003.

Gribbon, Michael J. *Walter J. Phillips: a Selection of His Works and Thoughts*. Ottawa: National Gallery of Canada, 1978.

Josephy, Alvin M. *The Artist was a Young Man: The Life of Peter Rindisbacher*. Fort Worth: Amon Carter Museum of Western Art, 1970.

Kane, Paul. *Wanderings of an Artist among the Indians of North America*. Dover Publications, 1996.

Leighton, David S. R. and Peggy Leighton. *Artists, Builders and Dreamers: 50 Years at the Banff School*. Toronto: McClelland & Stewart, c 1982.

Melnyk, George. *The Literary History of Alberta*, 2 vols. Edmonton: University of Alberta Press, 1999.